PROPAGANDA TECHNIQUE

IN THE

WORLD WAR

PROPAGANDA
TECHNIQUE

IN THE

WORLD WAR

Harold D. Lasswell

COACHWHIP PUBLICATIONS

Greenville, Ohio

Propaganda Technique in the World War, by Harold D. Lasswell
© 2015 Coachwhip Publications

Published 1927
No claims made on public domain material.

Harold Dwight Lasswell (1902-1978)

ISBN 1-61646-311-2
ISBN-13 978-1-61646-311-3

CoachwhipBooks.com

CONTENTS

Foreword   7

1 || The Matter in Hand   9

2 || Propaganda Organization   19

3 || War Guilt and War Aims   48

4 || Satanism   74

5 || The Illusion of Victory   95

6 || Preserving Friendship   105

7 || Demoralizing the Enemy   151

8 || Conditions and Methods of Propaganda   173

9 || The Results of Propaganda   197

Bibliography   205

Supplemental Material

Propaganda Behind the Lines // Street   215

Control of Propaganda . . . // Strong   229

Among the libraries which I have used, special acknowledgement is due to the *Musée et bibliothèque de la guerre* (Paris). Among the propagandists and journalists with whom I have consulted and debated, it would be invidious to distinguish. Within the academic ranks, I owe a personal and professional debt of formidable proportions to Charles E. Merriam, Chairman of the Department of Political Science of the University of Chicago, who has not only encouraged this, as indeed every effort to depart from the beaten path of formalism, but who has placed his special experience as a member of the staff of the Committee of Public Information in Italy during the War at my disposal. Quincy Wright, Professor of Political Science in the same institution, has rescued me from several mistakes. Imperfections of conception and execution are my own doing.

H.D.L.
Chicago

1
THE MATTER IN HAND

There are abundant signs of interest in international propaganda since the War of 1914. Several books have been published by men who held responsible propaganda posts during the War. Creel in the United States, Stuart in England, Nicolai in Germany, and Waitz and Tonnelet in France, have published much of their record to the world. Individual propaganda agents of high and low degree have written their memoirs, and international propaganda is alluded to in every reminiscence and apology of post-armistice times.

The professors and the graduate students and the publicists have swollen the flood of systematic speculation about, and systematic examination of, the subject. Among the conspicuous names in Germany, where the best work has been done, are Johann Plenge, Edgar Stern-Rubarth, Ferdinand Tönnies, and Kurt Baschwitz.[1] Research monographs of some value have been prepared by Schönemann, who wrote in German on the United States, Marchand, who wrote in French on certain aspects of German propaganda, Wiehler, who wrote in German on special problems, and several others. Démartial dissected his own French and Allied propaganda during the War in a brilliant contribution to the de-bunking of world opinion. Members of the new propaganda, or publicity, profession have begun to rationalize their own practices. The books by Bernays and Wilder and Buell are pioneers in this direction. Universities have begun to offer courses of lectures upon the new technique, and vast collections of War propaganda have been assembled at Stuttgart, Paris, London and Stanford.

There are many reasons why the role of propaganda in international politics, and especially in war-time, is receiving more careful scrutiny to-day than heretofore. There is a new inquisitiveness abroad in the world. Some of the people who in the years before the War were disposed to accept the changing tides of international animosity and friendship as inevitable manifestations of the cosmic fate, which commanded the sun to rise or the rain to fall, have become suspicious of the supernatural or the impersonal character of these events. A word has appeared, which has come to have an ominous clang in many minds—Propaganda. We live among more people than ever, who are puzzled, uneasy, or vexed at the unknown cunning which seems to have duped and degraded them. It is often an object of vituperation, and therefore, of interest, discussion and, finally, of study.

These people probe the mysteries of propaganda with that compound of admiration and chagrin with which the victims of a new gambling trick demand to have the thing explained. That credulous utopianism, which fed upon the mighty words which exploited the hopes of the mass in war, has in many minds given way to cynicism and disenchantment, and with these earnest souls propaganda is a far more serious matter. Some of those who trusted so much and hated so passionately have put their hands to the killing of man, they have mutilated others and perhaps been mutilated in return, they have encouraged others to draw the sword, and they have derided and besmirched those who refused to rage as they did. Fooled by propaganda? If so, they writhe in the knowledge that they were the blind pawns in plans which they did not incubate, and which they neither devised nor comprehended nor approved.

In the defeated countries, such as Germany, the military people have seized upon propaganda to save their own faces. They declare that their army was never defeated by the battering of Allied battalions, but that the nation collapsed behind their lines because all the alien and radical elements in the population were easy marks for the seductive bait of foreign propaganda. This is plausible to the public because people were everywhere warned during the war to beware the noxious fumes of enemy propaganda. The Germans were wrought up over "Reuter, the fabricator of War lies," Northcliffe, "The Minister of Lying," and the Allies, the "All-lies." They were, therefore, predisposed to attach very great importance to propaganda. Since the War Germany has been shorn of military strength, and must, therefore, rely upon subtler means of protecting and advancing its interests than armed coercion. Patriotic Germans are anxious to understand the nature of the non-coercive weapon which was wielded so successfully to their discomfiture in war-time, and there is to-day a more luxurious flowering of treatises upon international propaganda (its nature, limitations and processes) in Germany than anywhere else.

In some measure the present occupation with propaganda is due to the outright pacifists. There is a widespread belief that fighting is due to ill-will, and that, if war is to cease, there must be a "moratorium on hate." Can propaganda furnish a weapon of direct attack upon the psychology of nations, and expose the ways and means of sowing confidence where mistrust rankles?

This whole discussion about the ways and means of controlling public opinion testifies to the collapse of the traditional species of democratic romanticism and to the rise of a dictatorial habit of mind. As long as the democrats were in opposition, they were free to belabour the fact of an infallible though almighty king with the fantasy of an all-wise public. Enthrone the public and dethrone the king! Pass the sceptre to the wise!

Familiarity with the ruling public has bred contempt. Modern reflections upon democracy boil down to the proposition, more or less contritely expressed, that the democrats were deceiving themselves. The public has not reigned with benignity and restraint. The good life is not in the mighty rushing wind of public sentiment. It is no organic secretion of the horde, but the tedious achievement of the few. The lover of the good life no longer consults Sir Oracle; he pulls the strings of Punch and Judy. Thus argues the despondent democrat. Let us, therefore, reason together, brethren, he sighs, and find the good, and when we have

found it, let us find out how to make up the public mind to accept
it. Inform, cajole, bamboozle and seduce in the name of the public
good. Preserve the majority convention, but dictate to the majority!

To the sombre curiosity of the discouraged democrat must be
added the analytical motive of the social scientist. The division of
social thinking has at last reached a point which enables a few
people to achieve a fixed preoccupation with the explanation of
how the social wheels go round, wholly apart from any pressing
anxiety to steer them in any particular direction. Their business is
to discover and report, not to philosophize and reform. They are
more anxious to gratify their curiosity than to follow the footsteps
of the deity who created man in his own image.

The people who probe the mysteries of public opinion in politics must, for the present, at least, rely upon something other than
exact measurement, to confirm or discredit their speculations.
Generalizations about public opinion stick because they are plausible and not because they are experimentally established. They
fall by the wayside, when others, who have had experience with
the kind of fact which they purport to describe, disagree with the
original observer. Sometimes this disagreement is sharp and em-
phatic, because it comes from people who have tried to use existing notions about public opinion in their efforts to control it. This
is the engineering test. It is employed by propagandists and pub-
licity-men of all sorts and shapes.

Conjectures in the field of public opinion are particularly susceptible to engineering tests. But much of the literature of public
opinion is of such abstruse and indefinite character that it defies
empirical verification. There is a plethora of theories about something known as public opinion in general, and a paucity of hypoth-
eses about public opinions in particular. When the field of public
opinion is split into the problems of explaining and controlling
opinions about policies, attitudes toward persons and groups, and
attitudes toward the various modes of political participation, some
more tangible progress may be expected.

The role of opinion in international politics is peculiarly worthy of study, because it is a matter of growing importance. We are

witnessing the growth of a world public, and this public has arisen in part, because international propaganda has at once agitated and organized it. Interests overlap boundaries. It is a mere fiction that the citizens and the governments of each country refrain from meddling in affairs which are technically within the competence of another. In the summer of 1925, for instance, the German Reichstag was engaged in considering a proposal to levy protective duties upon agricultural and manufactured commodities. Theoretically, this is a domestic question, and is reserved for the exclusive determination of whoever happens to live inside the boundaries of the juristic entity called Germany. But in point of fact, external interests were affected, and they brought pressure to bear in their own behalf. American manufacturers, whose goods would be barred if the tariff went into operation, joined forces with British, French and German interests and sent their agents to Germany. They sought to reach the Press and to strengthen the hands of the elements inside Germany, who stood out against the bill.

Such private influencing as this is no longer the exception, but the custom. Corporations, for instance, find it convenient to subsidize newspapers abroad; and influencing is by no means confined to unofficial persons. Governments take an active hand in the game. The prestige-propaganda of the Japanese on the exclusion question, the "myth of a single guilty nation" propaganda of the Germans against the Versailles settlement, and the Soviet propaganda for American recognition are current cases. The new organs of international government are in close touch with interests inside each nation. The International Labour Office co-operates with those who wish to procure the ratification and the enforcement of the draft conventions of the International Labour Conference.

Official propaganda often takes the form of encouraging patriotic societies with branches abroad. The League of Germans Abroad claims to have 150 locals in Germany and in foreign countries, and the Union for Germanism Abroad says that it has over a million members in Germany and Austria. There are special organizations for Austria, Schleswig, the Saar Territory, Danzig, Czecho-Slovakia, Poland, the Tyrol, the Danube and overseas. These associations exist to keep alive a sentiment of cultural unity and may, in times of emergency, go further.

Governments smile benevolently upon certain international societies, such as the *Alliance Française* and the English-Speaking Union. They keep open channels of influence, which may be valuable in times of strain.

There are innumerable official and unofficial propagandas to instigate revolution, secession, or racial, cultural, geographical and religious unity. Such are suggested by these words: Communism, Irish Independence, Pan-Islam, Pan-Slav, Pan-America, Pan-Europe, League of Nations Union. There are propagandas on behalf of political personalities, for it is important to procure a favourable reception for every ambassador at a new post.

It is public opinion and propaganda in war-time which calls forth the most strenuous exertions. The conduct of war, conceived as a psychological problem, may be stated in terms of morale. A nation with a high morale is capable of performing the tasks laid upon it because of a certain momentum, which can only be measured when serious resistances appear. The conventional signs of high morale are enthusiasm, determination, self-confidence, absence of carping criticism and absence of complaint. Almost every fact may have its implication for morale. The calories in the official ration, the supply of cigarettes, the opportunities for recreation, the confidence of officers and public men, the smart demeanour of the troops, the mode of inflicting discipline; all this, and more, affects the fighting vim and tenacity of the military and civil population.

The problem of maintaining morale is only in part a problem of propaganda, because propaganda is but one of the many devices which must be relied upon. Its scope is limited though important. By propaganda is not meant the control of mental states by changing such objective conditions as the supply of cigarettes or the chemical composition of food. Propaganda does not even include the stiffening of morale by a cool and confident bearing. It refers solely to the control of opinion by significant symbols, or, to speak more concretely and less accurately, by stories, rumours, reports, pictures and other forms of social communication. Propaganda is concerned with the management of opinions and attitudes by the direct manipulation of social suggestion rather than by altering other conditions in the environment or in the organism.

Propaganda is one of the three chief implements of operation against a belligerent enemy:—

> Military Pressure (The coercive power of the land, sea and air forces).
> Economic Pressure (Interference with access to sources of material, markets, capital and labour power).
> Propaganda (Direct use of suggestion).

Negotiation is a method of influencing foreign states with which one is not in active combat. By negotiation is meant the official exchanges which look toward agreement. Mediation between contending parties and submission to arbitration are both commonly invoked. A government influences its own people by legislation, adjudication, policing, propaganda, and ceremonialism. For the soldiers, whom it has under the most complete control, it must make adequate provision of necessities and relaxation on pain of trouble. It drills them into a unified missile of destruction

During war much reliance must be placed on propaganda to promote economy of food, textiles, fuel, and other commodities and to stimulate recruiting, employment in war industries, service in relief work, and the purchase of bonds. But by far the most potent role of propaganda is to mobilize the animosity of the community against the enemy, to maintain friendly relations with neutrals and allies, to arouse the neutrals against the enemy, and to break up the solid wall of enemy antagonism. In short, it is the significance of propaganda for international attitudes in war which renders it of peculiar importance.

International war propaganda rose to such amazing dimensions in the last war, because the communization of warfare necessitated the mobilization of the civilian mind. No government could hope

to win without a united nation behind it, and no government could
have a united nation behind it unless it controlled the minds of its
people. The civilians had to be depended upon to supply recruits
for the front and for the war industries. The sacrifices of war had
to be borne without complaints that spread dissension at home and
discouragement in the trenches.

Now the civilians cannot be subjected to the same discipline as
the soldiers. The effect of the drill to which the soldier is subjected
is thus described by Maxwell:—

> the individual becomes highly imitative, conform-
> ing his movements in every respect to those of the
> drill-sergeants. He is not permitted to make the
> slightest alteration in the movements which he is
> shown, and is stopped again and again until at last
> his movements are satisfactory. At this stage in a
> soldier's training his behaviour is almost mechani-
> cal, and the unity achieved throughout the group is
> very little higher than that displayed by a machine.
> . . . The mere fact that each man acts like his neigh-
> bour enables the individual to rely upon the co-op-
> eration of his fellows with reference to the common
> end. On the parade ground each man soon discovers
> that every member of his unit is co-operating with him
> in the evolution in progress. In the trenches he is
> confident that the men on either side of him are doing
> the same, and that the divisions on the flanks of his
> own divisions are co-operating for the common end. It
> is through discipline that it is achieved (this co-opera-
> tion) in the Army, and the mutual trust engendered
> has the effect of welding what might otherwise be
> only a mechanical organization into a living unity.[2]

Active service brings with it a tendency to relapse to the primitive. Many observers have said that it is the simple bed-rock things
that matter most. It is food and drink and smokes and sleep and

warmth and shelter and creature comforts that bulk largest at the front. The human values and sentiments are left to atrophy for want of stimulation. The quiet influence of the presence of friendly scenes and faces is lost. The influence of certain of the more complex forms of religion is less.[3]

Military life approximates the aggregation of disciplined men in a dehumanizing environment. The civilian lacks the automatic discipline of drill and remains in an environment in which his sentiment-life (his *human* life) continues. Civilian unity is not achieved by the regimentation of muscles. It is achieved by a repetition of ideas rather than movements. The civilian mind is standardized by news and not by drills. Propaganda is the method by which this process is aided and abetted.

The intentional circulation of ideas by propaganda helps to overcome the psychic resistances to whole-hearted participation in war, which have arisen with the decay of personal loyalty to chiefs. Peace has come to be regarded as the normal state of society, and not war. There are ideologies which condemn war either as something bad in itself, or as the product of a detested order of society. Propaganda is the war of ideas on ideas.

This study is a preliminary and highly provisional analysis of the group of propaganda problems connected with the control of international antipathies and attractions in wartime. How may hate be mobilized against an enemy? How may the enemy be demoralized by astute manipulation? How is it possible to cement the friendship of neutral and allied peoples?

It is not proposed to write history, but to describe technique. When the war has receded further into the past, it will be possible to write at least a fragmentary history of the international propaganda of the time. The aim of the present inquiry is at once more modest and more ambitious than this. It is more modest in that it has chosen but a few of the facts which will be included in a comprehensive history. It is more ambitious in that it has undertaken to evolve an explicit theory of how international war propaganda may be conducted with success. It relies almost exclusively upon American, British, French and German experience.

Why not postpone the theory of method until the history is finished? The answer is that we knew enough about the history to justify a provisional study of technique, and a technical study at this time will perhaps improve the quality of the forthcoming history. After all, the relation between the student whose main interest is in the mechanism and the student whose chief concern is what happened in a particular circumstance is reciprocal. In a sense, the scientist and the engineer ask questions for the historian to answer, and the historian reports upon the probable influence of specific factors in a definite set of past circumstances. The lines are never mutually exclusive, for the historian is continually uncovering a new example of method, while the technical student is often able to plug a gap in chronology through his researches.

The procedure in this investigation has been to stick close to common-sense analysis. There are many seductive analogies between collective behaviour and the behaviour of individuals in a clinic,[4] but the analogies are too easily strained in the making. Clinical psychology is too rudimentary to carry an imposing superstructure. The present study goes no further than to develop a simple classification of the various psychological materials, which have been used to produce certain specified results, and to propose a general theory of strategy and tactics, for the manipulation of these materials. Subsequent inquiry and criticism may find other categories which are at once more accurate and suggestive.

Notes

[1] For the titles of their books, and the writings referred to elsewhere in this chapter, see the bibliography.

[2] *A Psychological Retrospect of the Great War*, p. 162.

[3] See Maxwell, as cited, 100.

[4] See, for example, Miss Playne's book called *The Neuroses of Nations*.

2

PROPAGANDA ORGANIZATION

Inside a democratic country there is a certain presumption against government propaganda. As Representative Gillett, commenting upon the Creel Bureau, said, admitting that it has not been conducted in a partisan spirit:

> That is the great danger of such a bureau as this, because we must all admit that if any administration has in its power a Bureau of Public Information, as it is called, but really an advertising bureau, a propaganda bureau, a bureau of publicity, to exploit the various acts and departments of the Government, it is a very dangerous thing in a Republic; because, if used in a partisan spirit or for partisan advantage of the administration, it has tremendous power, and in ordinary peace-time I do not think any party or any administration would justify it or approve it.[1]

The truth is that all governments are engaged to some extent in propaganda as part of their ordinary peace-time functions. They make propaganda on behalf of diplomatic friends or against diplomatic antagonists, and this is unavoidable. While, therefore, the presumption exists against propaganda work by a democratic government, this statement should not be taken too literally.

During the war-period it came to be recognized that the mobilization of men and means was not sufficient; there must be a mobilization of opinion. Power over opinion, as over life and property, passed into official hands, because the danger from licence was greater than the danger of abuse. Indeed, there is no question but that government management of opinion is an unescapable corollary of large-scale modern war. The only question is the degree to which the government should try to conduct its propaganda secretly, and the degree to which it should conduct it openly. As far as the home public is concerned, there is nothing to be gained by concealment, and there is a certain loss of prestige for all that is said, when secrecy is attempted. The carrying power of ideas is greatly increased when the authority of the government is added to them. With certain insignificant exceptions (the smuggling of propaganda material into adjacent enemy countries), nothing is lost, if all propaganda operations in neutral and allied countries are carried on openly. Otherwise, indeed, suspicion and distrust may exist where complete confidence and understanding are indispensable. The United States Committee on Public Information was undoubtedly correct in notifying neutral governments of what they wanted to do inside neutral borders.

It is bad tactics, however, to announce blatantly to the enemy that a "Director of Propaganda in Enemy Countries" has been named. As Sir Herbert Samuel said in the House of Commons, when Lord Northcliffe was appointed to this post in 1918:

> Possibly the Germans may regard Lord Northcliffe, the proprietor of the *Daily Mail* and the *Evening News*, in much the same light as we may regard Count Reventlow. What should we think, if we heard that an official announcement had been made by the German Government, that they had appointed Count Reventlow as the Director to carry on propaganda in the United Kingdom, and in other Allied countries?[2]

Assuming, in principle, that propaganda should be conducted in the open by a belligerent government, the problem of organization presents itself. What agencies should carry on the work, and to what degree is unity of command practicable? The work of carrying on the war brings several government services into the active control of certain streams of information, and international attitudes are to some degree involved with the rest. There is the Foreign Office at home, and the Diplomatic and Consular staffs abroad. There is the War and Naval Department at home, and the Military and Naval Attaches abroad. There is the General Staff and the Field Headquarters. There are the various service ministries engaged upon problems of supply and internal regulation. The mere enumeration of these agencies is sufficient to remind one of the evident proposition that the influencing of attitudes is implicit in every function, and that it is incapable of complete segregation in anything like the degree to which, let us say, the purchasing of horses can be confined to a particular agency.

Disunity brings dangers. The Foreign Office and the Field Headquarters may hold out contradictory inducements to the enemy and cast the whole propaganda of demoralization into disrepute. The military people at home may announce the destruction of public buildings in the occupied zone, much to the consternation of the diplomatic representatives in neutral countries. There is always the possibility that bad news of different kinds may break simultaneously and produce an unwonted state of depression if each service gives its own news to the public. The news of a naval loss, a military loss and an aviation loss may come when there is a shortage of flour, and when there is a prickly set of wage and price problems agitating the prints at home. If this news were handled through a central clearing house, it could be distributed over a period of time and nullified by the more favourable aspects of the general situation.

Disunity leads to a considerable duplication of effort. If the military people publish the same pamphlet that the diplomatic service publishes, and distribute it through the military attachés abroad when the diplomatic attachés have already doled it out, no good purpose can be served. It is difficult to work out a revision of general policy in the light of propaganda efforts, where there is no continuing mechanism for keeping tab on the whole range of propaganda work. The backwardness of certain departments, which may be opposed to publicity, may produce a repercussion of uneasiness and distrust. There may be delay in shifting the personnel devoted to propaganda work to the sectors where the most effect can be secured.

Some of these dangers may be offset by the dangers of unity. Any scheme of unity runs the risk of antagonizing the *amour propre* of some service and of ruining morale. If the control of foreign and domestic propaganda were integrated too tightly in the hands of one man, the one or the other might suffer from the preconceptions of the responsible head. Their requirements are so different that only a rare combination of talents can be relied upon to develop both of them to the highest efficiency.

The balance seems to point toward unity as more desirable than disunity, but it seems to justify a scheme of organization which preserves a considerable degree of autonomy to the constituent services. What are the possible forms of organization? There might be a single propaganda executive. There might be a committee of executives, each responsible for some branch of propaganda work, such as propaganda against the enemy, propaganda in neutral and allied countries, propaganda among civilians, and propaganda in the fighting forces. In any case, the propaganda work in training camps, at the front, in rest camps, on shipboard, and in transit, would vest largely in the military and naval authorities. A third method is to arrange a common Press conference for all departments, but to leave all other forms of effort to the regular agencies affected, which would especially be the Foreign Office, General Headquarters, the War Department, and the Ministry of the Interior. Broadly speaking, the United States adopted the first expedient in the last war, Great Britain, the second, and Germany, the third.

A Committee on Public Information was appointed, by order of the President, soon after the entrance of the United States into the War. It was composed of the Secretaries of the Navy and War

Departments, the Secretary of State, and Mr. George Creel. This was equivalent to appointing a separate cabinet member for propaganda, in fact, and Mr. Creel was responsible for every aspect of propaganda work, both at home and abroad. One result of this method of organization was to confer upon the representatives of the Committee abroad something of the prestige of three great government departments, and to satisfy the self-esteem of each one.

While the American system sprang into existence at a single stroke, and remained substantially unaltered during the War, the British system went through a long and intricate series of changes. As Major-General Sir George Aston wrote:

> Party politicians are suspicious folk, unwilling to trust any Government with money to spend on propaganda, for fear that they will spend it in their own interest rather than the country's. So the Parliamentary War Aims Committee was established with representatives of all parties. The Committee was charged with Home Propaganda, and came in for much criticism.[3]

A small department was set up at Wellington House in the office of the Insurance Commissioners to prepare pamphlets and leaflets. Wellington House initiated the Bryce Report, which was one of the triumphs of the War, on the Propaganda front, but most of its material was put out as though it were a private and not an official agency. A films and wireless committee was later set up under Mr. Mair, but its relation to the Home Office and the Foreign Office was uncertain. A Press Bureau was improvised in August, 1914, and was later adopted by the Home Office. The Foreign Office was meanwhile engaged in the following activities, according to a statement in Parliament by the Under-Secretary of State for Foreign Affairs (Mr. Acland):

> We are taking steps to see that there is supplied to the Press in neutral countries not only news strictly

so-called, but also news which we take here to be
rived at this same method of organization.

so-called, but also news which we take here to be rather commonplace, but which is of real interest to other countries, as to the condition of this country, and information with regard to trade, and with regard to employment, and with regard to recruiting, and with regard to all such matters as to which the condition of this country is really of interest to our friends.[4]

In January, 1917, the Department of Information was organized. Colonel Buchan had charge of four widely scattered services, and was responsible to the war Cabinet and the Prime Minister. An Advisory Committee was established, which consisted of Lord Northcliffe, Lord Burnham, Mr. Robert Donald, and Mr. C. P. Scott. When Lord Northcliffe proceeded on his mission to America, Lord Beaverbrook was appointed to this Committee, and later, Sir George Riddell was added. Things were still at loose ends under this system, and Sir E. Carson, a member of the War Cabinet, was asked to co-ordinate the various agencies. The War Department had organized a separate service for the purpose of conducting propaganda against the German Army, and the civilian peoples. Finally, in February, 1918, Lord Beaverbrook was made Minister of Information, occupying the post of Chancellor of the Duchy of Lancaster. At the same time Lord Northcliffe was named Director of Propaganda in Enemy Countries, and Directors were appointed for neutral countries for intelligence, and for cinematograph propaganda. Lord Northcliffe was technically responsible to Lord Beaverbrook in respect of finance, but, in fact, he had the right of direct access to the Prime Minister and the War Cabinet. Confusion was worse confounded by locating the Enemy Propaganda Department in the British War Mission with which Northcliffe had been working for some months past. Informal conferences were inaugurated to co-ordinate efforts, and later a Propaganda Policy Committee was presided over by Lord Northcliffe. A working unity was actually achieved, although at the expense of many weary months and years of bickering and duplication.[5] The Italians arrived at this same method of organization.

The most important difference between the American and the British plan was that the latter put foreign and domestic propaganda in the hands of co-ordinate officials. When the technicalities of the matter are allowed for, the British system clearly made no distinction between Northcliffe and Beaverbrook, for instance, who both had direct access to the Prime Minister and the War Cabinet. The British, in effect, laid equal emphasis upon the necessity for departmental autonomy in dealing with home, empire, neutral, allied, and enemy propaganda. The extraordinary diversity of foreign interests to which the British were appealing probably justified this procedure, because the problems which were presented were highly distinct.[6] The Americans came into the War, when it was neither their business to win the neutrals, nor to play one group against another. They had a very simple propaganda message to get across (American preparations; a Wilsonian Peace), and it could be vested in one executive without much danger.

It was the Germans who had a minimum of co-ordinated propaganda effort. Each Department went ahead in its own way, and the only formal co-operation was in the Press conference, which met two or three times a week. The War Ministry, the General Staff, the Navy Department, the District Military Authorities, the Colonial Office, the Post Office, the Interior Department, the Treasury Department, the Food Ministry, and eventually, the Foreign Office took part. The chairmanship was passed round in a rotating system, and the co-operating journalists chose a committee to speak for them.

The Military Authorities had to build their work from the ground up.[7] At the outbreak of the War there was but a single official who had contact with the Press. But they soon evolved an extensive Press service to report military operations, to edit the Field Press, to control the admission of home papers to the army, and to carry on propaganda against the enemy.

The Foreign Office was slow in clearing for action, but in October, 1914, when the check on the Marne had deferred the prospects for peace, a special *Zentralstelle für Auslandsdienst* was created. This was a very busy bureau and published an imposing array of propaganda material.

As the War developed, the conflict between military and civil authorities became more and more acute. The military men went into a paroxysm of rage when the peace resolution was moved by Erzberger in 1917, as they had when Bethmann-Hollweg held out the olive branch in 1916. The military authorities had no patience with palaver about peace; they wanted a victorious peace of dictation. Ludendorff granted an interview to the Berlin Press in which these views were put before the people. Instantly the Left and Centre took up the challenge, and assailed the military for trying to interfere in politics. The Chancellor, to avoid being caught between partisan fires, refused, as had his predecessor, to create a separate Minister of Propaganda. The military authorities had proposed this on three different occasions, for they had already begun to feel the effects of Allied propaganda. At last the G.H.Q. tried to reach the home public directly by establishing a special Press service called the *Deutsche Kriegsnachrichten*, which, in spite of the opposition of the large papers, prospered. At the direction of General Ludendorff an elaborate plan of patriotic stimulation was drawn up. It was designed to reach the Civilian and the fighting population.[8]

There were other tentative gestures toward the formation of a special propaganda agency to co-ordinate German efforts at home and abroad, but all of them failed. Private Citizens organized the Wagner Culture Committee, to spread Pro-German propaganda very early in the War, but its work lacked both prestige and deftness. Germany suffered from the overzealous efforts of private persons to fill the gaps left by Government omissions. Professor Lamprecht spoke with contempt of the educated man who "obtained the largest possible goose quill, and wrote to all his foreign friends, telling them that they did not realize what splendid fellows the Germans were, and not infrequently adding that, in many cases, their conduct required some excuses. . . . The consequences were gruesome." In 1916, some of the civilian authorities commended the movement to form a *Deutscher National-Ausschuss*, but this was still a private venture. Chancellor Hertling at last took some steps toward unified control in August, 1918, but his measures were both inadequate and tardy.

The French kept their propaganda in the hands of the established diplomatic, military and naval agencies. Occasionally they supplemented the work abroad by sending out a High Commissioner, who combined propaganda, economic and other functions, as did the temporary war missions of all the allied powers. The *Maison de la Presse* had its agents attached to the legations abroad.[9]

When Allies are fighting together, the problem of coordinating their propagandas and their policies arises. Inter-Allied co-operation in the last War was in a rudimentary stage at the time of the Armistice. When Lord Northcliffe became head of the British Enemy Propaganda Department in February, 1918, he called a preliminary conference on inter-Allied propaganda. One of the participating experts, Mr. Wickham Steed of *The Times*, writes that M. Henri Moysset, chief private secretary to the French Minister of Marine, spoke as a French representative, and insisted upon the imperative necessity for creating a "Thinking General Staff" to unify the effort exerted by the Allies in enemy and neutral countries. The Conference did actually appoint Professor Borghese (Italy), Mr. Steed and M. Moysset, with the expectation that they would co-operate in Paris, but jealousy of Moysset is said to have prevented the full development of the work.[10] The Allies conducted a formal conference in August, 1918, and their most successful common venture was a Permanent Inter-Allied Commission at the Italian G.H.Q.

Although the problem of organizing international propaganda campaigns was not satisfactorily solved in the late War, the experience of the Allies in certain other projects was complete enough to reveal sound principles of administration. Sir Arthur Salter, who digested his experience with the Inter-Allied Shipping Control with such skill, has generalized the conditions of continuing co-operation upon executive matters between independent governments.

Contact, and indeed regular contact, must be established between the appropriate permanent officials
of the several national administrations. It is important that these officials should (where possible) continue to exercise executive authority in their own departments and, where geographical reasons prevent
this, that they should, at least, be specialists, and
continue to exercise a decisive influence on them.
The officials must enjoy the confidence of the respec-
tive ministers, must keep in constant touch with
their policy, must, within a considerable range, be
able to influence their action, and they must have
an accurate knowledge of the limits of their own influence.[11]

He declares that they must work together in sufficient intimacy
to develop trust or knowledge of the limits within which they may
trust one another, and that they must endeavour to develop such
relations as will enable them, without disloyalty to their own governments, to discuss policy frankly in the earlier stages before it
has been formulated in their own countries. The formal authority
may best be supplied by the occasional meeting of the responsible
ministers. Formal meetings of international representatives ought
to be solely for the purpose of ratifying agreements already arrived
at informally. Even minor negotiation should never be in the nature of a bargain.

Salter argues that the arrangement which he suggests, is an
appropriate solution of the role of committees in administration.

Nothing is so ineffective as a committee which consists of persons, each of whom has no specialized
function and no personal executive authority, and
yet tries to direct executive action. But if a number
of persons, each of whom has a direct executive authority, which he continues to exercise in his own
special sphere, meet from time to time, in order to

dovetail their common measures and adjust them to a common plan, and then return to their departments to put into effect what they have agreed the committee is an effective instrument of co-operative action.

Assuming that the problem of co-ordinating inter-ally propagandas can be satisfactorily disposed of, our attention may revert to the problem of domestic organization. Once agreed that unity should be attained, the issue then arises as to whether the propaganda organization should seek to work through the existing diplomatic machinery abroad, or whether it should assemble separate staffs for that type of propaganda work. The late War seemed to show that special *ad hoc* agencies should be established abroad, even though the diplomatic staffs were often resentful of their new colleagues in the foreign field. Mrs. Vira B. Whitehouse, for instance, was sent to Switzerland by the Committee on Public Information. The Legation met her cordially, but, owing to the vagueness with which her instructions were defined, refused to give her the recognition and the facilities which were indispensable to her work. It was only after a special trip to Washington that a long and vexatious campaign of polite sabotage was surmounted.[12]

The diplomatic service is less likely to possess the type of personnel necessary to cope with a new and experimental service, such as propaganda, than an agency whose staff is explicitly recruited for the purpose. In some cases, too, the gum shoe tradition is detrimental to efficiency. The tactics of the American Committee on Public Information, which explained its purpose to the neutral government in whose territory it wished to operate, shocked many diplomats, who were trained in stealthiness.

What about the personnel of the propaganda service? The director of each major branch ought to be a man whose prestige equals that of the policy-determining officials. Now policy and propaganda should work together, hand and glove. General Ludendorff, whose astute observations on propaganda have won general recognition, has written that "Good propaganda must keep well

ahead of actual political events. It must act as a pace-maker to
policy and mould public opinion, without appearing to do so."[13]
The worst thing possible is for the propagandists and the diplomats to contradict one another openly. As a member of the House
of Commons declared in discussing the problem: "Nothing can be
more serious than a double voice in our Foreign Affairs."[14]

It is important to give the propagandist a place, not only in the
actual execution of policy, but in the formation. Policies are not
safely formulated without expert information on the state of that
opinion upon which they rely for success. Those who are occupied
with propaganda live under circumstances in which the daily bal-
ancing and weighing of delicate currents of public sentiment is
their job. Now the full import of estimates of the state of public
opinion cannot be realized unless they are urged by personalities
whose prestige is at least the equal of those who have the deciding
hand in matters of policy. It is not necessary that the heads of the
propaganda services should formally occupy ministerial or cabinet
posts, but they should have ministerial or cabinet influence, in fact.

This, I submit, is a legitimate inference from the role which
Lord Northcliffe played in Great Britain. When he took over the
Enemy Propaganda work, he quickly became aware of the crucial
importance of forcing a decision upon certain hitherto uncertain
and contradictory questions of policy. The British Government had
joined others in making contradictory promises to the Italians, and
to the South Slavs, and it was high time for the obscurity to be
dispelled. He demanded prompt action by the Cabinet, and was so
successful that the scruples of Downing Street and of Italy were
swept aside in time for a great propaganda offensive, to be launched
against the Austro-Hungarian troops, which had the effect of forcing the postponement of the Piave offensive.

The offensive was timed for April. 1918, and, according to
Wickham Steed and Sir Campbell Stuart it was postponed until the
end of June, because of the demoralizing inroads of Allied propaganda on the Southern Slav regiments.

In the United States it was of no particular importance that
Mr. Creel lacked prestige. The foreign policy of the country was

made by President Wilson, and it happened to have great propaganda value.

Is it desirable for the leaders of propaganda to be recruited from among the most powerful newspaper proprietors and editors? The selection of such a man is certain to arouse nasty insinuations in the legislature. After the announcement that a number of editors and proprietors had been appointed to posts in the British service, a member of the House rose to inquire:

> Is it the intention of the Government to "nobble" every editor in London? (The editors of the *Express*, *Times*, *Daily Mail*, *Evening Post*, *Chronicle* and certain other leading papers were involved.)

Mr. Austen Chamberlain put the criticism with less brevity and more wisdom.

> As long as you have the owner of a newspaper as a member of your Administration, you will be held responsible for what he writes in the newspapers. You would not allow a colleague, not the owner of a newspaper, to go down and make speeches contrary to the policy of His Majesty's Government, or to attack men who are serving His Majesty's Government. You cannot allow them, instead of making speeches, to write articles or to permit the articles to be written in their newspapers. My right hon. Friend and his Government will never stand clear in the estimation of the public, and will never have the authority which they ought to have, and which I desire them to have, until they make things quite clear, open and plain to all the world and sever this connection with the newspapers.[15]

The Prime Minister, Mr. Lloyd George, minimized the force of this objection by directing attention to the fact that:

the rule which applies to all company directors and
professional men joining the Government must be
applicable also to newspapermen, and as soon as the
two Ministers were appointed, they gave up all direction of their papers.[16]

To this, Mr. Chamberlain replied by denying that the analogy
of a private company is applicable to the Press.

If its independence is supposed to have been sacri-
ficed by the acceptance of Ministerial obligations,
then the Press loses its freedom, and with its freedom loses its authority.

He deplored certain unfortunate coincidences. After an attack
in the Press upon certain ministerial colleagues:

the Government finds it impossible, thereafter, to
retain in office the officials who are specially attacked, and the people who are specially associated
with those attacks are shortly thereafter found, in
this case, on their individual merits, and that alone,
to be indispensable to the Government in particular
offices.[17]

Mr. Lloyd George replied to these insinuations by saying that
he knew there would be a row about these appointments, and that
he was right, but that he had found that only newspapermen could
really do the job.

It is true that newspapermen are the most desirable, but it is not,
therefore, necessary to choose one of the biggest owners and editors. If a less conspicuous man is selected, he is, however, liable to
snubs, as a mere second-rater. England chose her Hearst to conduct propaganda against the enemy; the United States chose a man
of tremendous energy, but little reputation. Any proprietor who
has had sufficient strength to make his mark has undoubtedly

contracted enough animosities to impair his usefulness, and the same thing is true of a journalist or editor. The sticking point is the one to which Mr. Chamberlain referred, and the humbler journalist is free from objection on this count. It would, therefore, seem that the balance of the scale on this particular matter inclines toward the American practice.

There is no doubt about the superlative qualifications of newspapermen for propaganda work. The stars in the Propaganda firmament during the world war were mostly journalists, though there were a few literary men, like H.G. Wells, and widely travelled and alert historians, like Seton-Watson. And the journalists who delivered the goods were not, primarily, the editorial writers. They were men whose primary business was reporting or editing the news. Northcliffe was essentially a reporter, and Steed had spent long years in the foreign service of *The Times*.

Newspapermen win their daily bread by telling their tales in terse, vivid style. They know how to get over to the average man in the street, and to exploit his vocabulary, prejudices and enthusiasms. As Mr. Spencer Hughes; remarked in the House of Commons, they are not hampered by what Dr. Johnson has termed "needless scrupulosity." They have a feeling for words and moods, and they know that the public is not convinced by logic, but seduced by stories.

What not to do has been nowhere better illustrated than in Germany. The Prussian officer who had charge of the propaganda work for the General Staff was a most sincere and conscientious gentleman. He had, however, a singular unfitness for his job, as this story will show. An American newspaperman in Berlin had known him for some time. Shortly after the Allies had created a tremendous uproar about the execution of Nurse Cavell, the French executed two German nurses under substantially the same circumstances. Not a murmur in the German Press. The American saw the official shortly afterwards and asked—

> Why don't you do something to counteract the British propaganda in America?
> Why, what do you mean?

> Raise the devil about those nurses the French shot
>   the other day.
> What? Protest? The French had a perfect right to
>   shoot them!

Which, of course, was probably true, but utterly irrelevant to propaganda. A Prussian officer simply could not look at the situation with the naïve indignation of an untutored civilian. But it was civilians whose opinions were ultimately deciding.

Propaganda personnel ought to be recruited from among those who possess intimate knowledge of the group to which they are supposed to appeal. "Hansi," whose real name was Waitz, was an Alsace-Lorrainer, who had fled to France in the Summer of 1914, to escape punishment at the hands of the German authorities for his seditious propaganda. He organized the French propaganda against the Germans, and his beautiful and highly idiomatic German was buttressed by a complete knowledge of local allusions. He very properly lays it down that propaganda should be well written for whatever audience it is intended.

Bismarck's sense of the important led him to take infinite pains in matters of style. Busch, his propaganda secretary, tells about an article which he read over to Bismarck.

> It was to be dated from Paris, and published in the *Kölnische Zeitung*. He said, "Yes, you have correctly expressed my meaning. The composition is good, both as regards its reasoning and the facts which it contains. But no Frenchman thinks in such a logical and well-ordered fashion, yet the letter is understood to be written by a Frenchman. It must contain more gossip, and you must pass more lightly from point to point. A Parisian Liberal writes the letter and gives his opinion as to the position of his party toward the German question, expressing himself in the manner usual in statements of that kind."[18]

Within recent years there has been a development which may transform the personnel question in the future. Propaganda has become a profession. The modern world is busy developing a corps of men who do nothing but study the ways and means of changing minds or binding minds to their convictions. Propaganda, as remarked in the opening pages of this study, is developing its practitioners, its professors, its teachers and its theories. It is to be expected that governments will rely increasingly upon the professional propagandists for advice and aid.

Yet another question of propaganda organization is the problem of co-ordinating the efforts of central and local branches of the service. Ambassador Bernstorff complains of the inadequacy of the material sent to America by the German in Berlin,

> the Press-service (German) never succeeded in adapting itself to American requirements. The same may be said of most of the German propaganda which reached America in fairly large quantities since the third month of the War, partly in German and partly in not always irreproachable English. This, like the Press telegrams, showed a complete lack of understanding of American national psychology. The American character, I should like to repeat, is by no means so dry and calculating as the German picture of an American business man usually represents. The outstanding characteristic of the average American is rather a great, even though superficial, sentimentality. There is no news for which a way cannot be guaranteed through the whole country, if clothed in a sentimental form. Our enemies have exploited this circumstance with the greatest refinement, in the case of the German invasion of "poor little Belgium," the shooting of the "heroic nurse," Edith Cavell, and other incidents. Those who had charge of the Berlin propaganda, on the other hand, made very little of such occurrences on the enemy

side, *e.g.*, the violation of Greece, the bombing of
Corpus Christi procession in Karlsruhe, etc. One
thing that would have exerted a tremendous influence in America, if its publicity had been handled
with only average skill, was the suffering of our children, women and old people, as a result of the British hunger blockade—that they have made no attempt to bring to the notice of the world.[19]

He also complains that Berlin sent arguments instead of news.

Here was the opinion of the man on the spot. He felt that the
men at the centre were messing their job. His own anxiety to take
advantage of what he calls the "sentimentality" of the American mind,
led him to encourage a movement which was ultimately ruined
because the central authorities failed to support it. Bernstorff tells
the story thus:

Since the *Lusitania* catastrophe I had adopted the
principle, and put it into practice as far as possible,
of leaving the propaganda to our American friends,
who were in a position to get an earlier hearing than
we, and in any case understood the psychology of
the Americans better than the Imperial German
agents. Indeed, the words "German propagandist"
had already become a term of abuse in America . . .
a "Citizen's Committee for Food Shipments" was
formed, whose activities spread through the whole
country and were avowedly pro-German. A special
function of the committee of Dr. von Mach as executive chief was a month of propaganda throughout
the country with the object of obtaining the means
to supply the children of Germany with milk. The
English control of the post even led to the bold plan
of building a submarine, to run the milk through the
English blockade. The propaganda was very vigor-
ously attacked by the greater part of the American

Press, but pursued its course unafraid, collected money, submitted protests to the State Department against the attitude of the Entente, and so on.

Dr. von Mach succeeded in bringing the matter to the notice of the President, who actively interested himself in it, and promised to see that the milk should pass the English blockade and reach Germany in safety. Accordingly, the State Department instructed the American Embassy in Berlin to issue a statement. Meanwhile, the well-known American journalist, McClure, returned from a tour of investigation in Germany, where he had been supported in every way by the German Government Departments. He gave a very favourable account of the milk question, as of the feeding of infants in general, and this gave rise to the first disagreeable controversy. McClure took up an unyielding attitude. Unfortunately, however, the State Department then published an equally favourable report, which, coming from the American Embassy and published with the approval of the Foreign Office in Berlin, caused the complete collapse of Dr. von Mach. This incident made a most painful impression in America, and led to a series of bitter attacks on Dr. von Mach and the whole movement, which was thus exposed in a most unfortunate light. The favourable report on the milk question was drawn up by a Dr. E. A. Taylor, and definitely confirmed and, indeed, inspired by the German authorities.[20]

The Ambassador related this incident to discredit the central authorities, but perhaps greater responsibility rested on him for pursuing a policy which he had reason to know was distasteful to those authorities. And in this case the better reason seems to be on the side of Berlin, for they knew that to advertise a milk shortage would be to encourage the tenacious fighting spirit of the Allies and, in particular, to tighten the economic boycott of Germany. The man on the spot, Bernstorff, knew the value of a sentimental appeal, and he was right in this; but he was unwilling to bend his judgment to that of the central authorities and to refrain from encouraging a certain type of propaganda, which was likely to produce more harm than good. This incident illustrates the necessity for harmonious relations between the men at the centre and the men at the circumference, for Bernstorff was right in some particulars, and the central authorities were right in others. In most cases, Bernstorff was better advised than Berlin. Harmonious relations depend upon congenial personnel and can be but slightly affected by the mechanisms of organization.

While the discussion of propaganda organization had thus far dwelt upon problems of administration, there is no question of organization of more interest to the student of political science than the proper relation between legislative control and propaganda departments.

Propaganda is likely to be abused to promote personal and partisan ends, and the line of distinction between a private advantage which is incidental to a legitimate public advantage, and a private advantage which brings no overwhelming public advantage, is difficult to draw. A member of the British Parliament once called attention to a laudatory illustrated biography of the Prime Minister which was being circulated at public expense as part of British war propaganda.[21] Of course, it could be said that confidence in the Prime Minister was peculiarly necessary to war morale, and that such an expenditure was fitting and proper. It could also be said that the tone of the book was too full of adulation to free it from partisan suspicion.

Mr. Creel once put his foot in it by thanking God that the United States had been unprepared for war. To the Republicans this seemed to be the baldest possible attempt to whitewash the Democratic administration, and a fiery controversy broke out on the floor of Congress. Mr. Rainey came to the aid of the besieged head of the Committee on Public Information, by reminding the House that the Republicans had possessed power for sixteen consecutive years, right down to the two years before the European War, and if the Chairman had returned thanks for unpreparedness, he was returning thanks for the Republicans even more than for the Democrats.[22]

Sometimes it appears to be in the public interest for current facts to be suppressed, but this is liable to the gravest abuse, for it is also to the interest of those in power, to suppress facts, in order to avoid criticism. Legislative bodies look with a suspicious eye upon any evidence of partisan concealment. During a time when the American aviation programme was an object of uneasy attention, certain aeroplane photographs were released by the Committee on Public Information with sub-titles of this nature: "Though hundreds have already been shipped, our factories have reached quantity production, and thousands upon thousands will soon follow." It was obvious that, if news of this character was circulated among the American people, the public would look with impatience upon the opposition Senators who were condemning the Administration for the inadequacy of its aviation policy.[23] The Republicans in the Senate turned their heavy artillery on the Committee. The Committee claimed to have based its optimism upon authorized information from the aeroplane authorities. This appeared to be the truth, but there was no doubt that the report conveyed an exaggerated idea to the public.

In another case there was good *prima facie* evidence for suspecting that the Naval authorities had used the Committee to mislead the public. On the fourth of July, 1917, the public was congratulated upon the fact that our transports had arrived on the other side, although "twice attacked by German submarines." A correspondent of the Associated Press, who was reported to have been aboard the transports, sent back a story to the effect that the sea had been smooth, and the voyage uneventful. Even such administration organs as the *New York Times* joined in the demand for an explanation. The Republicans launched into a terrific tirade against the Committee, the Navy Department and the whole Administration. It eventually appeared that the transports had gone over in four divisions, and that two of them had encountered no trouble, but that two had encountered submarines.[24] Here was a case in which public sentiment was genuinely disturbed by an apparent fabrication, and Congress did right in ventilating its suspicions. But it did so in an insulting manner, which was well calculated to diminish public confidence in the integrity and competence of those responsible for conducting the War.

As Winston Churchill has agreed, the reasons "certainly had weight"[25] which moved the censorship to discourage or forbid the "writing up" of any general other than the Commander-in-Chief in France and Britain. But the unavoidable result was to entrench the Commander-in-Chief in public esteem when good reason existed for removing him. The general public in Britain banked upon Kitchener long after the better informed were aware of the shortcomings of "Lord K of Chaos." The French people relied upon Joffre long after the experts began to take his stolidity for stupidity and his equanimity for insensitivity. Legislatures and cabinets were highly taxed in inventing adroit means of kicking these leaders upstairs, and clearing the road for more capable chiefs. They had to reconcile the diverging claims of competence and public confidence.

Still another danger of abusing propaganda agencies lies in the possibility that public propaganda may be misused for commercial and class purposes. An attack upon the British Ministry of Information was made in Parliament by Mr. Leif Jones, who pointed to suspicious circumstances. First he gave the business connections of the most prominent men in the Ministry:

> Lord Beaverbrook . . . is a director of seven companies (was said to have withdrawn from active control). . . . Mr. Snagge is Secretary to the Ministry. He is a director of nine companies, and chiefly interested in rubber. The Director of Information in Scandinavia and Spain is Mr. Hambro, a member of the House, a banker, a railway director. . . . Take the Director of Propaganda for Switzerland—Mr. Guinness, who is director of nine companies. . . . Colonel Bryan, who assists in American propaganda, is

director of six companies, mainly interested in ships and ship-building. Colonel Galloway, Assistant Director of Hospitality, is a director of five or six companies. . . . Mr. Cunliffe Owen is a director of thirty-six companies. I understand they are all tentacles of a great tobacco trust, of which Mr. Cunliffe Owen is vice-chairman. This gentleman is placed in charge of propaganda throughout Asia and the Far East, including Japan.

He then proceeded to the point of his remarks:

I have a record of a very extraordinary film which is being performed now. . . . The title of the picture was "Once a Hun, always a Hun." It first of all depicts two German soldiers in a ruined town in France. They meet a woman with a baby in her arms, and strike her to the ground. The two German soldiers then gradually merge into two commercial travellers, and are seen in an English village after the war. One of the travellers enters a small village general store, and proceeds to show to the shopkeeper a pan. The shopkeeper at the beginning is somewhat impressed by what is offered him for sale, when his wife comes in and, turning the pan upside down, sees marked on it "Made in Germany." She then indulges in a good deal of scorn at the expense of the commercial traveller and calls in a policeman, who orders the German out of the shop. A final notice, flashed on the screen, was to the effect that there cannot possibly be any more trading with these people after the war, and under this statement were the words, "Ministry of Information." The question of the policy of trade after the war has got to be decided by this country, but I hope the Ministry of Information does not intend to decide it before we have an opportunity even of discussing the Government policy.[26]

The attack was much more than a bare insinuation that capitalistic interests had suborned national propaganda. It alleges that the Ministry of Information was committing the country in advance to a policy which the legislature had hot yet decided upon. The famous pronouncement by Lord Northcliffe at the end of the War had something of the same significance. Northcliffe was a member of a committee appointed by the British Cabinet to develop a formula of peace terms (war aims). He met with the representatives of the War Cabinet, the Admiralty, the War Office, the War Aims Committee, and the Official Press Bureau. The agreed formula was first given out by Lord Northcliffe in an address before the United States' officers in London, on October 22nd, 1918. On the 4th of November they were published in *The Times* under the title "From War to Peace," from whence they were reproduced around the world.

It is always possible that propaganda will prejudice the position of a minority group in the community. The Irish members of Parliament protested against the Ministry on account of some aspects of its American propaganda. Mr. Devlin declared,

> One of the books, which has been published in America, is called "The Oppressed English," written by Ian Hay. This is a book, paid for by the Ministry of Information. Although it has been sent all round America, it has not been allowed in this country. (It is) a tissue of falsehoods from beginning to end.[27]

Since propaganda agencies on a large scale were novelties of the last war in democratic countries, the legislative control of their expenditures was poorly organized at first. The funds for British propaganda were mostly taken from the general vote of supply for "His Majesty's Foreign and other Secret Services." The Creel Bureau was at first constituted by Executive Order and financed from the $100,000,000 appropriation granted to the President for the general promotion of the defence of the country. When the abuse of the Creel Bureau reached the peak of insinuation and distrust, Mr. Creel decided to force an investigation by the Appropriations Committee, by applying to Congress for a specific appropriation. After a hearing, which consumed three days, the Committee endorsed an appropriation for a million and a quarter dollars, and commended the past record of the bureau.[28] In the future it will probably be possible to provide for propaganda work by direct appropriation from the beginning.

The legislatures discussed the details of propaganda administration rather freely during the last War. Mr. T. P. O'Connor was anxious to remove the vexatious system of censorship, which had been introduced at the outbreak of the War, and which had aroused so much opposition from American newspapermen. In September of 1914 he declared,

> There is no public opinion in the world which ought to be so well informed with regard to the causes of the War, or the incidents of this War, or the principles of this War, as the opinion of the United States of America.[29]

Complaints were often made that the British propaganda was lagging behind the German propaganda in neutral countries.

Congress was far from reticent in criticizing the work of the Committee on Public Information. Senator Lodge uttered a solemn warning against German peace propaganda, and attacked a book entitled *Two Thousand Questions and Answers about the War*, which had been issued by the Committee with an Introduction by Mr. Creel. An officer of the National Security League had characterized it as a "masterpiece of German propaganda," and Mr. Lodge called to it the attention of the Senate. The defence given by Mr. Creel was that he had written the preface without reading the book, which he received from Mr. Albert Shaw, who in turn had come into the possession of the manuscript from an Englishman of undoubted integrity; that he had become uneasy about the document when his attention had been called to certain passages, and was revising it.[30]

On another occasion, Senator Poindexter, who had acted as something of an atrocity hound during the War, accused the Committee of defending the Germans because a statement had been issued under its authority denouncing the story of an American sergeant, who had been crucified by the Germans.[31] Senator Lenroot, of Wisconsin, defended the Administration, saying:

> there was a general inference drawn that that (crucifixion and similar atrocities) was a general practice. If it was not true, I think it is the duty of the War Department to deny it. The parents of these boys are suffering agonies enough now, without being led to believe that unspeakable outrages are being committed upon all of our American soldiers who may be captured.

The legislative proceedings are full of attacks upon the personnel of the propaganda services. The tenor of much of this criticism may be gathered by perusing these Congressional remarks upon Mr. Creel:

> Mr. Penrose (Senator from Pennsylvania). I do not see why we should permit men like Mr. Creel, for instance, whose scurrilous and defamatory utterances on the Constitution of the United States were read in this body the other day, to be holding an office and publishing a publicity chronicle, when he is smeared all over with treason.[32]

> Mr. Longworth (Representative from Ohio). Mr. Speaker, if I have any apologies to make to this House or anybody for the opinion that I enunciated about this man who, the day before yesterday,

insulted the patriotism of the American people, and to-day insults the American Congress, it is that my language was far too temperate (applause).[33]

Mr. Sherman (Senator from Illinois). Congress is stigmatized as a slum by a public officer created by an Executive Order, and paid by an appropriation made by the body he traduces. . . . After this, any servile deputy candle-snuffer is at liberty to revile us at pleasure. Any gangrened egotist afflicted with an ingrowing conceit may hereafter spurn Congress, and demand appropriations to feed him with the complacent assurance that precedent now justified everything.[34]

The immunities of Congress were used so recklessly that Mr. Creel was led to remark,

The heavens may fall, the earth may be consumed, but the right of a Congressman to lie and defame remains inviolate.[35]

Lord Northcliffe and the others in England came in for the severest censure, but Parliament conducted itself with more restraint and dignity than Congress.

It is abundantly clear from this review of the relations between legislatures and propaganda bureaux that there is bound to be ample opportunity for misunderstanding, criticism and suspicion. Unless the legislature is informed and critical, the propaganda branches may be perverted to partisan, personal and class ends; if the legislature is superfluously critical, the confidence of the public in its leaders may be destroyed, and morale impaired. It is humanly improbable that a satisfactory middle course can be steered, since this depends upon the voluntary restraint of the legislature. The only hope lies in confidential and informal relations between administrators and legislators, supplemented by an appeal to publicity when the legislator can justify such conduct to his own conscience. Personal explanations at the dinner table, the clubhouse, the lounge, or the street corner, are the lubricants of the great and complicated machinery of government.[36]

This completes our survey of the problem of organizing a war-time propaganda service to influence international attitudes. The succeeding chapters will outline the nature of the psychological appeals which appear to be necessary to accomplish the purpose of such a mechanism—the instigation of animosity toward the enemy, the preservation of friendship between allies and neutrals, and the demoralization of the enemy.

Notes

[1] *U.S. Cong. Rec.*, 65th Cong., 2nd Sess., p. 7915.

[2] 103 *H. C. Deb.*, 5s., col. 1410, 27 February, 1918.

[3] "Propaganda and the Father of It," *Cornhill Magazine*, N.S., v. 48: 233-241.

[4] 66 *H. C. Deb.*, 5s., col. 549, 9 September, 1914.

[5] The attitude of the Foreign Office clique toward the Beaverbrook ministry is reflected in the comments of the anonymous author of *The Pomp of Power*. He says that a group of experts on foreign affairs refused to work under the direction of Beaverbrook and migrated to the Foreign Office. Beaverbrook relied upon Canadians "whose experience of foreign affairs and whose knowledge of foreign languages was as limited as his own." Beaverbrook has told his own story in *Politicians and the Press*. Lord Bertie, British Ambassador to France, lamented that for two years (until 1917) the Foreign Office failed to establish a Press bureau in Paris. (*Diary*, 1914-18, II: 203.)

[6] This will appear especially in connection with a later point.

[7] Nicolai complains that the Reichstag failed to vote them enough money to develop a satisfactory Press section before the war, because "in peace times the Press was conceived as a partisan instrument." Nicolai, *Nachrichtendienst, Presse u. Volksstimmung*. p. 53.

[8] The memorandum of July 29, 1927, is printed in Nicolai, p. 119 ff.

[9] A committee to conduct artistic propaganda abroad was formed in the spring of 1918 under the direction of the Minister for Education and Fine Arts. Besides the *Maison de la Presse* there were unofficial members from organizations like the *Chambre syndicale de la haute couture*. *Journal Officiel*, 8th March, 1918.

[10] Steed, *Through Thirty Years*, II: 196.

[11] J. A. Salter, *Inter-Allied Shipping Control*, p. 257.

[12] *A Year as a Government Agent* tells the story.

[13] See *Meine Kriegserinnerungen*, pp. 284-313.

[14] 109 *H. C. Deb.*, 5s., col. 987.

[15] 103 *H. C. Deb.*, 5s., col. 657.

[16] 104 *H. C. Deb.*, 5s., col. 40.

[17] 104 *H. C. Deb.*, 5s., col. 76.

[18] Busch, *Bismarck*, I : 8.

[19] *My Three Years in America*, p. 53.

[20] Bernstorff, p. 259.

[21] 109 *H. C. Deb.*, 5s., col. 978.

[22] *U.S. Cong. Rec.*, 65th Cong., 2nd Sess., p. 4859.

[23] *U.S. Cong. Rec.*, 65th Cong., 2nd Sess., pp. 4254 ff.

[24] U.S. Cong. Rec., 65th cong., 1st Sess., pp. 4811 ff.

[25] Winston Churchill, The World Crises, 1916-18, I;

[26] 109 *H. C. Deb.*, 5s., cols. 95 ff.

[27] 109 *H. C. Deb.*, 5s., col. 1029.

[28] *H. Doc.*, No. 1168, 65th Cong., 2nd Sess.; *U.S. Cong. Rec.*, 65th Cong., 2nd Sess., pp. 7910 ff.

[29] 66 *H. C. Deb.*, 5s., col. 759.

[30] *U.S. Cong. Rec.*, 65th Cong., 2nd Sess., pp. 1037 ff.

[31] Same, pp. 9056 ff.

[32] *U.S. Cong. Rec.*, 65th Cong., 2nd Sess., p. 4827.

[33] Same, p. 4974.

[34] Same, p. 8990.

[35] Creel, *How We Advertised America*, p. 52.

[36] The problem of arriving at a financial estimate of what may be accomplished by propaganda is broached in a succeeding chapter.

WAR GUILT AND WAR AIMS

So great are the psychological resistances to war in modern nations that every war must appear to be a war of defence against a menacing, murderous aggressor. There must be no ambiguity about whom the public is to hate. The war must not be due to a world system of conducting international affairs, nor to the stupidity or malevolence of all governing classes, but to the rapacity of the enemy. Guilt and guilelessness must be assessed geographically, and all the guilt must be on the other side of the frontier. If the propagandist is to mobilize the hate of the people, he must see to it that everything is circulated which establishes the sole responsibility of the enemy. Variations from this theme may be permitted under certain contingencies which we shall undertake to specify, but it must continue to be the leading *motif*.

The governments of Western Europe can never be perfectly certain that a class-conscious proletariat within the borders of their authority will rally to the clarion of war. Before 1914 the growth of the Social Democrats in Germany, the vogue of anti-patriotism in France, and the rising star of the labourers in England, filled the governing classes with foreboding. It was freely predicted that mobilization could be paralysed by a general strike, and that social revolution might raise its ominous head.

To the uncertainties of proletarian sentiment must be added the vagaries of conciliatory opinion. When the crisis of 1914 arose in Great Britain, it was at once evident that powerful elements in the Cabinet, the Liberal Party, the literary and even the financial world were opposed to intervention to aid France. The columns of the *Daily News*, a Left Wing Liberal organ, the *Manchester Guardian*, another Liberal paper, and the *Labour Leader* were flooded with letters, editorials and manifestos of protest against the idea of British participation in the impending struggle on the continent.

Let us remember, admonished the *Daily News* on the 29th day of July,

> that the most effective work for peace that we can do is to make it clear that not a British life shall be sacrificed for the sake of Russian hegemony of the Slav world.

On the following day it wrote that

> the free peoples of France, England and Italy should refuse to be drawn into the circle of this dynastic struggle.

On the first of August, the *News* published a bitter protest against the policy of intervention, under the well-known initials, "A.G.G." The title was "Why we must not fight."

> For years under the industrious propaganda of Lord Northcliffe, Mr. Strachey, Mr. Maxse, and the militarists, this country has been preached into an anti-German frame of mind that takes no account of the facts. Where in the wide world do our interests clash with Germany? Nowhere. With Russia we have potential conflicts over the whole of South-Eastern Europe and Southern Asia.

The Bishop of London, J. Ramsay MacDonald, Keir Hardie, Thomas Hardy, J. J. Thomson, Gilbert Murray, and scores of lesser celebrities protested against British aid to France and Russia on many different grounds. Most of these men were not proletarian internationalists, and they found reasons to object to war on grounds of the national interests of England. Most of them implied that war might, under some circumstances, be legitimate, but in the hour of decision they shrank from believing that the hour had come. Now, it is hard to conceive of an international complication in which divergent interpretations of national interest, nurtured by aversion to war and ruthlessness, will not precipitate dissent and controversy. The conciliatory frame of mind is prone to temporize and find good reason for delay.

Certain business and banking interests, when pulled up short by the prospect of imminent war, try to put on the brakes. That such international bankers as the Speyers and the Bonns were restraining influences during the first and second Moroccan crises is generally known. A less successful instance of such pressure upon those who wield political power is revealed by Wickham Steed, of the London *Times*. In the midst of the crisis in 1914 the financial editor of that paper, Mr. Hugh Chisholm, was urgently invited to call upon the head of one of the largest financial houses in the City. The financier told him flatly that the pro-war editorials in *The Times* must cease. They were hounding the country into war. The City of London was on the verge of a disaster, such as the world had never seen. Strict neutrality was the only course for England to adopt. He produced a message which he had just written to the head of the Paris house of his family, in which the alarming statement was made that the writer had only a billion pounds in the Bank of England and £800,000 in the Union of London and the Smith's Bank with which to meet engagements, and that the margin about obligations was so slight that the Paris house must refrain from drawing cheques or bills upon him. *The Times*, it may be added, did not succumb to this pressure, although certain members of the Cabinet were strongly moved by it.[1]

Every resource must be exploited if such inconvenient currents are to be turned aside. The identification of a particular foreign nation as the enemy may be established by three lines of inference. It invariably mobilizes first, in the days of crisis (either openly or secretly), and commits acts of war, and by doing so, reveals a criminal anxiety to press matters to a finish. More than that, it invariably incriminates itself by endeavouring to maneuver our government into the position of an aggressor during the feverish negotiations preceding the final break. Behind all this, there invariably stands a record of lawlessness, violence and malice, which offers unassailable proof of a deliberate intent to maim or destroy us.

A typical bill of indictment is the one drawn up by *Le Petit Journal*, one of the "Big Five" of the Paris Press, on the 3rd of August. It gave its version of the war under the heading, "Machiavellian Duplicity." Germany secretly connived at the formulation of an unacceptable ultimatum to Serbia. She perfidiously protested her desire for peace. She tried to divide the Allies by urging France to apply the pressure to Russia which she refused to apply to Austria. She tried to maneuver France into the position of an aggressor in the eyes of England, by asking France to denounce the Alliance with Russia, or to declare her willingness to fight with Russia. Germany opened hostilities against France and violated French territory before she broke off diplomatic relations. She violated the neutrality of Belgium in the face of a solemn promise to protect it. In so doing, she was acting in complete harmony with her historical traditions of ruthless and barbarous dealing. Frederick the Great and the robbery of Maria Theresa are earnests of this.

These indictments come with peculiar weight from historians and from other men who are credited in the public mind with the single-minded pursuit of truth. German scholarship leaped to the colours in the last War in the famous and unforgettable manifesto, signed by ninety-three of her most illustrious intellectuals. Attached to the document were such names as Ehrlich, Behring, Röntgen, Ostwald, Harnack, Schmoller, Brentano, Nernst, Hauptmann, Sudermann, Eucken, Wundt, Eduard Meyer, Lamprecht, Wilamowitz, Humperdinck, Reinhardt and Liebermann. Serious historians and journalists combined to elucidate the responsibility of Germany's enemies in such co-operative ventures as *Zum geschichtlichen Verständnis des grossen Krieges* by A. O. Meyer, Graf Ernst Reventlow, R. Nebersberger, C. H. Becker, G. Küntzel and F. Meinecke (2 Aufl., Berlin, 1916). The forward policy of Russia in Europe, since her humiliation in the East at the hands of Japan, the lust for revenge in France, and the jealousy of Germany's expansion by England were the cardinal points in interpreting the War. The immediate diplomacy of the conflict showed that Russia, secretly encouraged by France, had seized upon the Serbian complication to provoke a general war. Russia had mobilized first, and had actually invaded German territory, as, indeed, had the French, before the severance of diplomatic relations. The envious English, ostensibly neutral, but bound by secret understandings, had grasped their opportunity to crush the competitor, whose naval and commercial supremacy must be forestalled at all costs of morality and decency.

The crisis burst on France and Belgium with such paralysing suddenness and such devastating consequences, that there was little need for elaborate rationalizations about the instigator of the War. The Germans had to explain the war in the West, because they were in foreign territory, and, therefore, *prima facie* the aggressor. It was in Britain, with its territory intact and the issue of war or peace undetermined for many agonizing hours after the die was cast on the continent, where discussion and rationalization played an influential part. Masterly appeals to the national interest, after the style of *The Times* on 31st July, were necessary to carry conviction to the more articulate elements of the community that Germany should be treated as an immediate and overwhelming menace. It argued:

> A German advance through Belgium to the north of France might enable Germany to acquire possession of Antwerp, Flushing, and even of Dunkirk and Calais, which might then become German naval bases against England. That is a contingency which no Englishman can look upon with indifference. But if it is merely a contingency, why should England not wait until it is realized before acting or preparing to act? Because in these days of swift decision and swifter action, it would be too late for England to

act with any degree of success after France had been defeated in the North. . . . Even should the German navy remain inactive, the occupation of Belgium and Northern France by German troops would strike a crushing blow at British security. We should then be obliged alone and without Allies to bear the burden of keeping up a Fleet superior to that of Germany and of an army proportionately strong. This burden would be ruinous.

In the United States, where the issue of war or peace hung in the balance longer than in Great Britain, the disagreement over which group of belligerent powers was the enemy drew forth an unparalleled mass of rationalizations, suitable for circulation by the protagonists of either set. The historians and the other seekers of the truth were no more reticent than their German colleagues in putting the blame on the enemy for the calamity of war, once war came. The curious fact that in such emergencies the truth seekers find different truths, and that the differences are territorially segregated according to national boundaries, is once more exemplified in the Oxford War pamphlets, the Princeton symposium, or the Chicago war series, when they are placed side by side with the German literature alluded to above. The facility with which sincere and dextrous hands may shape cases on either side of a controversy, leaves no doubt that, in the future, the propagandist may count upon a battalion of honest professors to rewrite history, to serve the exigencies of the moment, and to provide the material for him to scatter thither and yon.

There are, no doubt, profound psychological dispositions, which facilitate the work of the propagandist in fastening war guilt upon the technical enemy. Just what these tendencies are is a matter of obscurity and dispute, but perhaps the most ingenious explanation is the one put forward by Baschwitz, who describes the mind of the public as in conflict between the disagreeable fact of war and the wish to believe that the good is triumphant in the universe. It must, therefore, be that one's own nation is vindicating

the right against the wrong.[2] Speculations of this sort are hazard-
ous in the extreme, and the propagandist is content to accept the
aid of his anonymous allies, while he busily multiplies the evidence
of the responsibility of the enemy. He instigates or welcomes such
a windfall as accrued to the cause of the Entente in the last War,
when an eloquent volume, *J'accuse* (Lausanne, 1915), came from
the pen of Richard Grelling, a native of Switzerland and close student of Germany. He bestirs himself to counter-attack against such
telling thrusts, as did the Germans who brought Grelling's son,
Kurt, to publish *Anti-J'accuse* at Zurich, in 1916. He scans the
horizon for new material as the War evolves, as did the Germans
when they scrutinized the captured Belgium archives for material,
which might incriminate the Entente, and broadcasted everything
which seemed to do so.

Now the task of the propagandist is just begun, when he fas-
tens the guilt of willing the War upon an opposing nation. No
sooner is the enemy located than the nation discharges its energies, churned in the crucible of hours and days of suspense, in
instantaneous movements of defence and counterattack. In the very
act of delivering the blow the nation calls for unity and victory. It
is the business of the propagandist to amplify and repeat the call.

As early as the 29th of July, 1914, the London *Times* called upon
all parties to "Close Ranks." The Kaiser united his people behind
him, when he declared that he knew no party more. The Fascio
came in Italy and the *"Union sacrée"* was proclaimed in the French
Parliament. The sensational appeal of Gustave Hervé to the ranks
of Labour was broadcasted far and wide. Hervé was a notorious
sans-patrie who had belittled patriotism as an implement of capitalistic exploitation. On the very brink of the War he changed the
name of his paper, *La Guerre Sociale*, into *La Victoire* and pleaded
with all the ardour of his fervent spirit for unity:

> Amis socialistes, amis syndicalistes, amis anar-
> chistes, qui n'êtes pas seulement l'avant-garde
> idéaliste de l'humanité; mais qui êtes encore le nerf

et la conscience de l'armée française, la patrie est
en danger!
    La patrie de la Révolution est en danger![3]

The call of the Empire—"Your King and Country calls you"—
buried the hatchet in Ireland and brought recruits from all over
the British dominions. The work of the Overseas League and the
Victoria League in strengthening the ties of friendship and affection was vindicated. In order to illustrate the unity of the Empire,
a number of profusely illustrated volumes were put out, showing
the history of British beneficence and the degree of Empire co-
operation at the front. There is *India and the War*, for example,
edited with an introduction by Lord Sydenham (1915), which glo-
rifies British rule in India, and has page after page of coloured pictures, showing Indian regiments in native uniforms.

The call to unity is essentially a call to history, and the memory
of a common past has powerful sentimental value. *La Libre Pa-
role* for the second of August, 1914, thus admonished its readers:

> Haut les coeurs! La France de Jeanne d'Arc, de Louis
> XIV et de Napoléon, la France de Bouvines, de
> Valmy, de Jéna, et de Montmirails n'a rien perdu de
> ses antiques vertus.

None of the sentiments which are deeply imbedded in the social tradition can afford to be neglected in justifying belligerent
idealism through murder and hate. To the historical may be usually added the religious vocabulary. Never have these chords been
strummed with greater dramatic sense than by Kaiser William II.,
as he looked over the surging throng in the Lustgarten on that
epochal July night and said:

> A fateful hour has fallen for Germany.
>   Envious peoples everywhere are compelling us
> to our just defence.

The sword has been forced into our hands. I hope that if my efforts at the last hour do not succeed in bringing our opponents to see eye to eye with us and in maintaining peace, we shall with God's help so wield the sword that we shall return it to the sheath again with honour.

War would demand of us enormous sacrifices of property and life, but we should show our enemies what it means to provoke Germany.

And now I commend you to God. Go to church and kneel before God and pray for his help and for our gallant army.

Even such exuberance of sentiment as the Credo for France, prepared by M. Henri Lavedan, has its place:

I believe in the courage of our soldiers and in the skill and devotion of our leaders. I believe in the power of right, and in the crusade of civilization, in France, the eternal, the imperishable, the essential. I believe in the reward of suffering and the worth of hope. I believe in confidence, in quiet thought, in the humble daily round, in discipline, in charity militant. I believe in the blood of wounds and the water of benediction; in the blaze of artillery and the flame of the votive candle; in the beads of the rosary. I believe in the hallowed vows of the old, and in the potent innocence of children. I believe in women's prayers, in the sleepless heroism of the wife, in the calm piety of the mother, in the purity of our cause, in, the stainless glory of our flag. I believe in our great past, in our great present, and in our greater future. I believe in our countrymen, living and dead. I believe in the hands clenched for battle, and in the hands clasped for prayer. I believe in ourselves, I believe in God. I believe, I believe.[4]

This sort of verbal delirium is capable of very remarkable things, as when Albert de Mun, the venerable Catholic leader, solemnly implored God to "aid the sons of Clovis," alluding to one of the barbarous teutonic chieftains of early French history.[5] Graceful phrasemongers like Maurice Barres, who believed the spirit of France to be a "grave enthusiasm, a disciplined exaltation," can be trusted to furnish volatile words acceptable to less religious minds.

For the preponderating majority in any community the business of beating the enemy in the name of security and peace suffices. This is the great war aim, and in single-hearted devotion to its achievement they find that "peacefulness of being at war," of which Principal Jacks once wrote.[6] In 1915, he glanced back over the first twelve months of the Great War, and observed that "the life of Great Britain has been acquiring a unitary aim of purpose. The aim itself is warlike; but it has been attended with some increase of mental peace." He cast a jaundiced eye upon the pre-war world and wrote, "Regarded from the moral point of view, the scene was one of indescribable confusion. It was, in fact, a moral chaos. Our 'inner state,' in consequence, was marked by profound unrest." People were once uncertain of life, but now they had found a mission. The propagandist, indeed, can always count upon the state of mind which is here so gracefully expressed. Men with uncongenial spouses, wives with uncongenial husbands, youths with suppressed ambition, elderly men with their boredoms and faint yearnings for adventure, childless women and some wifeless men, the discredited ones who pine for a fresh deal in the game of life; all, and many more, find peace from mental fight in the intoxication of life in one historical hour and for one historic goal.

This simple cry for unity and victory (with accompanying peace) is not enough. What form shall the victory take? There are inquiring minds who push behind the formula of victory and seek to prescribe what shall be meant thereby. Indeed the whole function of war aims is to arouse ambition and to fortify the resolution of the community to overcome every resistance to fulfilment. The enemy must be made to appear as more than a menace to the social heritage; the enemy is an obstacle to the realization of new national

values. For the diplomatically-minded the war may become a war
to expand the national influence in terms of lands and concessions
and ports. This section of opinion in Germany gorged itself upon
visions of a humiliated Britain, shorn of her fleet, and upon dreams
of a partitioned France and Russia. In Britain the most popular
war aim among these circles was the scrapping of the German Navy.
For the French Victory meant the restoration of Alsace and
Lorraine, and the partition of Germany.

But the propagandist must never permit himself to forget that
in the complex communities of our time there are minds who find
no peace in war. Graham Wallas testified not for himself alone,
when he commented on Professor Jacks' article and said, "I should
choose the unrest of thought because I desire that the war should
come to an end the instant its continuance ceases to be the less of
two monstrous evils, and because I believe that our national policy
should, even during the fighting, be guided not only by the will to
conquer, but also by the will to make possible a lasting peace."

Here is the mind for which war is a loathsome abomination,
and which steadfastly refuses to believe that the defeat of a particular enemy is enough to make it worth getting on with. The
primitive man, overtaken by catastrophe, hunts high and low for a
scapegoat and a messiah. The scapegoat is the person who got him
into the mess and the messiah is the person who will get him out.
History is the story of the struggle of devils and deliverers. This
primitive pattern of thought leads to the interpretation of war as
the struggle between a good and a bad collective person. Cleave to
the good and punish the bad. Such a formulation is by no means
acceptable to the sophisticated few, who have come to believe that
persons (individual or "collective") act as they do, because of the
tenacious grip of circumstances. If things have gone badly in the
past, the explanation is to be found in impersonal forces. If it is
hoped to produce better behaviour in the future, some fundamental forces must be adjusted. It is no good wreaking vengeance for
the past; it is only profitable to take precautions for the future and
to modify the conditions which have played havoc with the past.

The propagandist who deals with this new pattern of thought must be subtler than when he copes with the punitive pattern of mind. If the adherents of the former are to join in condemning the enemy, it must be because they see in him the most powerful obstruction in the path toward the realization of new world conditions. If their allegiance is to be won for the war, they must be furnished with war aims of a highly rationalized and idealistic type.

Propaganda of this sort played a decisive role in the late struggle for world supremacy, and the reasons are evident. If we examine the currents of public opinion in England during the weeks immediately preceding the crisis of 1914, we cannot fail to remark the numerous signs of specifically anti-war agitation. In the London *Daily News* for the 15th of July an editorial was printed under the title, the "Octopus of Militarism," which declared the business of the armament makers to be

> cosmopolitan in its operations and soulless in its motives. It works upon the fears and hates of ignorant people, uses the Press as the instrument of its purposes, and makes tools of the diplomats and statesmen, many of whom are financially interested in its success.

A few days later it addressed itself to the subject again, asking

> Why has the one (the duel) been abolished, and the other (war) left? There is only one answer—that there is money in armaments and no money to speak of in duelling.

During the same weeks the new book by H. N. Brailsford, called *The War of Steel and Gold*, was running the gamut of the reviews. Polemic had not yet subsided over Norman Angell's thesis in *The Great Illusion*.[7] The quiet influence of John A. Hobson and of many other publicists in Liberal and Labour ranks helped to drive home

the economic interpretation of war. Their writing was less tinc-
tured by doctrinaire formulas than the corresponding work on the
continent.

If anything, the socialists of France and Germany were more
vociferous than the English in denouncing war and war-makers.
But when the crucial moment came, the evidence of the culpabil-
ity of the enemy was so overwhelming, that they joined the War.
This decision split the Social Democrats in Germany, and left a
discontented fraction in France, and as the War wore on, the dis-
comforts of combat favoured the recovery of the old uncompro-
mising attitude. The Socialist and Democratic papers in Germany
became thorns in the side of the Imperial Government. A similar
evolution went forward in France. Such Liberal elements as those
associated with the personalities of Leon Bourgeois and
Estournelles de Constant were allied to the workers in their very
keen regret at the turn of affairs, and after the first shock of battle
wore away, a certain recovery set in, much as it had in Germany.

While concessions were actually made to this type of sentiment
in France and Germany, it was in England and in America that the
most notice was taken of it. In both countries there was a period of
hesitation before battle. H. G. Wells may be taken as an example
of the pacifistically inclined Liberal, more gracefully articulate than
most, whose support of the War came at the cost of inner struggle,
and whose enthusiastic aid in a prolonged contest depended upon
an elaborately rationalized cluster of war aims. Writing in the London *Daily Chronicle* for August 20th, 1914, he said:

> A war that will merely beat Germany a little and re-
> store the hateful tension of the last forty years is not
> worth waging. As an end to all our efforts it will be
> almost an intolerable defeat. Yet unless a body of
> definite ideas is formed and promulgated now things
> may happen so.

Wells, of course, saw in "German militarism" one of the most
colossal obstacles to the achievement of a better world order. His

attitude of mind is precisely the one to be striven for by the inventor of war aims; set up an ideal which will arouse the enthusiasm of those elements in the nation whose support is desired, and make it clear to them that the chief immediate stumbling block is the military enemy. This permits the scrupulous to kill with a clean conscience; or, at least, to admonish the younger to do so.

When the Bolsheviki published the diplomatic correspondence winch they found in the archives of the Tsar's government after the second revolution, a most embarrassing situation confronted the Allied Statesmen. For the Bolsheviki revealed for the first time to the world that the Allied governments had carved up large blocks of the world and raffled them off to one another. This raised some very disconcerting questions for those who had been talking about this War as different from every other war, since it was a war to end war and to make the world safe for democracy. By treaties signed in 1915, and subsequently, the possessions of the enemy powers were allotted to their future owners, without so much as a pretence at plebiscite or international control. In spite of the efforts of the Allied governments to suppress the knowledge of these incriminating documents in Great Britain, word soon reached the British labour leaders, and they bestirred themselves to force a show-down from the government. Mr. Lloyd George made a sensational speech on the fifth of January, 1918, in which he came out four-square for a peace acceptable to the conciliatory elements of the public. The secret history of this speech was not generally known until the publication of Woodrow Wilson's papers after the War. Among them is published a secret cablegram from Balfour, British Minister for Foreign Affairs, to the American State Department. Here is the dispatch:

> Following for information of the President, private and secret:—
> Negotiations have been going on for some time between the Prime Minister and the Trade Unions. The main point was the desire of the Government to be released from certain pledges which were made

to the Labour leaders earlier in the War. This release is absolutely indispensable from the military point of view for the development of man power on the Western Front. Finally the negotiations arrived at a point at which their successful issue depended mainly on the immediate publication by the British Government of a statement setting forth their war aims. This statement has now been made by the Prime Minister. It is the result of consultations with the Labour leaders as well as the leaders of the Parliamentary opposition.

Under these circumstances there was no time to consult the Allies as to the terms of the statement agreed upon by the Prime Minister and the above-mentioned persons. It will be found on examination to be in accordance with the declarations hitherto made by the President on this subject.

Should the President himself make a statement of his own views which in view of the appeal made to the peoples of the world by the Bolsheviki might appear a desirable course, the Prime Minister is confident that such a statement would also be in general accordance with the lines of the President's previous speeches, which in England as well as in other countries have been so warmly received by public opinion. Such a further statement would naturally receive equally warm welcome.[8]

A point to be remembered by the working propagandist is that Liberal and middle-class people are likely to give their approval to war aims of a political or juristic character. The Labour ideology is more or less coloured by philosophies of economic determination which wound the property sentiment of the possessing classes. If the problem of reconstructing the world is to be shorn of an apparent class bias, it must be conceived as a problem of a politico-juristic nature, for talk about world legislatures and courts tends to ingratiate itself where proposals for the administration of raw materials by world action, and for the use of the world taxing power to level up existing inequalities of opportunity, are suspect. Phrases like "World Organization," "The United States of the Earth,"[9] "The Confederation of the World,"[10] "A World Union of Free Peoples," or "A League of Nations," slide trippingly from the tongue.

A war to vindicate international law thus has the sanction of bourgeois morality about it and avoids anything which tinges of a class issue. In the last War this idea figured heavily. Those who were arguing for British participation in the War, on grounds of national self-interest (vide *The Times*) chucked this article of faith out of the window, and transformed the War into a holy crusade for the Law of Nations when the news came that the Germans were marching into Belgium. The French organized a Committee for the Defence of International Law, headed by M. Louis Renault, of the Institute. The Germans were staggered by this outburst of affection for international law in the world, but soon found it possible to file a brief for the defendant. The cross-bill alleged that Belgium had not really been neutral, for the papers captured in her archives had revealed secret military conversations with the French and the British. The British, moreover, were reckless of the law of contraband and were invading the rights of neutrals on the high seas. The Germans, therefore, discovered that they were really fighting for the freedom of the seas and the rights of small nations to trade, as they saw fit, without being subject to the bullying tactics of the British fleet. The Allies had already declared a war for the liberation of oppressed peoples, by which they understood at first no more than Belgium and Alsace and Lorraine. Later, the implications of this phrase were extended to cover the nationalities in the Austro-Hungarian Empire and the Poles in Germany. The Germans replied by saying that they, too, were fighting to liberate the oppressed, and, by this, they meant Ireland, Egypt and India.

A propagandist must always be alert to capture the holy phrase which crystallizes public aspiration about it, and under no circumstances permit the enemy to enjoy its exclusive use and wont. There are some holy phrases which have subversive connotations, unless they are promptly interpreted in a broad sense. When the members of the Union of Democratic Control in Great Britain began to say that they wanted the War to end secret diplomacy and to democratize foreign policy, they were talking about conditions in England as much as about conditions elsewhere. But the phrase was caught up by astute men, and turned into a criticism of the enemy.[11] It is the business of idealistic war aims to be invidious at the expense of the enemy.

Should there be a next general war, war aims of an idealistic character will probably be just as important as they were in the last one. International organizations are still so weak that at least one other war could be fought on the pretext of strengthening them. Should the existing League stigmatize any group of nations, there is no question that this group would be the target of a very dangerous idealistic propaganda. It should have little trouble, however, in explaining to the satisfaction of its own people, at least, that it is fighting for a more elevated conception of public right than its enemies.

So much for the war aims intended to appease the scruples of a Liberal conscience. Another class of war aims of a general character, can reach a wider constituency. The collective egotism, or ethnocentrism, of a nation, makes it possible to interpret the war as a struggle for the protection and propagation of its own high type of civilization. When a nation is engaged in battle with a people whose technological equipment is less destructive than its own, this form of self-flattery is obviously founded upon clear differences. The "whiteman's burden" has been carried lightly on the shoulders of the British in India and Africa, and of the Americans in Cuba and the Philippines. But at first sight it would appear paradoxical that a war between nations of Western Europe should also assume the form of a war to save civilization. Their similarities are so much more fundamental than their differences that a visitor from another planet would undoubtedly bracket them together.

The explanation is to be found in the rise of literacy. Literacy and elementary instruction have opened the cultural heritages of the nation to a larger portion of the community than ever before. It was the "Yellow Press," which popularized the idea in every country, but it was the wise men who used their acumen to prove it. On the 8th of August, 1914, the London *Evening Standard* shouted "Civilization at Issue," and the theme reverberated ever after. "Guerre contre les barbares," was simultaneously declared in France, while in Germany, the defence and nurture of *Kultur* became a duty and privilege of all good Germans. The consensus of German opinion is set out in a swollen flood of print, from which the following worthy specimens may be culled:

> Karl Lamprecht, *Krieg und Kultur* (Leipzig, 1914).
> Otto von Gierke, *Krieg und Kultur* (Berlin, 1914).
> Eugen Kühnemann, *Vom Weltreich des deutschen Geistes* (München, 1914).
> Oskar Fleischer, *Vom Kriege gegen die deutsche Kultur* (Frankfurt, 1915).
> Ernst Troeltsch, *Der Kulturkrieg* (Berlin, 1915).

In this list appear, among lesser luminaries, the foremost jurist and two of the most brilliant historians of the world. They were all convinced that the traditional Germany of philosophers and poets (*Denker und Dichter*) had of late added unto it, the practical gifts of political sagacity, exemplary fecundity, unremitting industry and monumental research, all of which compared more favourably with the atheism, sterility and giddiness of the decadent Latins, not to mention those sordid sportive, dawdling British. A brilliant example of this sort of thing is the volume called *Händler und Helden*, by Werner Sombart, the distinguished authority on modern capitalism. The title of the book explains its animus: Traders and Heroes. The former are the British and the latter are the Germans. He advances the thesis that every war may be analysed into a war of beliefs. The present War is a struggle between the sordid British and the self-sacrificing, loyal, courageous and obedient Germans. The Englishman is incredibly narrow, utterly incapable of rising above the "realities" of the moment, as a glance at their philosophers from Bacon to Spencer will prove. To the trader life is but a series of bargains, and even science is commercialized. The whole empire is a great trading enterprise and the empire's wars are wars of pecuniary calculation. The Germans will never be conquered by this damning taint of commercialism, and their spirit will stamp it from the world. The war is a war of German Kultur, which must not be denied and cannot be denied by the trader.

The war can likewise be a war of race. Not only did the Germans of certain strata declare a war of Kultur, but they declared a war of race, and in this they were joined by certain elements elsewhere. The elements of the extreme right in France cherished the myth of a pure Gallic race, and *La Croix*, in its issue for August 15th, 1914, found that the heroic exertions of war are the

> ancient élan of the Gauls, the Romans and the French resurging within us. The Germans must be purged from the left bank of the Rhine. These infamous hordes must be thrust back within their own frontiers. The Gauls of France and Belgium must repulse the invader with a decisive blow, once and for all. The race war appears.

Urbain Gohler published *La race a parlé* at Paris in 1915.

While war aims of this species are certain of a general vogue, they need re-enforcements of a more tangible and intimate kind. The nation as a whole, is divisible into an almost infinite number of constituent groups, which are in possession of special aspirations of their own. The war ought to be interpreted to them as something in which they have a stake, not only as members of the general group. The war ought to be fought to save business, family and church, and to add to prosperity, security and faith. Each interest should be encouraged to formulate war aims which point to the enemy of all who is, in fact, quite as much the enemy of each.

For the sake of the business men the war must appear as a profitable enterprise. L. G. Chiozza Money, M.P., published a statement in the London *Daily Chronicle* for August 10th, 1914, which is a pattern for this sort of thing. He wrote

> Our chief competitor both in Europe and outside it will be unable to trade, and at the conclusion of the War the unmistakable antagonism which German aggression is everywhere arousing will help us to keep the trade and shipping we will win from her.

Sidney Whitman published a pamphlet, called *The War on German Trade. Hints for a Plan of Campaign* (London, 1914). Meanwhile, the economic groups of Germany swarmed with visions of tangible expansion in every direction. The Bund der Landwirte, der Deutsche Bauernbund, der Vorort der christlichen Bauernvereine, der Zentralverband deutscher Industrialer, der Bund deutscher Industrialer, and der Reichsdeutsche Mittelstandverband, joined in a monster petition on May 20th, 1915, to the Chancellor, in which they explained what they wanted.

The annexationist claims were the whole of Belgium, Northern France to a line established from the mouth of the Somme straight eastward to the Belgian boundary, along the Maas, to its juncture with the Mosel in the Pagny-Toul region, thence through Lunéville east, along the Vosges to Belfort. The Departments of Pas de Calais and du Nord, half the Meuse Department, the greatest part of Meurthe and Moselle, part of Vosges and the Territory of Belfort, were thus contemplated additions to Germany. In the East a part of Liviand, the largest and most densely inhabited part of Kurland, most of the Kovno district, the entire district of Suwalki, half of Lomza, all of Ploczk, a small slice of the Marschau district, half of Kalisch, a fourth of Pietrokoc, a small piece of Kielce—a total of 80,000 square kilometers, and five million people—were the annexationist claims. Adding this to the 50,000 square kilometers and the eleven million people demanded in the West, it appears that the German industrial and agrarian organizations were committed to the incorporation of 130,000 square kilometers and sixteen million non-Germans into the Imperial jurisdiction. The inhabitants of these areas were to be deprived of any political participation in the internal politics of Germany, and the large and middle-sized properties were to be transferred to German citizens at the cost of the defeated opponents of Germany.

Since the flaming vocabulary of religion still has the power to move the hearts of many men, it is a poor propagandist who neglects the spiritual and ecclesiastical interpretation of the War by the spokesmen of every sect. Each religious body must be brought to see in the discomfiture of the enemy, a triumph for its gods and priests and dogmas. Copious examples of the formulas which are appropriate to this end are to be found in the religious Press of every belligerent country. *La Croix*, the organ of the French clericals, identified the progress of France in the late War with the Kingdom of God. Writing in the feverish days of August, 1914, shortly after the alleged capture of Mulhouse by the French, it shouted,

> The story of France is the story of God.
> Long live Christ who loves the Franks![12]

The Holy War, "La Guerre sainte," had been proclaimed the day before by *L'Echo de Paris*, when it reported how waves of spontaneous applause had broken out during solemn services at the Madelaine. *La Croix* published an interpretation of the War on August 15th. It is first of all a war of revenge, this revenge which we have desired for 43 years.

It is a colossal

> duel between the Germans against the Latins and the Slavs.

It is a contest of

> public morals and international law.

And, as a final climax,

Is it not a war of Catholic France against Protestant Germany?

The Catholics of France were so zealous in the prosecution of the War that they aroused the suspicion of the radical elements in the country and quite a controversial literature sprang up. The pamphlet, *Les curés ont-ils voulu la guerre?* (Did the priests want war?), precipitated an acrimonious controversy.[13]

The German Catholics bitterly resented the attempt of the French clericals to monopolize the War. A literary relic of this dispute is the volume of able essays edited by Georg Pfeilschifter, *Deutsche Kultur, Katholizismus and Weltkrieg. Eine Abwehr des Buches "La Guerre allemande et le catholicisme."* (Freiburg, 1916.)

The churches of practically every description can be relied upon to bless a popular war, and to see in it an opportunity for the triumph of whatever godly design they choose to further. Some care must, of course, be exercised to facilitate the transition from the condemnation of wars in general, which is a traditional attitude on the part of the Christian sects, to the praise of a particular war. This may be expedited by securing suitable interpretations of the war very early in the conflict by conspicuous clericals; the lesser lights will twinkle after. It was of some advantage to the war party in Britain to have such a statement as the following, from the Bishop of Hereford:

Such a war is a heavy price to pay for our progress toward the realization of the Christianity of Christ, but duty calls, and the price must be paid for the good of those who are to follow us. That better and happier day when the people now under militarist rule shall regulate their own life is doubtless still so far away that an old man like myself can hardly hope to see it dawning, but amidst all the burden of gloom and sorrow which this dreadful war lays upon us we can at least thank God that it brings that better day a long step nearer for the generation in front of us.[14]

The patriotic chorus of the gentlemen of the cloth in Germany reverberates again through the pages of the anthology prepared by Professor Bang during the War, and called *Hurrah and Hallelujah!* (New York, 1917.) Bang was a Danish professor of theology and took the pains to collect some of the German gems. Pastor Traub, P. de Lagards, and scores of other clericals unwittingly contributed to this book. All of it seems to be the grossest blasphemy to the enemies of Germany and the sincerest reverence to the friends of the German cause. Only the Liberal minority protests in Germany or elsewhere against the outpourings in its own behalf.[15]

The number of possible re-interpretations of a war is limited only by the number of special interests whose allegiance is offered or sought. To the economic and ecclesiastical groups already referred to could be added a constellation of artists, scientists, teachers, or sportsmen without end. The members of the talkative professions (preachers, writers, promoters) depend for a living upon their capacity to arouse an emotional response in the breasts of their clientele. When the public is warmed up to fight, the clerical who treats the matter coldly is committing suicide, just as is the writer or the promoter. The circularity of response is established, for one interstimulates the other. The actor is the slave of his audience, though the audience is bound in temporary servitude to the actor.

Promoters can be relied upon to re-interpret the war aims of the groups with which they are identified. Thus certain musical promoters discovered that the War was really a war between German and British music. As Isidore de Lara wrote:

> The hour has come to put aside and to veil with crape the scores of the men who have crystallized in so unmistakeable a manner the spirit of the modern Huns. . . .
>
> The future belongs to the young hero who will have the courage to exclude from his library all the works of Handel, Mendelssohn, Wagner, Brahms and Richard Strauss . . . who will draw from the

depths of his own being tone pictures of all that is
beautiful in the wonderful poetry of Great Britain,
and find the vigorous rhythms that will tell of the
dauntless spirit of those who go to death singing
"Tipperary."[16]

Under the stress of war the nurses of the scrawny infant known
as "Opera in English," were able to procure solid nourishment for
their charge. To them, opera in German was a profanation, and the
"Ring" was pronounced with the accent of Belgravia or not at all.

Certain American educators took advantage of the War to
gather steam behind their pet projects of educational reform. The
baneful influence of the German common school model upon
American education was held up for universal execration, and the
war for these educators became a sort of crusade to make the world
safe from the *volksschule* and for the Junior High School.[17]

Over in Germany the tailors and dressmakers declared war
upon the immoral fashions of decadent Paris and perfidious London. No longer was the matchless frame of the Fräulein to appear
ridiculous in the simpering fluffs of Paris. She must be free and
independent of the passing whims of Parisian mistresses.

In short, the active propagandist is certain to have willing help
from everybody with an axe to grind in transforming the War into
a march toward whatever sort of a promised land happens to appeal to the group concerned. The more of these sub-groups he can
fire for the War, the more powerful will be the united devotion of
the people to the cause of the country, and to the humiliation of
the enemy.

Notes

[1] Steed, *Through Thirty Years*, II: 8.
[2] See Baschwitz, *Der Massenwakn*, passim.
[3] *La Guerre Sociale*, July 31, 1914.
[4] Translated in John Buchan, *History of the War*, Chapter XXII.
[5] *Le Gaulois*, August 5, 1914.

[6] *New Republic*, September 11, 1915.

[7] See, incidentally, his forcible letter in the *Times* of August 1, 1914, against intervention.

[8] R. S. Baker, *Woodrow Wilson and the World Settlement*, 1: 40.

[9] See August Forel's pamphlet, *Die Vereinigten Staaten der Erde*, Bern u. Lausanne, 1914/15.

[10] See Louis Junod, *La confédération mondiale: Une alliance pour l'unification d. peuples*, Genève, 1914.

[11] The Union of Democratic Control was organized in England by E. D. Morel, A. Ponsonby, and several others shortly after the outbreak of the War. It was instigated by indignation at the fact that the British Cabinet had secretly entered into engagements on the side of France which constituted in fact a commitment in advance to join in the War against a supposedly attacking Germany. It is interesting to note that the Bund Neues Vaterland, which was organized about the same time in Germany, spoke exactly the same language, and was quite unaware that the Union of Democratic Control in England was in existence.

[12] "L'histoire de France est l'histoire de Dieu, Vive le Christ qui aime les Francs!" August 8.

[13] See Edouard Poulain, *Réfutation décisive* (1, *globale*, 2, *détaillée*); *onze rumeurs inflammées sur le clergé français* (Paris, 1916); Paul Feron-Vrau, *Les catholiques et la presse*.

[14] *London Times*, August 12, 1914.

[15] See Hans Fülster, *Kirche und Krieg*, Heft 8 in *Kultur und Zeitfragen*.

[16] "English music and German masters," *Fortnightly Review*, 103 :847-853.

[17] Friedrich Schönemann in *Die Kunst der Massenbeeinflussung in den Vereinigten Staaten von Amerika*, Berlin and Leipzig, 1924, shows how every agency was mobilized to carry propaganda in the United States during and directly after the War. The school, the church, the women's club, the newspaper, the movie, the business club, the Ku Klux Klan, the American Defense Society, the National Security League, the American Legion, the "hereditary" patriotic societies (Sons of the American

Revolution, etc.) all played their active part. Although the book is written in evident bitterness of spirit, it is an excellent piece of pioneering. This study avoids duplication as much as possible.

4
SATANISM

When the public believes that the enemy began the War and blocks a permanent, profitable and godly peace, the propagandist has achieved his purpose. But to make assurance doubly sure, it is safe to fortify the mind of the nation with examples of the insolence and depravity of the enemy. Any nation who began the War and blocks the peace is incorrigible, wicked and perverse. To insist directly upon these qualities is merely a precaution, and its chief effect is to make it more certain that the enemy could be capable of so monstrous a thing as an aggressive war. Thus, by a circularity of psychological reaction the guilty is the satanic and the satanic is the guilty.

The themes to be selected for emphasis depend upon the moral code of the nation whose animosity is to be aroused. But there are certain common denominators which can be counted upon to work in any situation. The opposing nation is nearly always demonstrably overbearing and contemptuous. The French Press was full of scornful thrusts at the presumptuous "Herrenvolk" just across the Rhine. These insolent and ridiculous people even took for their name a word "Allemagne," which, literally transcribed, is supposed to mean "all people!" "Deutschland über alles" provoked exactly the same indignation in Downing Street and Fleet Street that "Rule, Britannia" did in the Wilhelmstrasse and the Linden. Recruiting was stimulated in Great Britain at one time by playing up the alleged remark of the Kaiser, who referred to "the contemptible little English army."

The enemy is not only insolent. He is sordid. The Germans were perfectly sure that British envy was the root of the War, and, as for the United States, the economic motive was all too plain. As Charles A. Collman wrote in *Die Kriegstreiber in Wall Street* (Leipzig, 1917), the American manufacturers and bankers stayed out of the War, until their best customer, Great Britain, was threatened with insolvency, whereupon they proceeded to stampede the American public into the War, barely in time to save their accounts. The House of Morgan, with its overdraft to the British government of $400,000,000, was faced with certain ruin, having overstrained its credit to supply the British with munitions. Only the diversion of the first Liberty loan proceeds to Morgan saved him. The British Chancellor of the Exchequer, Bonar Law, made a clean breast of the British position in a speech which he delivered July 24th, 1917:

> Indeed, it is an open secret that we had spent so freely of our resources that those available in America had become nearly exhausted when our great ally entered the struggle.

In December, 1916, the bare announcement that Germany was making overtures of peace sent stocks hurtling down. Bank credits were sharply curtailed and the Allied governments were able to renew their bills with the most extreme difficulty. The news of the diplomatic break with Germany on the 4th of February, 1917, sent Bethlehem Steel up 30 points. American industries, already geared for production to supply the Allies, had faced liquidation, readjustment and even ruin at the whispers of peace; they were able to breathe easily once more. Mr. Henry P. Davidson, a partner in J. P. Morgan and Company, had been one of the most active opponents of Germany's "insincere" peace offers; he had wished for American participation in the War in order to "cleanse us from our selfishness."[1]

The enemy is inherently perfidious. M. Felix Sartiaux wrote in the *Morale Kantienne et morale humaine* (1916) that

> One of the most subtle tendencies of the German
> character is the hypocritical lie, which appears under
> the guise of naïve sincerity, and justifies itself by the
> most incredible sophisms. . . . The judgment of a
> Latin historian, Villeius Peterculus has often been
> quoted. He found the ancient Germans a race of
> "born liars."[2]

The enemy conducts a lying propaganda. This theme is of particular importance. Unfavourable reports about allies, the heads
of the army, the conditions at the front, and the bureaucracy are
certain to leak past the censorship, or to spring full-blown inside
the ramparts. Psychological barriers as well as physical barriers
must be interposed between dangerous news and subversive responses. This psychological barrier consists in the suspicion that
unfavourable news is likely to be a cunning specimen of enemy
propaganda. If this supposition can be planted firmly in the public mind, a mighty weapon has been forged against disunity and
defeatism.

The Germans were aghast at the efficiency of Allied propaganda
and they undertook to steel their people against it by protesting
loudly against the official French and British Press and Press services. Rudolf Rotheit declared that one of the conditions of peace
must be the emancipation of the World Press from the clutches of
enemy telegraphic agencies. He wrote *Die Friedensbedingungen
der deutschen Presse—Los von Reuter und Havas* (Berlin, 1915).
Even the schools had such copying exercises as "Reuter's Agency,
the fabricator of War lies." The British Press was the theme of Paul
Dehn's study, entitled *England und die Presse* (Hamburg, 1915).
The Germans took Northcliffe as the symbol of the British Press
and poured vials of abuse on his head.

The cry of German propaganda in France was loud and insistent. Certain newspapers, even in the capital, were suspected of
contaminating the French mind to suit German purposes. A more or
less typical exposure of German methods is contained in *Le Matin*
for October 24th, 1917. M. Louis Forest accuses the Germans of

spending money to influence the Press abroad. He calls attention to the book of an Alsatian, which had exposed the German system before the War. Even during the Franco-Prussian War, the Germans had their friends in Parisian newspaper offices. After reviewing the evidence of past and present activity, he draws this conclusion

> everyone can determine for himself whether the present German system is new or old. If to us it appears new, it is because we are ignorant of such things.[3]

The enemy is quarrelsome, crude and destructive. MM. Tudesq and J. Dyssord published *Les Allemands peints par eux-mêmes* in November, 1917. Heine was the authority for the remark that

> Christianity has softened to a certain degree this brutal belligerent ardour of the German, but has been unable to destroy it entirely.

Especially, exclaim the French editors, their proclivity to destroy cathedrals, which has been amply confirmed by the bombardment of Rheims, the burning of Belgian churches and of cathedrals in Lorraine. Goethe had acknowledged that

> We, the Germans, are of yesterday. For a century it is true that we have made substantial progress in civilization, but centuries will yet pass before our peasants will have the ideas or the spirit of a civilization sufficiently advanced to enable them to render homage to beauty as did the Greeks.

Schopenhauer blushes to belong to their race.

The enemy is atrociously cruel and degenerate in his conduct of the War. A handy rule for arousing hate is, if at first they do not enrage, use an atrocity. It has been employed with unvarying success in every conflict known to man. Originality, while often advantageous, is far from indispensable. In the early days of the War of 1914 a very pathetic story was told of a seven-year old youngster, who had pointed his wooden gun at a patrol of invading Uhlans, who had dispatched him on the spot. This story had done excellent duty in the Franco-Prussian War, over forty years before. But many of the most successful tales have a far more venerable history. There is one about the Turks, which had rattled down Christendom since the first crusades. According to this account, a tub full of eyes was discovered at a certain point, where captives were being tortured for the amusement of Turkish generals.

Stress can always be laid upon the wounding of women, children, old people, priests and nuns, and upon sexual enormities, mutilated prisoners and mutilated non-combatants. These stories yield a crop of indignation against the fiendish perpetrators of these dark deeds, and satisfy certain powerful, hidden impulses. A young woman, ravished by the enemy, yields secret satisfaction to a host of vicarious ravishers on the other side of the border. Hence, perhaps, the popularity and ubiquity of such stories.

While all atrocity stories show a family resemblance, and the old stand-bys can be relied upon, no classification should be regarded by the practical propagandist as more than suggestive. A certain fringe of novelty is always permissible, because the conditions of warfare are never precisely the same. Since the discovery of germs the enemy may be accused of infecting wells, cattle, and food, not to speak of wounds. A booklet on *Microbe-Culture at Bucharest* was put out in London in 1917, and covered the subject very nicely. If the enemy shows signs of believing that a campaign of frightfulness is sound military strategy, there need be no hesitation about calling God and man to witness that such an abomination is the new-born creation of the diabolical enemy. It was the absence of any opportunity for effective contradiction in wartime which made it possible for Professor Lavisse, for instance, to proclaim in the *Pratique et doctrine de la guerre allemande* that

> Not one of our military writers taught the doctrine of the *guerre atroce*.

After peace came it was possible for another Frenchman, Démartial, to procure a hearing in the interest of veracity and to recall attention to a three-volume tome (*Vaincre*) by the French officer Montaigne, in which this thesis was defended:

> Terrify; and in order to terrify, destroy. One sets out to kill, one shoots to kill, one leaps at the throat of the enemy but to kill, and one kills until there is nothing left to kill.[4]

Americans did not think it worth while to recall the theory of war entertained by General Sheridan. He visited Bismarck at the field headquarters of the Prussian Army in France, in 1870, and declared,

> The proper strategy consists in the first place in inflicting as telling blows as possible upon the enemy's army, and then causing the inhabitants so much suffering that they must long for peace, and force their government to demand it. The people must be left nothing but their eyes to weep with over the war.[5]

It was likewise perfectly safe for President Poincaré to flay the barbarous Germans for dropping bombs upon defenceless women and children. Very few among the Allied peoples knew, and very few of them, had they known, would have cared, that on the 26th of June, 1916, French and English aviators dropped bombs upon Karlsruhe, killing or wounding 26 women and 124 children, or that on the 22nd of September, 1915, the Allied bombers had taken a toll of 103 victims in a raid upon the same city. In the fever of combat the news of the slaughter of enemy noncombatants is apt to be met by the exulting cry that the "whelps and dams of murderous foes" are no more, to quote a chivalrous line of Swinburne, when he heard about the frightful mortality in the concentration camps for Boer women and children in South Africa.

It was equally safe for the Allies to declare that it could only have occurred to a German Hun to organize a campaign of systematic

destruction of machinery, warehouses, bridges and railroads in a
region from which they were retreating. There was no one to call
attention to the recommendations of the *Engineer*, a reputable
British technical periodical, in its issue for September 25th, 1914,
to the effect that the army ought to break up the equipment and to
raze the factory of every German industry which the fortunes of
war might bring into their hands. German competition after the
War would thus be seriously crippled.[6] Nor was the destruction by
the Allies of the oil properties during their retreat through Rumania conspicuously interpreted to the people as other than a smart
stroke to cheat the enemy.

A catalogue of the crimes which the enemy has been held to
have perpetrated in the past ought to stimulate the ingenuity more
than the imitativeness of the propaganda expert. The suggestions
referred to here are by no means exhaustive. During the late War
innumerable schemes for classifying enemy outrages were invented. As a random sample one may select the first large and important atrocity brochure put out by the French Government.[7]

German sins were sorted into bins which were labeled thus:

1. Violation of the neutrality of Luxemburg and Belgium.
2. Violation of French Frontier before the Declaration of War.
3. Killing of prisoners and wounded.
4. Looting, arson, rape, murder.
5. Use of forbidden bullets.
6. Use of burning liquids and asphyxiating gas.
7. Bombarding of fortresses without notice and of
   unfortified towns; the destruction of buildings
   consecrated to Religion, Art, Science and Charity.
8. Treacherous Methods of Warfare.
9. Cruelties inflicted on civil population.

Dr. Ernst Müller-Meiningen, a member of the German Reichstag, compiled the sins of the Entente in *Der Weltkrieg und der*

Zusammenbruch des Völkerrechts, which had passed through a third revised edition by the middle of 1915. The general scheme of organization is indicated in the Table of Contents:

1. The Neutrality of Belgium (How Belgium connived secretly with the Allies).
2. Mobilization and the Morality of Nations.
3. Violation of the Congo Acts. The Colonial War.
4. The Employment of barbarous and warlike tribes in a European War.
5. The Violation of the Neutrality of the Suez Canal.
6. The Breach of Chinese Neutrality by Japan and England's Assault upon Kiao-Chau.
7. The use of Dum-Dum Bullets and the like.
8. Treatment of Diplomatic Representatives by the Triple Entente Countries in Violation of International Law. Acts of Diplomatic Representatives of the Triple Entente in Violation of International Law.
9. Non-observances and Violations of Red Cross Rules on the Part of the Triple Entente States.
10. Franc-Tireur Warfare and the Maltreatment of the Defenceless before and after the Declaration of War. Also the Imprisonment of Civilians.
11. Unlawful and Inhumane Methods of Conducting War Practised by the Hostile Armies and the Governments of the Triple Entente and Belgium.
12. The Russian Atrocities in East Prussia in especial.
13. Jewish Pogroms and Other Russian Atrocities in Poland, Galicia, the Caucasus, etc.
14. The "Spirit" of the Troops of the Triple Entente. Plundering, and Destruction of their own country's Property. Self-Mutilations. Verdicts upon the Troops of the Triple Entente by their own Officers.

15. The Destruction and Misuse of Telegraph Cables.
16. Further Details as to the Vendetta of Lies of the Press of the Triple Entente. A Method of Waging War contrary to all International Law. The French "Art of War."
17. The Bombardment of Towns and Villages from Aeroplanes. The use of shells that develop Gas.
18. English Business Moral and the Code of English Creditors. Deprivation of the Legal Rights of Germans in Russia and France.
19. Breaches of Neutrality on the Seas by England and the Other States of the Triple Entente. Contraband of War. Blockades, etc.

(Condensed.)

The quantitative methods of modern social science were applied to the atrocity problem as the War went on. In a report prepared for the Serbs about Austro-Hungarian atrocities the first plate, which summarizes the investigation is entitled, "Statistics of Atrocities." It is limited to the districts of Potzerie, Matchva, Yadar and certain others. Women and children are recorded in parallel columns, and the number of cases relating to each item is recorded. The items are:

Executed or otherwise shot, Bayoneted or knifed, Throats cut, Killed, Burnt alive, Killed in massacre, Beaten to death with rifles or sticks, Stoned to death, Hanged, Disembowelled, Bound and tortured on the spot, Missing, Carried off as prisoners, Wounded, Arms cut off or broken, Legs cut off or broken, Noses cut off, Ears cut off, Eyes gouged out, Sexual parts mutilated, Skin torn in strips, Flesh or scalp removed, Corpses cut into small pieces, Breasts cut off, Women violated.

Certain special items, such as the use of explosive bullets, which were not susceptible of statistical treatment, were dealt with in qualitative terms.[8] To the impact of the quantitative method is added the dramatization of the individual case. The book is copiously embellished with horror-photographs of mutilated corpses and devastated villages.

There is a certain technical advantage in varying the form of the atrocity account. Sometimes a victim may be permitted to tell his own story, as in the case of a distinguished Belgian scholar who was condemned by the Germans to forced labour and told his experiences in *Through the Iron Bars* (London, 1917). William Caine published an alleged interview with a victim of the German invasion, called *Monsieur Sagotin's Story* (London, 1917). The misadventure of a single person was related by W. T. Hill in *The Martyrdom of Nurse Cavell*.[9] The neutral witness always speaks with some authority, and Dr. De Christmas testified to the sad lot of the French prisoners in Germany as he visited them. His was called *Le Traitement des Prisonniers Français en Allemagne* (Paris, 1917). Admissions by an enemy are always useful, and the French published the captured diary of a non-commissioned German officer, in which the cruelties perpetrated by officers on soldiers and civilians were written down. The diary was edited by Louis-Paul Alaux, and published in 1918, under the title *Souvenirs de guerre d'un sous-officer allemand*. The record of a *German Deserter's War Experience* was published in New York, 1917.

An excellent device which was used by the British to lend weight to their stories of German atrocities was to constitute a commission of men with international reputations for truthfulness to collect evidence and deliver findings. The British, with an eye not alone upon their own populace, but upon the American people, delivered a stroke of genius by appointing the so-called Bryce Commission. The Evidence and Documents laid before the Committee on Alleged German Outrages (London, 1915) was the magnum opus of the War on this front. The brochure on German War Practices, which was published by the Committee on Public Information in the United States in 1916, was one of the last of the innumerable versions of this report.

Yet another form in which propaganda complaints may be made against the enemy is in the controversial statement or pamphlet. Dr. Max Kuttner remonstrated with a former pupil of his who had lent his pen to the French "calumnies" in a little booklet called *Deutsche Verbrechen?* . . . (in reply to) Joseph Bédier, *Les crimes allemands d'après temoignages allemands* (Bielefeld und Leipzig, 1915). Had not this Frenchman once been taught the importance of weighing evidence? Hubert Grimme took a similar line in his remarks on *Ein böswilliger Sprachstumper* (Münster, 1915). Nobody ever supposed that these pamphlets would produce repentance in France, but they serve to keep alive the spirit of virtuous indignation in Germany. To ask whether the Germans were criminals was like announcing a sermon on the subject, "Are Churchmen Hypocrites?" The answer is a flattening and resounding negative which readily passes over into an indignant criticism of the perfidy of those who dare insinuate such a thing.

Before taking leave of the unsavoury subject of atrocities another principle must be brought out. It is always difficult for many simple minds inside a nation to attach personal traits to so dispersed an entity as a whole nation. They need to have some individual on whom to pin their hate. It is, therefore, important to single out a handful of enemy leaders and load them down with the whole decalogue of sins.

No personality drew more abuse of this sort in the last War than the Kaiser. The London *Evening News* christened the Kaiser the "Mad Dog of Europe" on the 6th of August, and the "War Lord" a little while thereafter. Austen Harrison wrote about *The Kaiser's War* (London, 1914). The *Liberté* of Paris took pains in the issue of November 24th, 1916, to identify William II. with the Beast of the Apocalypse, as foreseen by St. John. It appeared that upon the basis of researches, conducted by an English savant, the number of the Beast was 666, and the Kaiser's number was just this. The word Kaiser has six letters. Place them one beneath the other in a column. At the left of each number, record the place in the alphabet, which is occupied by each of these letters. Thus "K," the eleventh letter in the alphabet, is placed beside six, to make 116. The completed columns sum up to 666, the mystic number.[10]

It would be possible to multiply the individual adjectives which can serve as the themes for injurious propaganda against a nation, but it is now more to the point to suggest some of the methods by which the whole of the indictment can be presented synthetically. There are some, who do not hesitate to indict a whole civilization at a single gesture, and these mentalities may be relied upon to furnish systematic treatises upon such subjects as *Civilisés contre Allemands*. This particular book was published in Paris in 1915, by the Frenchman, Jean Finot, who had published an excellently objective treatise on race prejudice before the War. In the same strain wrote the eminent historian, Ernest Lavisse, in his *Kultur et Civilisation* (1915), and André Saures in *Nous et Eux* (1915). Mr. Rudyard Kipling said in the columns of *The Morning Post* (London) of June 22nd, 1915:

> But, however the world pretends to divide itself, there are only two divisions in the world to-day— human beings and Germans.

In what purported to be a scientific treatise on the Instincts of the Herd in Peace and War (London, 1917), Trotter solemnly said,

> The incomprehensibility to the English of the whole trend of German feeling and expression suggests that there is some deeply-rooted instinctive conflict of attitude between them. One may risk the speculation that this conflict is between socialized gregariousness and aggressive gregariousness.[11]

Mr. John Cooper Powys replied to Professor Münsterberg under the title, *The Menace of German Culture* (London, 1915). The Germans were heaping up a vast literature of self-exaltation about the theme, Kultur. An inspection of this list of selected titles from German output will reveal something of its scope and purport:

Herm. Cohen, *Ueber das Eigentümliche des deutschen Geistes* (Berlin, 1915).

E. Bergmann, *Die weltgeschichtliche Mission der
deutschen Bildung* (Gotha, 1915).

Rudolf Eucken, *Die weltgeschichtliche Bedeutung
des deutschen Geistes* (Stuttgart, 1914).

R. v. Delius, *Deutschlands geistige Weltmacht-
stellung* (Stuttgart, 1915).

J. A. Lux, *Deutschland als Welterzieher* (Stuttgart,
1914).

Herausgeg. v. Karl Hönn, *Der Kampf des deutschen
Geistes im Weltkrieg. Dokumente des deutschen
Geisteslebens aus der Kriegszeit* (Gotha, 1915).

German assurance and self-esteem was buttressed by the testimony of a cloud of foreign witnesses. Björn Björnson, Scandina-
vian writer, paid a tribute called *Vom deutschen Wesen. Impres-
sionen eines Stammesverwandten*, 1914-17 (Berlin, 1917). Hous-
ton Stewart Chamberlain, ex-patriated Englishman, rallied to the
defence of the *Deutsches Wesen* (München, 1916). In his earlier
writings he had exclaimed, "If there is in the world a peaceful, well-
behaved, pious people, it is the Germans. In the last forty-three
years, not a single man in the whole country has desired war—no,
not one." England had been led into the War by the unscrupulous
machinations of a King who was a tool of a cunning diplomat. England was no longer the land of liberty, but the slave of a vicious
oligarchy.[12] Ferdinand Tönnies, a celebrated German sociologist,
brought together all the imperialistic utterances of British statesmen in his book about England.[13] The business of editing antholo-
gies of incriminating remarks thrived all during the War. Jean
Ruplinger published a collection of German War utterances, under
the title, *Also sprach Germania*. The book appeared in Paris in
1918, with a preface by Edouard Herriot. William Archer compiled
the *Gems of German Thought*, which was published in 1917.

A great mass of specialized studies upon different features of
the life and character of another country is welcome in war. The

aged philosopher and psychologist Wilhelm Wundt compared the philosophical ideals of every nation, greatly to the advantage of Germany, in a brochure entitled, *Die Nationen und ihre Philosophie* (Leipzig, 1914). In particular, Baron Cay von Brockdorff took care to expose the truth about Bergson, as he saw it, in *Die Wahrheit über Bergson* (Berlin, 1917). In the United States, John Dewey unintentionally did great service to those who were drumming up sentiment against Germany by ringing the changes on certain aspects of German philosophy in his book on *German Philosophy and Politics* (New York, 1915), which had a new vogue when America went to War. If the history of Prussia was interpreted as a record of ruffian robberies by Allied scholars, the story of British imperialism was a stench in the nostrils of the Germans. Some incriminating morsels were assembled in books about Persia and India, such as the *Englische Dokumente zur Erdrosselung Persiens* (Berlin, 1917), and *Indien unter der britischen Faust* (Berlin, 1916). The real meaning of political freedom was clarified by A. O. Meyer, who discovered that real freedom was in Germany and not in England, and wrote *Deutsche Freiheit und englischer Parlamentarismus* (München, 1915). The Belgian Fr. De Hovée intended to compliment the British educational system, when he compared it to the disadvantage of the German system, by writing that its aim might be summarized in the slogan

Be good, my pretty maid, and let who will be clever.

His book was *German and English Education* (London, 1917). While Germany was yet at peace with America, Dr. Karl Henning published a scurrilous pamphlet on America, called *Die Wahrheit über America* (Leipzig, 1915) which was subsequently useful when War came. Henning devoted most of his attention to the family and the educational system in the United States. He combed the reports of some of the municipal vice commissions for juicy stories about sex offences committed by children and reproduced these as typical of the standards of American life. One prize exhibit was a letter, which he said was in his possession, and was written by an eight-year old girl to a boy of the same age. It was:

Dear Arthur,—I will come over to-night, shall I? Do
you love me? I love you very dearly and to-night we
will go to a show and stay till midnight and we will
dance at a theatre for a long time and then we will
come home and you can sleep with me till morning
and next Sunday we will go horse-riding. Your sweet-
heart, M. (Page 54.)

Now monographs of every variety reach a certain restricted
audience, and if the wider circles of the public are to be touched
by synthetic representations of the life of another country, the form
must be personal and dramatic and literary. Of this sort of thing a
book put out in England during the War may well serve as a model.
It was plausible, well-written, and utterly devastating. I have been
told by more than one member of the German propaganda service,
that they considered it the best piece of propaganda work gotten
out by the Allies in the course of the War. This was *Christine*, by
Alice Cholmondeley (New York, 1917). It purported to be an authentic collection of letters written by a music student in Germany
to her mother in England. The girl was a talented violinist and in
May, 1914, went over to study with a great German master. She
was bubbling with enthusiastic anticipation of art and life in Germany. She wrote her Berlin letters from an address in
Lützowstrasse, where a Pension was known to be.

All is buoyance and happiness until, by degrees, German civilization begins to make itself known to her. The police are boorish
and haughty. Her music master is secretly scornful of the whole
German régime. The talk at the Pension is about clean Berlin, and
slummy London. She is held more or less personally responsible
for the Boer War. She is pestered by all sorts of irritating rules
and regulations, for she is not allowed to practise on the Sabbath.
Rules are typical of Germany, and she finds a girl acquaintance
celebrating the birthday of her father, whom she despised, five
years after his death. Her lamp is taken away at 10 p.m. and she is
left with a candle. Snobbishness abounds. A Countess patronizes

the arts, but will not permit her daughter to become contaminated. A young German of high birth longs to become a musician, but the caste conventions make an officer of him. The children kill themselves in Germany because of overwork in the schools. She is elbowed by men and boys when she walks abroad alone. The pros and cons of Weltpolitik follow her everywhere. An ominous sense of impending war pervades everything. The lower classes grovel in servile respect before the upper classes. The drill, perhaps, does it. Unmarried girls are not supposed to ask questions in conversations, but to keep discreetly silent and unobtrusive. A rural pastor lectures her on the English love of money bags. She meets a staff officer, who ominously advises her to ask the Council of her Sussex village to straighten the road for heavy traffic. An expectant mother prays for a boy baby, so that she can be the mother of a soldier. She finds the German aristocrats so middle class. She becomes engaged to the charming young officer with musical frustrations. As the international crisis approaches, she sees wild orgies of joy at the imminence of War. Her violin master has his mouth stuffed by receiving a Royal decoration. Her marriage is blocked by the superior officer of her betrothed. She flees to escape internment and is stopped on the border. A young subordinate forces her to wait in the sun for two hours, and she gets double pneumonia, dying at Stuttgart on the 8th of August, 1914. All the facts about German life are floated in a wave of gush about music and mother. The whole thing is marvellously executed, and the book had a tremendous circulation among women and school children in Allied and neutral countries. It is typical of the circumstantial-sentimental type of thing which can be placed in the fiction columns of a woman's magazine or in the book stalls. By such a thing does the opposing nation become His Satanic Majesty, the Enemy.

The cult of satanism thus arises and feeds on hate. Vengeance is Mine, saith the Lord, and the Lord is working through us to destroy the Devil. The stirring stanzas of Lissauer's famous "Hymn of Hate" expose all this in its pristine nudity.

> Hate by water and hate by land;
> Hate of the heart and hate of the hand;
> We love as one, we hate as one;
> We have but one foe alone,—England.

All the specific means of conquering the Evil One are, and should be, glorified. The cult of battle requires that every form of common exertion (enlistment, food-saving, munition making, killing the enemy) should have the blessing of all the holy sentiments. In Christian countries precautions must be taken to calm the doubts of those who undertake to give such a book as the Bible an inconvenient interpretation. It is always expedient to circulate the arguments of the preachers and priests who are willing to explain how you can follow Jesus and kill your enemies. There are always enough theological leaders to undertake the task, since it is only the small sects, usually regarded as fanatical, who see any serious difficulty in the problem. In the German war literature are to be found many books which were written to remove doubts from those hesitant souls, who hated to shoot worse than they hated the English. Theodore Birt reassured the Christians who were perplexed by the exhortation to "Love your enemies" in *Was heisst "Liebet eure Feinde"? Ein Wort zur Beruhigung* (Marburg, 1915). W. Walther wrote a popular treatise for the benefit of the Lutherans. It is called *Deutschlands Schwert durch Luther geweiht* (2 Aufl., Leipzig, 1915). Otto Albrecht found a forecast of victory in Luther, *Eine Kriegspredigt aus Luthers Schriften* (1914).

It is also useful to justify war in general on ethical rather than exclusively religious grounds. The eminent Rudolf Eucken praised the moral power of war in *Die sittlichen Kräfte des Krieges* (Leipzig, 1914), and Theodor Elsenhaus lauded it as a great teacher in *Der Krieg als Erzieher* (Dresden, 1914). Theodor Kipp saw no antithesis between the idea of might and right, the important thing being to make the right mighty, as he contended in *Von der Macht des Rechts* (Berlin, 1914).

The justification of war can proceed more smoothly if the hideous aspects of the war business are screened from public gaze.

People may be permitted to deplore war in the abstract, but they must not be encouraged to paint its horrors too vividly. In fact, there is place for such items as this one, which appeared in the American Press during the early days of the Spanish-American War:

> DEATH RATE HAS GROWN LESS. Fearful Record of Trafalgar's Days has never been equalled. Machine Gun's Moral Effect. Modern guns less destructive than flint locks, dart, or javelin.[14]

Better yet, of course, is the interpretation of the war in terms of heroism, good fellowship, smartness and picturesqueness. In the late War, an artist like Muirhead Bone could be relied upon to present *The Western Front* in softened sketches. The humorous magazines and books help to banter away the realities of battle and they profit from the impulse to turn one's head away from a spectacle which, if completely realized, might well prove unbearable. A Bruce Bairnsfather is worth at least an Army Corps.[15] Popular accounts of how the military machinery works give the public a sense of knowing just how things get on; of course, the writers should be careful to keep too much blood from getting mixed in the story. Such writers as Bernard Shaw, H. G. Wells, and Arthur Conan Doyle, were sent to visit the British officials and they came back with discreet accounts of how they felt about it. Ludwig Ganghofer described all the German fronts in a series of books.

It is the letters and books written by actual fighters to which the most importance is attached. Harold R. Peat (*Private Peat*) and Sergeant Guy Empey (*Over the Top*) explained the actual conduct of modern war to Americans. Donald Hankey (*A Student in Arms*) was a soldier who saw the War through the lenses of a moral and religious idealist, and his book struck many responsive chords in America and England. This same quality pervaded the work of certain other writers, such as *Carry On?* by Coningsby Dawson. A whimsical, determined note in Ian Hay's *First Hundred Thousand* sent it through the English-speaking world, as soon as it fell from the Press.

Tales of individual adventure kept the old spell of romance about war. One soldier told *Was ich in mehr als 80 Schlachten und Gefechten erlebte* (Berlin, 1916). Pat O'Brien told how he escaped from the Germans in *Outwitting the Hun* (New York, 1916). Dr. Th. Preyer tells how he managed to return home from New York in *Von New York nach Jerusalem und in die Wüste* (Berlin, 1916). Paul Konig related the exploits of the submarine which crossed the Atlantic in *Die Fahrt der Deutschland* (Berlin, 1917). Marcel Hadaud caught the atmosphere of air battle in *En plein vol* (Paris, 1916). The *Zeppeline über England* met with a warm reception in Germany in 1916, as did *Kapitän-leutnant Freiherr von Förstner als U-Bootes Kommandant gegen England*. Von Mücke's story of the *Emden* was one of the most popular books of the War. Kurt Agram told the sensational story of the 100,000 Germans, who were banished to Siberia by the Russian Government, and of how he managed to escape, in *Nach Sibirien mit* 100,000 *Deutschen*. How he managed to reach the Fatherland from the besieged colonies was the theme of Emil Zimmermann, *Meine Kriegsfahrt von Kamerun zur Heimat*.

Special collections of letters from the front were prepared in all countries. *Der deutsche Krieg in Feldpostbriefen, Soldier's Tales of the Great War*, and similar collections ran into several volumes. Special volumes were continually appearing, such as Charles Foley, *La vie de la guerre* (Paris, 1917), in which the War letters first published in *L'Écho de Paris* are brought within one cover. Sketches of the front were always welcome when done with any literary skill, and Henry de Forge, *Ah! la belle France!* (Paris, 1916), Maurice Grandolphe, *La marche à la victoire* (Paris, 1915), or Max Buteau, *Tenir. Récits de la vie de Tranchées* (Paris, 1918) were ample to satisfy the demand.[16]

Professional people of various kinds are able to reach their own public, and should be encouraged to write. Aug. A. Lemaître, pastor at Liévin, and of Swiss origin, gave his story of *Un an près des champs de bataille de l'Artois* (Edité par la société centrale évangélique, Paris). J. Emile Blanche's *Cahiers d'un artiste* (Paris, 1917) touched the artistic fraternity. Teachers, doctors and nurses, not to speak of engineers and chemists, belong to the ranks of those, who can usually describe what they see, with some reserves about the unpleasant.

During the first few weeks of the War those elements in the business community who required some coddling before they would face realities, were fed on such catchwords as "Business as Usual." This phrase sprang up quickly in England, where it had a short vogue before succumbing to facts and ridicule. Mr. Tom Bruce Jones brought out a pamphlet on *The Danger of Britain's Invasion, and how it may be met whilst carrying on "business as usual"* (Falkirk, 1914). On the 11th of August, the phrase appeared in the London *Daily Chronicle* in the letter from H. E. Morgan of W. H. Smith and Sons. Thus are all barriers down to the glorification of all the means necessary to the overcoming of evil by force.

Notes

[1] These interpretations, which were current in Germany during the World War, can be read in English in J. K. Turner, *Shall It Be Again?* and L. E. Rowley, *War Criminals* (Privately Published, Lansing, Michigan, 1924).

[2] Page 408.

[3] This may be read now with a certain amusement, for the Russian documents have revealed the extent to which the Russian government bought a large percentage of the French Press support which it enjoyed in pre-war days. See the *Livre Noir* in particular, and the subsequent articles in *L'Humanité*.

[4] Cited on page 19 of G. Démartial, *Comment on mobilisa les consciences.* "Umano," an Italian jurist, publishes an anonymous collection of statements by public men during the War which he regards as unfounded in connection with his diffuse yet interesting study called *Positiva scienza di governo*, 1922.

[5] Busch, *Bismarck*, I: 128.

[6] Cited by Démartial as cited, p. 24.

[7] République Française, *Documents rélatifs à la guerre* 1914-15. *Rapports et Procès-verbaux d'enquête de la commission*

instituée en vue de constater los actes commis par l'ennemi en violation du droit des gens. Paris, 1915.

[8] Kingdom of Serbia, *Report upon the atrocities committed by the Austro-Hungarian Army during the first invasion of Serbia*, by R. A. Reiss, London, 1916.

[9] The German public believed that Miss Cavell was a spy, incidentally.

[10] Repeated in Graux, *Les fausses nouvelles de la grande guerre*, I: 282. Former Ambassador J.W. Gerard criticized the Kaiser in *My Four Years in Germany*, New York, 1917, and *Face to Face with Kaiserism*, New York, 1918. The dentist Arthur N. Davis wrote about *The Kaiser as I Knew Him*, New York and London. 1918.

[11] Page 174.

[12] His earlier essays were published in England in 1915 under the title of *The Ravings of a Renegade*.

[13] An English edition was brought out in New York in 1915 under the title, *Warlike England As Seen by Herself*.

[14] Louisville *Courier-Journal*, June 26, 1898.

[15] See, for instance, *Bullets and Billets*, N.Y., 1917.

[16] Boyd Cable performed the difficult task of squeezing stories out of official communiqués. In his *Between the Lines* and other books, a dull, dry extract from an official despatch was polished up into a story.

5

THE ILLUSION OF VICTORY

The fighting spirit of a nation feeds upon the conviction that it has a fighting chance to win. The enemy may be dangerous, obstructive, and satanic, but if he is sure to win, the morale of many elements in the nation will begin to waver and crumble. The animosity of a discouraged nation may be diverted to a new object, and the nation may be so busy hating the ruling class of its own country or its own allies, that it simply ceases to hate the technical enemy, and military collapse ensues.

The illusion of victory must be nourished because of the close connection between the strong and the good. Primitive habits of thought persist in modern life, and battles become a trial to ascertain the true and the good. If we win, God is on our side. If we lose, God may have been on the other side. To bow to necessity is to bow to the right, unless the universe is itself evil, or unless this can be interpreted as a temporary tribulation meted out to punish us for past sins or to cleanse us for future glory. In any case, defeat wants a deal of explaining, while victory speaks for itself.

The state of public expectation about the issue of the War depends upon the answer to the query, what is the relative strength of our side, and the enemy's side? From the propagandist point of view there are several striking examples of the way this question ought not to be answered. To insist upon the feebleness of the enemy, and to foster public expectation of his imminent collapse is to encourage hopes which may be indefinitely deferred, with the resulting danger of disenchantment, depression and defeat. During

the first month of the late War Paris was left without exact news of
the position of the struggling armies, and the most feverish
rumours filled the void. Paris expected immediate victory. Had not
von der Goltz admitted that the enervating life of the cities had
already fostered the decadence of Germany? Had not General Keim
declared that Germany could never have won in 1870 but for the
circumstance that she outnumbered the French by one-third, a
disparity which the presence of the English and the Belgians had
now overcome? Were not Italy, Holland and Portugal on the verge
of casting in their lot with the Entente? Were not enemy prisoners
begging bread for themselves and oats for their horses? Were not
strikes and riots breaking out in Berlin? Were not the soldiers
driven to battle by their Prussian officers at the point of the pis-
tol? Were not they deserting in droves, and had not a single French
soldier on patrol frightened fifty Germans into surrender? Were
not our horses drinking at the brooks in Lorraine?

After the report that Müllhausen had been captured on the 9th
of August no more specific information was published until much
later about the theatre of the War. Of what then did the newspapers write? Dr. Graux, a physician, kept a diary of War rumours,
which has been published in five volumes. He answers the question thus:

> Of German atrocities? That, alas, was true. But also
> of the correspondence of soldiers, a religious cer-
> emony at the Kremlin, the findings of a military com-
> mission of inquiry at Belfort, our manner of treat-
> ing prisoners, the Crown Prince's wound—a false re-
> port—war correspondents, the prohibition of Rus-
> sian exports, Swiss neutrality, German bluff, a pa-
> triotic address by M. Clémentel, the ambulance of
> Madame Messimy, of Swiss volunteers, *les prom-
> enades de Paris*, the conquest of Togo, Red Cross
> supplies, Americans maltreated in Germany![1]

But where were the Germans?

It was not until the 20th that the *Matin* began to break the news. Its headline read

ARE THEY AT BRUSSELS?

As the truth began, in part, to filter through, wild rumours clouded the sky. Alarmists saw Germans in the Bois de Boulogne. On the 27th there appeared no official communiqué, and on the 28th the newspapers tried to plug the gap by prophesying that

THE TSAR SOON DICTATES
CONDITIONS TO GERMANY.

On the 29th the front seemed to be on the Somme, and on the 30th the facts came out. Hopes were meanwhile nourished on the report that "Turpinite," a new and deadly explosive, would annihilate the invader.

In Berlin the first twenty-five days of the War were passed in a joyous delirium. The papers were congested with news of captured soldiers, captured guns, captured flags. More material of war was taken than in the whole campaign of 1870. The fall of Paris was but a matter of days.

The exaggerated optimism of those days reverberated in an undertone of accusation all during the War. Had not the public been grossly misled by its leaders? The proper way to manage the public, of course, is to insist upon the *ultimate* success of our cause. Both the French and the German commands were saved from complete loss of confidence by the thesis of "surprise attack" by the enemy, and this is an excellent theme for the propagandist to foster. If you win, you can afford to let the "surprise attack" slip out of mind, but if you are embarrassed, it is a very present help in time of trouble. The civilian population is ready to accept this thesis, because it knows perfectly well that it was plotting no war and, therefore, that the enemy must have been.

Among the Allied powers the official thesis was that Germany, armed to the teeth and crouched to spring, had suddenly, to the consternation of the peaceful and unprepared world, invaded Belgium and swept through Northern France before the pacific and astonished Allies could recover from the shock sufficiently to stem the attack.

So far as the truth is concerned, the fact seems to be that the talk about "surprise attack" and "unpreparedness" was grossly exaggerated for the purpose of covering up the failure of French strategy and of preventing the total eclipse of civilian morale. Such, at least, is the thesis of Jean de Pierrefeu, who, as the maker of official communiqués at General Headquarters during the War, was in a favourable position to ascertain the truth. After having connived at deception for the years of the War, he had undertaken to reveal the truth as he saw it in a book called *Plutarch Lied* (*Plutarque a-t-il menti?*). He says that the French General Staff had known for years that the German attack would be by way of Belgium, and that they had planned their strategy with this in mind, but that they were beaten in open combat, because their plan miscarried. The High Command kept indispensable reinforcements from the Left, which was crumpling before the Germans, on the supposition that a French attack through Alsace would enable them to imperil the communications of the German armies in the West. The French were hurled back in Alsace, swept aside in the West, their whole plan of campaign smashed into bits, and their very existence saved only by a boneheaded play on the part of the Germans.[2]

The thesis of surprise attack is rendered plausible to the civilian population by rumours of enemy spies. Spy hunts are due to great excitement in the presence of a huge, new danger, which is magnified by the sense of personal frustration produced by the sense of inability to do anything effective toward dispelling the menace. The peasants of Germany were excited by the wild tales of yellow automobiles which were supposed to be dashing from France across Germany, laden with gold for Russia. They stretched iron chains across the roads and made it unhappy for many a poor tourist. Military despatch riders in Great Britain were frequently stopped and lodged in gaol during the feverish days of the War.

The spy mania is a great inconvenience to many people, but it helps to arouse the community to a deeper sense of the necessity for joint action in the crisis. Such books as that of William Le Queux, *Britain's Deadly Peril* (London, 1915) project the spy fear further into the conflict.

The theory of surprise attack must be associated with the thesis of our brilliant resistance to temporarily overwhelming odds, if undue pessimism is to be averted. Our ultimate success is assured. Our reserves of men and material and foreign friendship are greater than those of the enemy. On these points, foreign testimony is particularly reassuring. The French encouraged themselves by publishing the *Voix italiennes sur la guerre de* 1914-15 and the *Voix de l'Amérique latine* (Preface by Gomez Carillo) in 1916. The English collected *Sixty American Opinions on the War* (1915), and welcomed Roosevelt's *Why America should join the Allies* (1915). Ramsey Muir wrote an introduction to the English edition of *The War and the Settlement*, by Rignano, the eminent Italian philosopher (1916). The Germans favoured the War correspondents of foreign countries before the Allies woke up to its importance, and they were usually sure of a rich harvest of clippings for reproduction in the home Press. Sven Hedin, a Swede, wrote *With the German Armies in the West*, which was widely translated. The Germans were assured of the active aid and sympathy of the Germans in the United States, according to the book by Karl Junger, called *Deutsch-Amerika mobil . . . !* (Berlin, 1915). A Swiss neutral, Dr. J. Strebel, told the Germans about some encouraging signs of future collapse, which he had observed in Allied countries. His *Reisebilder* was put out at Lucerne and Berlin in 1915. A Swiss neutral, Paul Balmer, told the French about some encouraging signs of future collapse which he had observed in Germany. His *Les Allemands chez eux* was put out at Paris in 1915. An American pacifist had seen suffering in Germany at first hand, and wrote *Short Rations* (by Madeleine Z. Doty) which was published in New York in 1917.

Such cumulated fact and opinion may be supplemented by prophecy. The famous *Almanach de Madame de Thèbes* nourished the morale of certain classes of the French public in the critical days of 1914. The *Figaro* published a prophecy on the 19th of August, 1914, which was supposed to date from the year 1600. A certain Friar John foresaw that an Anti-Christ by the name of William the Second would succumb in the same territory where he forged his weapons. Essen and Westphalia were undoubtedly meant.

Occasionally, a prophecy will inadvertently work both ways. The Germans launched a prediction that victory would rest with three emperors and three kings, which clearly referred to Germany, Austria, Turkey, Bavaria, Saxony and Bulgaria. The Entente was able to match this array with Russia, India, Japan, Belgium, Italy and Serbia.[3]

Prophecies for the more sophisticated members of the community take on subtler forms. Thus Professor Lanessan took a hand in explaining *Pourquoi les Germains seront vaincus*, (Paris, 1915). In 1916 Lloyd George was said to have remarked to Emile Vandervelde of Belgium that—

> England declared war in 1914, began it in 1915, developed it in 1916 and will finish it in 1917.

It seems that in the main, however, the canny Welshman confined himself to the excellent formula:

> We will finish the War when we have attained our objective.

There is a great advantage in having certain unofficial interpreters of the War to the public who can be relied upon to present matters in their most flattering light. Frank Symonds in the United States, Colonel Repington in England and Commander Rousset in France secured the confidence of the public and were of the greatest assistance to the authorities, for they were cogs in the machinery by which those interpretations least damaging to public morale were circulated. They were able to explain why retreats were "strategic retirements," and how evacuations could be "rectifications of the line."

One of the questions which rises in the conduct of the War is how to handle the news of losses. The possible policies vary all the way from complete suppression to immediate disclosure. When Winston Churchill was at the Admiralty he was characterized by the Chief Naval Censor as

> a bit of a gambler, *i.e.*, he would hold on to a bit of bad news for a time on the chance of getting a bit of good news to publish as an offset, and I must say that it not infrequently came off! On the other hand, there were days when it did not, and then there was a sort of "Black Monday" atmosphere about—a bad "settling day" sort of look on all our faces.
>
> After he left I always pleaded for the immediate publication of disasters or, at any rate, that they should be made known as soon as the number of casualties had been reported and the relatives informed; and this soon became more or less the practice.[4]

The British followed the policy of complete silence when they lost the battleship *Audacious* on the 27th of October, 1914, by a mine off the Irish coast. It was never officially acknowledged while the War lasted, and was solemnly reported after the armistice. The Germans were able to make a great deal of capital out of the reticence of the British in the early days, and it was not until the Jutland affair that the British were able, by a daring stroke, to recapture confidence at home and abroad. The Germans announced by wireless on the 31st of May that they had won a great naval victory. Damaged ships and messages to relatives began to come along the east coast of England, and silence was no longer feasible. The official communiqué for the 2nd of June made a clean breast of the British losses as so far reported. The shock was stupendous. When the enemy losses began to come in later in the day, the general consternation was somewhat assuaged. The Germans were slowly constrained to admit the truth.[5]

It is probably sound, on the whole, to reveal losses when they come, and to trust to the ingenious multiplication of favourable news to neutralize the effect. Special problems arise in connection with losses which are known only in a general way to the enemy. Brownrigg opposed the publication of British losses of merchant ships from enemy submarines and mines on the ground that the enemy would, in this way, be supplied with precise information that he would not otherwise get. The public demand for enlightenment on the progress of the submarine war was so insistent that a compromise was ultimately arrived at. At first, the number of ships lost per week was announced, with no further particulars, and later, the tonnage lost per week was substituted for the number of ships. This suggests a sound principle in dealing with such matters. When the losses are of such a character that the enemy cannot be entirely certain of them, the disclosure ought to take a summary and not a particularized form. A definite total is necessary in order to allay the wild exaggerations of alarmist whispers.

Another problem which arises in the conduct of war is how to treat new devices of warfare which it is proposed to introduce. Every new innovation by a belligerent is likely to be welcomed at home as a promise of victory, and to be condemned abroad as a crime against humanity. But there are exceptions to this rule, and for the sake of squeamish souls at home, who may deplore the introduction of particularly devastating measures, a careful campaign of preparation should be launched. If it is reported that the enemy has just adopted a new device, cries will arise instantly for its adoption as a measure of justifiable reprisal. Aerial bombardment and the use of gas were supposed by both the Allied and the German publics to be the product of the nefarious genius of the other side. The submarine was defended in Germany as a reply to the brutal British blockade which had so far disregarded the bounds of international law as to become a weapon of attack against the old and the very young, the women and the children, rather than against the fighting men. The Government defended the order to sink without warning, by telling how the Allies took advantage of the kind heart of a certain submarine commander. An English sailor, dressed in women's clothes, and with a bundle which appeared to be a baby, stood on the deck of a boat which a submarine had just stopped. The submarine came up to take off the unfortunate woman before sinking the ship, when the disguised sailor suddenly dropped a bomb on the submarine, destroying it instantly.

For those very numerous members of the nation who visualize war as a battle of goliaths, the propaganda of confidence in leaders is indispensable. It is a reassuring experience to read a well-written biography of a public character. Otto Krack wrote a popular *Life of Ludendorff*, and Harold Begbie glorified Kitchener in his book, *Kitchener, Organiser of Victory*. *General Paul von Hindenburg* was written up by Bernard von Hindenburg.

Reports of heroic achievement in routine or exceptional jobs strengthen the assurance of ultimate victory. To the tales from the trenches must be added the less dramatic tale of how the country is solidly behind the front in food saving, munition making, and relief work. Rudolf Hans Bartsch took a trip around Germany and described Das deutsche Volk in schwerer Zeit, a volume which was reassuring to the men at the front and encouraging to the civilians.

The will to win is intimately related to a chance to win. The thesis of ultimate victory is indispensable to the conduct of war, if discouragement is not to sap determination and to precipitate internal friction and strife.

Notes

[1] The record of the first few days is found in Graux, *Les Fausses Nouvelles de la Grande Guerre*, vol. 1.

[2] For the pre-war literature which forecasted and analysed the strategy of the War, see John Bakeless, *The Origin of the Next War*, ch. X. For another side of a controversial issue, see Philip Neame, *German Strategy and the Great War*.

[3] Graux, as cited, I: 244.

[4] Rear-Admiral Sir Douglas Brownrigg, *Indiscretions of the Naval Censor*, p. 13.

[5] Brownrigg tells the story from the British point of view in Chapter 4 of the book cited.

6
PRESERVING FRIENDSHIP

One prerequisite of a solid front against the enemy is cordial relations among allies. It is particularly important that allies should stimulate one another by emphasizing their strenuous exertion in the prosecution of the war. During the last War the effective entry of America into the struggle came before Italy had recovered from the collapse of Caporetto. Weary and discouraged, the Italian people were cynical of America's whole-hearted sincerity in making war. The Americans, so it was whispered about, are an industrial people, who have forgotten how to fight. They are unwilling to forsake their prosperous jobs for a post of danger. America had no army, did not want one, and could not raise one if she tried. Supposing that an army were actually raised, the submarines would sink all transports capable of bringing it to Europe. And, anyhow, American officers and soldiers were too inexperienced to matter much. [1]

The ringing keynote of American propaganda in Italy was, therefore, the invincible determination of America to smash the Central Powers, as revealed by her war preparations. The New York Office of the Committee on Public Information prepared items of news which were distributed through the Agenzi Stefani, the largest Press Association. These items had to do with military preparation, ship building, food conservation, Liberty Loans, Red Cross and other civilian services. A special mimeographed news letter was addressed to influential Italians.

Italian journalists were selected to tour America and report their impressions. Italians who lived in America were encouraged to write letters home, telling about the great American effort. Newspapers were induced to cooperate, pamphlets and booklets were put in print, Americans (especially of Italian origin) were sent over to speak, and motion picture reels and lantern slides were furnished in great profusion. American photographs and postcards, ribbons and buttons, posters, flags, music and exhibits were multiplied everywhere. A detachment of real, live American soldiers was brought to Italy, less for fighting than for exhibition purposes, and they aroused tremendous enthusiasm as the advance guard of America's contingent.

The dominating theme in all this was America's strenuous effort to win the War. The head of the Mission to Italy writes,

> Our only inaccuracy consisted in understating the magnitude of American preparations. We felt that since Americans had a reputation as boasters it would be better to understate than to overstate, and were greatly pleased to receive, after having been in Italy for some months, a friendly criticism from an Italian who declared that the information that we were furnishing did not reveal the full strength of America's effort.

Strenuousness in the conduct of the war is not, of itself, sufficient to arouse the enthusiasm of an ally, if there is any reason to suspect that the war aims of one ally are at cross purposes with those of another. The English were continually forced to deal with an undercurrent of suspicion in France that victory would be used to the disadvantage of France. Persistent rumours crept about that the English were not only planning to stay in Calais, as shown by the fact that they were building quarters of permanent material, but that they were chiefly instrumental in prolonging the War for the sole purpose of using French blood to drown a dangerous commercial rival. In the hard winter of 1917 Mr. Wickham Steed, of the London *Times*, was appalled to discover how much headway had been made by the insinuation that a favourable peace could be secured at any time, if England were willing to return the colonies which she had taken from Germany.

Steed seized the opportunity in one of his lectures to explain that the former colonies of Germany could never be disposed of at the arbitrary whim of Downing Street. The British Empire was no longer, strictly speaking, an Empire; it had become a Commonwealth of Nations, whose component members had spilt their blood in these former German territories, and would never consent to permit Downing Street to use them as mere bargaining points. Steed believed that it was only by explaining the constitutional facts of the British Empire that the rumour could be squashed once and for all.[2]

Some of the lukewarmness of Italy toward American participation in the War was due to the widely circulated assertion that America had entered the War to capture the commercial supremacy of the world. The American plan was to loan vast sums to the impoverished Governments of Europe and, once the War terminated, to demand compensation of an unspecified, but alarming kind. This subtle campaign of insinuation and suspicion was met by a vigorous Wilsonian propaganda, which dwelt upon the disinterested and humanitarian character of America's war aims.

The French were grieved to discover that American opinion was by no means united in support of the thesis that Alsace and Lorraine should be handed over to France at the end of hostilities. The French War Mission to the United States busied itself to convert the Americans, and the French High Commissioner, M. Tardieu, strained every nerve in this direction. A few months after his arrival in May, 1917, he takes pleasure in recording,

> this state of opinion was entirely changed. I venture
> to believe that the activities of my co-workers and
> myself, the 15,000 lectures in English where young
> officers, with all the authority of their war record
> and of their wounds, presented the pitiful situation

of the captive provinces, had something to do with this transformation. (He organized an Association of Alsatians and Lorrainers in America.) Thousands of huge posters, reproducing Henner's *Alsacienne* with the text of the Bordeaux protest had carried the meaning and scope of our claim to every State in the Union.[3]

The process of "selling" one country to another is illustrated by the campaign to secure American support, which was waged by the friends of Lithuania in 1919. The Lithuanian National Committee retained a public relations counsel to conduct a campaign which was practically tantamount to encouraging an ally to accept the aims (complete independence) desired by its minor partner. The following moves were made by the public relations counsel:

He had an exhaustive study made of every conceivable aspect of the problem of Lithuania from its remote and recent history and ethnic origins to its present-day marriage customs and its popular recreations. He divided his material into various categories, based primarily on the public to which it would probably make its appeal. For the amateur ethnologist he provided interest and accurate data of the racial origins of Lithuania. To the student of languages he appealed with authentic and well-written studies of the development of the Lithuanian language from its origins in Sanscrit. He told the "sporting fan" about Lithuanian sports, and he told the women about Lithuanian clothes. He told the jeweller about amber and provided the music lovers with concerts of Lithuanian music.

To the senators he gave the facts about Lithuania which would give them basis for favourable action. To the members of the House of Representatives he did likewise. He reflected to those communities whose crystallized opinions would be helpful in guiding other opinions facts which gave them basis for conclusions favourable to Lithuania.

A series of events which would carry with them the desired implications were planned and executed. Mass meetings were held in different cities; petitions were drawn, signed and presented; pilgrims made calls upon Senate and House of Representatives Committees. All the avenues of approach to the public were utilized to capitalize the public interest and bring public action. The mails carried statements of Lithuania's position to individuals who might be interested. The lecture platform resounded to Lithuania's appeal. Newspaper advertising was bought and paid for. The radio carried the message of speakers to the public. Motion pictures reached the patrons of moving picture houses.

Little by little, and phase by phase, the public, the Press, and the Government officials acquired a knowledge of the customs, the character, and the problem of Lithuania and the small Baltic nation that was seeking its freedom.

When the Lithuanian Information Bureau went before the Press Associations to correct inaccurate or misleading Polish news about the Lithuanian situation, it came there as representative of a group which had figured largely in American news for a number of weeks, as a result of the advice and activities of its public relations counsel. In the same way, when delegations of Americans, interested in the Lithuanian problem, appeared before the members of Congress or officials of the State Department, they came there as spokesmen for a country which was no longer ignored.[4]

This sort of propaganda needs to be supplemented by constant assertions of respect and esteem. The Allies observed one another's chief holidays. The American 4th of July was spread far and wide in Europe. American propagandists staged a great demonstration in honour of Italy's entry into the World War (May 24th). The public addresses and statements issued by the Inter-Allied War Missions consisted in fulsome phraseology which rang true in moments of profound emotional agitation.[5]

Each ally ought to re-enforce the themes of domestic propaganda at every point. They must stimulate each other to realize that their own interests are at once threatened and obstructed by the enemy. It was failure on this point that may have been partly responsible for the defection of revolutionary Russia from the ranks of the Entente. Colonel Robins was sent over to Russia to aid Colonel Thompson of the American Red Cross, and his version of what happened in Russia is a matter of public record in the hearing conducted before a Senatorial investigating committee. Colonel Robins went out to see what the soldiers were thinking, and when he came back, Colonel Thompson asked him:

> "Now, this thing is cutting deep, is it not—this thing that is going through Russia—this defeatist culture?" I said: "Yes, Colonel; and it tends to disorganize the whole Russian social fabric." He said, "Well, what about the Allied propaganda?" I said "Colonel, that is worse than nothing." The Allied propaganda at that hour, Senator Overman, was this: Pictures and written words about how great France is, how tremendous England is, how overwhelming America is. "We will have 20,000 airplanes on the front in a few weeks. In a few months we will have 4,000,000 soldiers. We will win the war in a walk." The peasant moujik said: "Oh, is that so? Well, if the Allies are going to win the war in a walk, we who have been fighting and working a long time will go back and see the folks at home"; and the real effect of the

Allied propaganda was to weaken the morale instead of strengthening it, if I am any judge of the facts.

It was agreed among us that there was an answer that was close to the ground, and that was genuine— an effort to interpret this to revolutionary Russia, cursed by the Tsar's espousal of the Allied cause in the first instance, and by all the cross-currents that followed; that, although it was not possible at all, I knew, to get that massed revolutionary mind to think as we thought as Allies, it was possible to get them to fight Germany to save the Revolution; and if they served the cause, we did not care anything about what they thought, and we said, This is the situation: We have got to interpret the holding of the front and the defeat of German militarist autocracy into terms of saving the Revolution; and it happens to be true. We have got to say that, if the German militarist autocracy wins, the Russian Revolution is doomed. We have got to picture it until the average soldier and peasant sees behind the German bayonets the barons and feudal landlords coming to take back the land; behind the German bayonets the feudal masters of industry coming back to transmute the 8 hours and 15 roubles of the Revolution back to the 2 roubles and 12 hours of the semi-slave days before the Revolution in the factories, mills, and mines. We have got to have them see that behind the German bayonets are the grand dukes coming to destroy their local self-governing soviets and revolutionary councils. If we do that, we can save the situation.

In the second or third conference on this matter the question of money came up. It was a large enterprise. "How are you going to do it?" Well, it was perfectly apparent that you could not do it. There was no machinery to do it, no American or Allied bureau to do it. The Allies shared in the common curse of the autocracy in the mind of peasant Russia. It had to be Russian, and it had to be revolutionary.

There was in the Winter Palace at that time Madame Breshkovsky, that old and yet heroic figure, possibly the greatest revolutionary figure at that time. Madame Breshkovsky, after 40 years of service in Russia for the Revolution, was now at the Winter Palace in Petrograd, having come back from Siberia in a triumphal journey with great celebrations, having been received in Petrograd by one of the greatest gatherings in the history of that city—this old peasant woman and revolutionist received in the great railroad station in the chamber of the Tsar, honoured by the ministers of the government, and all that sort of thing. She was now in the Winter Palace, in the Grand Duke's suite that looked out over the Neva to Peter and Paul, where she had been three years a prisoner. It was a dramatic, a tremendous setting. I had known her, known her for 12 years, known her when she was in this country; had helped her in some of her work at that time. I knew Nicholas Tchaikovsky, a thoroughly sincere and genuine revolutionist, and at that time the head of the Peasant Co-operative in Russia.

It was agreed by Col. Thompson that there should be organized a committee on civic education for free Russia. Madame Breshkovsky should be chairman of the committee; and as members there should be Nicholas Tchaikovsky; Lazaroff, the Russian revolutionist, who had been head of the milk station or dairy in Switzerland, which was really an underground station for the Russian Revolution, for many years, and well known with credit through service to his country; Gen. Neuslakovsky, the most trusted member of Kerensky's general staff, who was in active co-operation with this committee from the military angle; and David Soskice, Kerensky's private secretary. They were to form the committee on "Civic education in Free Russia." The programme was this: "We will begin by buying some newspapers, and with other publicity we will prepare simple statements in peasant patois and in the general terms of the Russian peasant's and workingman's mind, by Russian peasants and workmen, not by intelligentsia. We will send into the ranks and into the peasant villages this new gospel of fighting German militarist autocracy; not to serve the Allies but to save the Revolution.[6]

Colonel William B. Thompson spent one million dollars of his own money on this sort of propaganda in an effort to stave off the defection of Russia.[7]

At the first of the War the keynote of the Allied propaganda was very properly the thesis of ultimate victory against an aggressive Germany. It required all the ingenuity of the Allied representatives in Russia to bolster the Russian morale during the months of August and September when the French and British armies were recoiling before the German avalanche. The French Ambassador, writing in his diary of those days, records:

> I have seen to it that these events should be presented by the Russian Press in the most suitable (and perhaps the truest) light, *i.e.*, as a temporary and methodical retirement, a prelude to a *volte-face* in the near future for the purposes of a more formidable and vigorous offensive. All the papers support this theory.[8]

He was confronted by this situation:

> Financial circles in Petrograd are in continuous communication with Germany through Sweden, and all their views on the war are inspired by Berlin.

The thesis they have been expounding during the last few weeks bears a thoroughly German stamp. We must see things as they are, they say. The two groups of belligerents must realize that neither will ever succeed in vanquishing and really crushing the other. The war will inevitably end in arrangements and compromise. In that case, the sooner the better. If the hostilities continue, the Austro-Germans will organize an enormous fortified line around their present conquests, and make it impregnable. So in the future let us give up these futile offensives; with the inviolable protection of their trenches, they will patiently wait until their disheartened adversaries moderate their demands. Thus peace will inevitably be negotiated on the basis of territorial pledges.

. . . I never fail to reply that it is our enemies' vital interest to obtain a swift decision, because, when all is said and done, their material resources are limited, while ours are practically inexhaustible. In any case the German General Staff is condemned by its theories to preserve an offensive strategy.[9]

There are circumstances in which the unity of operations is seriously prejudiced by stimulating the self-confidence of an ally. The Germans were fearful lest the Austrian and Hungarian authorities might grow too sanguine of the future and resent their subordination to the northern ally.[10]

The propaganda which is directed to disaffected groups inside a nation may be powerfully reinforced by inter-Allied co-operation. The Catholics of Italy were not only subjected to the appeals of certain Italian leaders who were friendly to the Allies, but from such men as Cardinal Gibbons, Cardinal Farley and Cardinal O'Connell, of the American hierarchy. The Labour groups of Italy were reached, not alone by pro-Ally leaders at home, but by a visiting selection of Radicals from abroad. The Americans brought over Alexander Howat ("the man who never lost a strike") and John Spargo.

Inter-Allied propagandas of friendship require a reciprocal control of attitudes. Most of the friendly sentiments toward an ally are manufactured by one country among its own population. The stimulation of pro-ally emotions at home is more important than the stimulation of pro-ally sentiments abroad. The themes to employ are identical with the ones which have already been enumerated in connection with the problem of arousing an ally.

Sometimes the business of retouching the figure of an ally in the public mind is a delicate and precarious operation. Arthur Meyer frankly marvelled at the extent of the rapprochement between France and England, for he could remember when the children of Paris were chanting the couplet:

> Jamais, jamais en France
> L'Anglais ne règnera![11]

Sometimes a frank apology helps, as when the celebrated writer, Pierre Loti, of the French Academy, published in the *Figaro* his plea to Serbia:

> Pauvre, petite Serbie, devenue tout à coup martyre et sublime, je voudrais au moins lui ramener les quelques cours français que mon dernier livre a peut-être éloignés d'elle.[12]

The most delicate problem was how to evoke a pro-Russian response in the ranks of the British public. For many years the traditional menace to the Empire had been Russia, and not Germany, and the stories of Russian absolutism froze the blood of a nation inoculated with parliamentarism. The success in revamping the public attitude was indeed notable, and Basil Thompson, head of Scotland Yard, looks back upon it rather cynically from the vantage ground of subsequent years:

> It is strange, now, to think that in March, 1915, Russia was thought in England to be breathing a new

inspiration to the West. It was said that the Crusader spirit was alive again, that the whole Russian nation was inspired with a determination to rescue Constantinople for Christianity, and to win again the holy sepulchre; . . . vodka was prohibited with the unanimous approval of the nation; . . . crime had almost disappeared among the peasants. . . If they were successful in the war they were told that there would be a struggle between their religious idealism and their high ethical instincts and the monster of western materialism from which, so far, they had kept themselves clean. All this was honestly believed by persons who thought they knew Russia; now, after a short six years, their voices are heard no more.[13]

When a bond of traditional friendship unites two countries, it is simple to invoke it for emergencies. In this style does Gaston Riou welcome the Americans in his *Lafayette, nous voilà!* (Paris, 1917.)

Important as the maintenance of friendly relations between the nations fighting on one side really is, the crucial problem for the outcome of the war often is the attitude of the neutrals. The essential problem in controlling neutral attitudes is to lead the neutral to identify your enemy as his enemy and your aims as his aims.

There is an imperceptible slant in the war news, which comes from one side rather than another, which leads to the propagation of a powerful bias toward the contending nations. Almost inadvertently one comes to speak of "our victory," "the enemy retired," or "our lines held." The fact that England controlled the cables to the United States was a precious advantage in her favour. The Germans were never able to perfect their wireless service to the point of competing with the cables on a plane of equality. Less from original bias than from a subtle entanglement in the bias of the news, there appeared in certain New York papers headlines of this character, even when the Germans were pounding down through Belgium and northern France:

BELGIUM BEATS GERMANS;
ENGLISH ARMY TO AID HER.
GERMANS LOSE THOUSANDS IN BELGIUM.
ROUT OF GERMANS IN BELGIUM
TURNED INTO A SLAUGHTER.

The direct representation of the other side as an enemy of the neutrals may take a multitude of forms. As early as 1915 a book was devoted to the horrible fate of America in case Germany should win the War. In J. Bernard Walker's *America Fallen: A Sequel to the European War*, the Germans sack New York (London, 1915). This time-honoured device was employed at the time of the Franco-Prussian war to incite England against Germany. In *Blackwood's Magazine* for April, 1871, appeared an article called "The Fall of England, or the Battle of Dorking," which was reprinted as a pamphlet and sold broadcast.

The Germans found it impossible to raise the claim that Great Britain intended to attack America, since the British were obviously very much engaged in Western Europe. Instead, they insinuated that the attack upon America would come by the characteristically English method of indirection. Japan would do the will of England. What other interpretation, indeed, could there be placed upon the Anglo-Japanese Alliance? Why is Japan

feverishly engaged in ship building and has now under way 168,000 tons of shipping?

We Americans feel safe, peaceful and conceited as we sell to Europe tools with which they murder each other, and as we say to ourselves, "We are too big to be in danger."

We would feel differently if we knew that Japan, representing all Asia, all the yellow race, had decided that the moment had arrived to make the attack, and to make both sides of the Pacific Japanese.[14]

Jefferson Jones viewed *The Fall of Tsingtau* (New York, 1915) with alarm, and the book was of some aid in arousing suspicion of the Japanese.

The heterogeneous composition of the American community lent itself to special propagandas. It was possible to arouse the Jews against the Russians, the Irish against the British, the Westerners against the Japanese, and (for some time) the Italians against the French. The Entente could appeal to the English, French, Scotch, Welsh, Russian, Serbian, Rumanian elements, and, after the growth of anti-Austro-Hungarian sentiment, to the South Slavs and the Czecho-Slovaks and the Poles.

The hereditary enemy of America, the *Erbfeind*, was England, and upon the anti-English chord the Germans strummed incessantly. It was England who burned Washington in 1814, and drew from Jefferson the bitter saying that

> It was reserved for England to show that Napoleon
> in atrocity was an infant compared to her ministers
> and generals.

It was moreover, the dastardly English who stirred up the Indians to massacre the Americans who lived on the frontier during the Revolutionary War, and the War of 1812. Perfidious Albion is still trying to put something over, and Mr. O'Reilly, through the hospitable columns of the Hearst press, asked:

> Are we not being bribed to sacrifice our own best
> interests as well as our moral scruples, and to send
> arms to England, so that then she can exterminate
> the Germans and obliterate Germany, and possess
> herself of Germany's commerce and colonies?[15]

The Central Powers were set forth as the champions of the traditional American principle of a free sea. This thesis was argued in William Bayard Hale's pamphlet, *American Rights and British Pretensions on the Seas.*[16] The British offset this appeal by exposing the German plans to expand into South America after the War, regardless of the Monroe Doctrine, and to conquer the world for German trade, by cementing a European bloc.[17] The British likewise rose to assert that they were fighting a war of democracy versus militarism and autocracy, and they published General Bernhardi's *Germany and the Next War*, to convict the whole nation. A brilliant rationalization such as that of H. G. Wells in *Mr. Britling Sees it Through*, won a large audience in America.

Hand in hand with other plans must go the systematic vilification of the enemy. During the Franco-Prussian War the French raised a great outcry in England at the proposed bombardment of Paris, bitterly assailing the Germans for their barbarous indifference to the priceless treasures of civilization. Bismarck was quite aware of the importance of this appeal to neutral sentiment, and instructed one of his propaganda secretaries to draft an article for the Press on this theme:

> If the French wanted to preserve their monuments and collections of books and pictures from the dangers of war, they should not have surrounded them with fortifications. Besides, the French themselves did not hesitate for a moment to bombard Rome, which contained monuments of far greater value, the destruction of which would have been an irretrievable loss.[18]

When the London *Standard*, which was hostile to the Germans during the War of 1870, printed a story by the Duc de FitzJames, in which various Prussian abominations at Bazeilles were described, Bismarck dictated an answer to be transmitted to the English Press. He argued that the horrors of the War were not horrors of the Germans, but of the foolish stories of Prussian cruelty which frightened the peasants into deserting their homes where they would have been secure. He attacked the reliability of the Duc as witness.[19]

During the same War, the French prepared a pamphlet for circulation at home and abroad which was entitled *La Guerre comme la font les Prussiens*. Bismarck instructed Busch,

> Please write to Berlin that they should put together
> something of this description from our point of view,
> quoting all the cruelties, barbarities and breaches
> of the Geneva Convention committed by the French.
> Not too much, however, or no one will read it, and it
> must be done speedily.[20]

During the World War the neutrals were deluged with propaganda stuff, in which the sins of the enemy were exposed to public gaze. Besides the appeal to the general sentiment of the neutral nation, hosts of special appeals were launched. The Germans circulated an appeal to Protestants in neutral countries to rise and protest against the mistreatment of missionaries by the English. Rev. W. Stark prepared a pamphlet on *The Martyrdom of the Evangelical Missionaries in Cameroon*, 1914, (Berlin, 1914). Such damages as were inflicted in the occupied territories to churches were assigned to the Germans. The Catholics, as the chief sufferers, organized a special propaganda committee to work on foreign Catholic opinion. The nature of its work appears from the following list:

> René le Cholleux, *Notre Dame de Brébières;
> l'Allemagne et les Allies devant la conscience
> chrétienne* (pref. Mgr. Alfred Baudrillart).
> La Guerre Allemande el le Catholicisme.
> Raoul Narsy, *Le Supplice de Louvain.*
> *L'Éveil de l'Ame française devant l'appel aux armes.*
> L'Abbé Pasquier, *Le Protestantisme Allemand.*
> L'Abbé E. Foulon, *Arras sons les Obus.*

Mgr. Pierre Batiffol published his letter, *A un neutre catholique* in 1915, for the edification of the non-combatants. The French Protestants followed the example of their Catholic brethren, and established a committee for foreign propaganda and advertised *Nos sanctuaires dévastés*. The Italians used the same weapon in the pamphlet, *Austrian Barbarities against Italian Churches* (Florence, 1917).

This atrocity propaganda was conducted with great ability in America, particularly by the Allies. A mass meeting at Carnegie Hall in New York protested against the treatment of the Belgians, December 18th, 1916. Rector Manning presided, and there were addresses by the Hon. James M. Beck, Alton B. Parker, Elihu Root, and telegrams from Theodore Roosevelt, Joseph H. Choate, and Archbishop Ireland. An appeal from Cardinal Mercier was read, and the whole affair procured the widest publicity in the Press.

The Russian Government went so far as to address a special memorandum to neutral powers, for the purpose of protesting against the alleged slanders which the Central Powers were industriously circulating about the conduct of her troops. She likewise objected to the *Violations of Laws and Rules of Warfare, committed by German and Austro-Hungarian troops in Russia* (1915). The Germans were outmanoeuvred by the British, who secured the services of the former Ambassador Bryce to serve on an atrocity commission. The protest which the Kaiser addressed to the President of the United States against the franc-tireur excesses of the Belgians proved ineffectual. They compiled a mass of material for the purpose of incriminating the Belgians, such as the *Völkerrechtswidrige Rührung des belgischen Volkskrieges*, put out by the Foreign Office, May 10th, 1915. They advertised the misdeeds of the invading Russians in East Prussia, and sharply criticized the mistreatment of German civilians and military prisoners abroad.[21] The Belgians replied officially to the charges lodged against them, but one of the best indirect replies was a study made by Fernand van Langenhove, Scientific Secretary of the Solvay Institute of Sociology at Brussels, on *The Growth of a Legend. A Study, based upon the German accounts of Francs-Tireurs and "Atrocities."* The English version of the work had a Preface by the eminent American social psychologist, J. Mark Baldwin, a diligent Francophile during the entire War.[22] With the air and method of a serious study in collective psychology the book treated the franc-tireur stories as legends.

For circulation in America the Germans prepared an appeal to race prejudice, called *Employment contrary to International Law*

*of Coloured Troops upon the European Arena of War by England
and France* (Berlin, 1915).

Indeed, everybody took a whirl at blackguarding his enemies
and whitewashing himself. All the minorities in America had their
special propaganda, issuing such things as *Austro-Hungarian
Judicial Crimes* (Chicago, no date), prepared by the Jugo-Slav
Committee in North America. As late as 1918 the Bulgarians tried
to reach the neutral world with a defence and a counter-thrust by
publishing *Les Atrocités Serbes*, by M. D. Sopiansky (Lausanne,
1918). The most important feature, of course, was to secure the
services of an eminent neutral to testify to his own countrymen.
Mary Roberts Rinehart (*Kings, Queens and Pawns*, 1915) and
scores of publicists gave their pens to the Allied cause; fewer helped
to expound the German viewpoint.

The other side is a nefarious plotter and liar, unworthy of confidence. Frederick William Wile endeavoured to expose *The German-
American Plot, the record of a great failure* (London, 1915), and
every idea which convenienced the plot was dubbed with the damning epithet, "Pro-German." The Germans poured out the same dark
hints and insinuations about the members of the American Press
and public who dared disagree with them. The American Truth
Society wrote about the Treason Press, and in this indictment they
meant nearly all the American Press of metropolitan standing, except Hearst and the Chicago Tribune. It goes without saying that
ex-President Roosevelt came in for vile abuse from the German
sympathizers. Everybody tried to tar the other fellow with the same
stick. Rumours of propaganda and bribery fell thick and fast.

Direct appeals to neutral opinion continued all through the
conflict. In 1914 James Bryce discussed the *Neutral Nations and
the War*. The Germans used one of their Swiss connections to publish an exposure of *Comment l'Angleterre combat les neutres*
(Zurich, 1917); to which the British replied in William Archer, *An
die Neutralen! Aufruf zur Geduld* (1917). Max Gaetcke discussed
Der grosse Raubkrieg und die Interessen der neutralen Mächte
(Karlsruhe, 1916), while the French contributions to this literature

included Henri Hauser, *La Guerre et les Neutres. Etude sur le sentiment démocratique dans ses rapports avec la guerre européenne* (Paris, 1917), and Ernest Lémonon, *Les Alliés et les Neutres*, 1914-16 (Paris, 1917).

To the general appeals were added the special appeals. The French Federation of Schoolteachers prepared a message, *To the Schoolmistresses and Schoolmasters of all countries*. The famous *Aufruf Gelehrter Deutschen*, which came early in the War, provoked the professors abroad to feverish hyperactivity. One of the numerous replies was intended for consumption in Southern Europe and South America. A manifestation was held at the Sorbonne on the 12th of February, 1915, and the addresses which were delivered were printed under a favourite title with the French, *La civilisation latine contre la barbarie allemande*. For the sake of interesting the wage earners, an *Appeal of the Belgian Workmen to the Workmen of all Nations* appeared in London in 1916, and a year later, *The Condition of the Belgian Workmen, now Refugees in England*.

Besides the direct themes of the order hitherto enumerated neutral opinion may be reached by indirect ones. The neutral must be confident of the ultimate success of your side. Georges Hoog published his *Lettres aux neutres sur l'union sacrée*, to impress the neutrals with the solidarity of his country. Books of type of Robert Grant, *Their Spirit. Some Impressions of the English and French during the Summer of* 1916, reassure the friends of one side and affect the indifferent. The heroism and determination of a belligerent can be illustrated in military and civilian war letters, such as *War Letters from France* (edited by A. de Lapradelle and Frederick Coudert, New York and London, 1916). The pictorial medium was chosen by the Information Department of the British Foreign Office, to impress the neutrals with British strength, and the film called *Britain Prepared* was widely circulated.[23]

The crucial importance of the foreign correspondent is alluded to by Theodore Roosevelt in his letter to Sir Edward Grey, bearing the date, January 22nd, 1915:

There have been fluctuations in American opinion
about the war. The actions of the German Zeppelins
have revived the feeling in favour of the Allies. But I
believe that for a couple of months preceding this
action there had been a distinct lessening of the feeling for the Allies and a growth of pro-German feeling. I do not think that this was the case among the
people who were best informed, but I do think it was
the case among the mass of not very well-informed
people, who have little to go upon except what they
read in the newspapers or see at cinematograph
shows. There were several causes for this change.
There has been a very striking contrast between the
lavish attentions showered on American war correspondents by the German military authorities and
the blank refusal to have anything whatever to do
with them by the British and French Governments.
Our best war correspondent on the whole, is probably Frederick Palmer. He is favourable to the Allies.
But it was the Germans, and not the Allies, who did
everything for him. They did not change his attitude,
but they unquestionably did change the attitude of
many other good men. The only real war news, written by Americans who are known to and trusted by
the American public, comes from the German side;
as a result of this, the sympathizers with the cause
of the Allies can hear nothing whatever about the
trials and achievements of the British and French
armies. These correspondents inform me that it is
not the generals at the front who raise objections, but
the Home Governments, and in consequence they get
the chance to write for their fellow-countrymen what
happens from the German side, and they are not
given a chance from the side of the Allies. I do not
find that the permission granted them by the Germans has interfered with the efficiency of German

military operations, and it has certainly helped the Germans in American public opinion. It may be that your people do not believe that American public opinion is of sufficient value to be taken into account, but, if you think that it should be taken into account, then it is worth your while considering whether much of your censorship work and much of your refusal to allow correspondents at the front has not been a danger to your cause from the standpoint of the effect on public opinion without any corresponding military gains. I realize perfectly that it would be criminal to permit correspondents to act as they acted as late as our own Spanish War, but as a layman, I feel sure that there has been a good deal of work of this kind of which I have spoken in the way of censorship and refusing the correspondents permission to go to the front, which has not been of the slightest military service to you, and which has had a very real effect in preventing any rallying of public opinion to you.[24]

One of the most subtle and effective forms of indirect propaganda is the encouragement of everything which draws the neutral into some form of *de facto* co-operation with the belligerent. This may be done in part by playing up the instances in which a neutral citizen takes arms on behalf of one or the other belligerent. This phase of propaganda was discussed in the following letter to the London *Times*, dated December 26th, 1916, by an American partisan of the Entente. It was called "British Publicity in the United States," and read thus:

France has known how to reach the sympathy of Americans, and her publicity has been extraordinarily effective. It has been personal and it has evoked enthusiasm. It has been written to a great extent by American soldiers in the French army, each of whom is an endorsement of France. The presence of every American participant is widely advertised by the French. He is decorated wherever there is the least occasion for doing so. He is encouraged to write of his experiences. Articles and books by American soldiers of France are published by the score. Alan Seegar's Poetry of the Foreign Legion is widely known in America, and his death was as much regretted in the United States as that of Rupert Brooke in England. Robert Herrick, one of our best novelists, joined the American Ambulance with the avowed purpose of writing a series of books from the viewpoint of a participant. I was permitted to write and publish the *Note-book of an Attaché* without ever submitting it to the French censor. There are only about 500 Americans in the French army. Yet in the United States we hear something about them every day. The newspapers are full of their doings every item of news from them is justly considered as an endorsement of France. In consequence of France's shrewdly-managed publicity America is whole-heartedly pro-French.

Because Ian Hay was a participant in the War, albeit not an American one, the publication of his book in the United States, and his extended speaking tour, shared with the books and speeches of Frederick Palmer the distinction of being the only redeeming bits of British propaganda. . . . Bruce Bairnsfather's drawings and Raemaeker's cartoons, still too little known in the United States, would prove an invaluable influence to mould public opinion.[25]

Further than this, if the neutral power can be drawn into some form of non-military participation with a belligerent, his sympathies are likely to crystallize about the object of his assistance. This is the inner significance of the tremendous campaign to secure aid for Belgian widows and orphans in America, of which one memento is the pamphlet known as *The Need of the Belgians*, prepared by an illustrious galaxy of literary stars, among whom were Thomas Hardy, May Sinclair, Arnold Bennett, Will Irwin, John Galsworthy, Anthony Hope, A. W. Mason, and George Bernard Shaw. The Committee for Belgian Relief was the sponsor for this and other details of the campaign.

The Allies succeeded in forging bonds of economic interest between themselves and America, and against this the Germans waged a propaganda offensive from the start, realizing what its implications were to be for American attitudes. William Bayard Hale wrote *The Exportation of Arms and Munitions of War* in 1915, arguing that the Allies were getting most of the benefit because of the British control of the sea, and that it was tantamount to becoming a silent partner in the Entente. His booklet was published under the auspices of the Organization of American Women for Strict Neutrality, organized for propaganda purposes.

The German propagandists took particular care to reach out for the women on this particular issue. A memorandum of one of the conferences of the New York bureau contains these items:

> *May 24th*, 1915.
> All preparations are made for carrying through the project of poster advertising. The pamphlet entitled "Thou Shalt Not Kill," written by Mr. Hale, has been printed and will be sent out. Signatures to a petition to Congress collected by the ladies now number 200,000, and will in time perhaps reach 600,000. The ladies have applied for assistance in their campaign to a number of persons named by Mr. Hale. It is suggested that it be put up to the ladies to address the petition to the President and Congress, and not wait until the collection of signatures is complete before sending it to Washington, but send them, at once, in batches of about 10,000.

Mr. Hale reports that Mrs. Hale is busy upon propaganda against the exportation of horses. Mr. Claussen undertakes to have a correspondingly touching scenario (story of former fire-brigade mare slaughtered in Flanders) written.[26]

Some editorials of William Randolph Hearst were collected under the title, *Let us promote the world's peace, not promote the world's warfare* in 1915. Martin Ilsen argued the illegality of the Ammunition Trade in 1915, and the American Independence League broadcasted a statement by Charles Nagel on the *Traffic in Arms and Ammunition*. The National German-American Alliance published an open letter by Dr. Charles J. Hexamer to the Committee on Foreign Relations in which these points were reiterated. The American Truth Society (catering to the Irish) sought to expose the *Peril of American Finance. The British Raid upon our Resources* in 1915.

As Ambassador Bernstorff has remarked, the economic question was necessarily the centre of gravity of active propaganda in America. He shrewdly comments upon the skill of the English in applying trade restriction to America. They encroached upon the freedom to trade inch and inch, and only as they stepped in to supply the market which they curtailed. Bernstorff remarks:

It is characteristic that the declaration of cotton as unconditional contraband was made public on the very day on which the American Press was in a state of great excitement over the Arabic case, so that this comparatively unimportant incident filled the front pages and leading articles of the newspapers, while the extremely important economic measure was published in a place where it would hardly be noticed.[27]

The Germans formed an association of Americans to protest against the cotton contraband, but it did little good. The cleverest move of the economic propaganda of the Germans was the provoking of "Issues," which Bernstorff has defined as

> the attempt by carefully construing individual incidents to make clear to public opinion the fundamental injustice of the English encroachments and their far-reaching consequences in practice. The most important case in this direction is that of the *Wilhelmina*. According to the prevailing principles of international law, foodstuffs were only conditional contraband. They might be imported into Germany if they were intended for the exclusive use of the civil population. As, however, England succeeded in restraining the exporters from any attempt to consign foodstuffs to Germany, especially as, in view of the enormous supplies that were being forwarded to our enemies, they had little interest in such shipment, the question never reached a clear issue. Herr Albert, therefore, induced an American firm to ship foodstuffs for the civil population of Germany on the American steamer *Wilhelmina*, bound for Hamburg, by himself undertaking the whole risk from behind the scenes (Albert was the German purchasing agent in America).

This scheme went on the rocks because the English, after capturing the ship, declared a blockade, and the decision ceased to matter. It was one of the "Issue" boats that put up a problem to the British which Ambassador Walter Hines Page was able to solve. The *Dacia*, a ship of former German ownership, which had transferred to American registry on the outbreak of war, was outfitted with crew, flag and cotton by Mr. E. N. Breitung, of Marquette, Michigan, and, after great advertisement, sailed for Germany. A terrific row would have broken out if the British captured the ship, and Page's inspiration was to allow a French warship to capture it.

This went through on schedule and not a chirp was raised in America.[28]

Neutrals may eventually be drawn into the war by direct insti-gation. The outside propagandist may circulate such pronounce-ments as those of Roosevelt, who favoured the Allies, and they may encourage the activity of the war party. In Italy, the pro-Ally sen-timent was whipped to the exploding point by d'Annunzio. The story is told thus by Thomas Nelson Page, American Ambassador to Italy, 1913 to 1919.

> It had for some time been contemplated to unveil a statue to Garibaldi and "the Thousand" at Quarto, the little port near Genoa from which they had sailed on the 5th of May, fifty-five years before, for the wresting of the Sicilians from a foreign yoke and the uniting them to the kingdom of Italy. Great prepa-rations were made for the celebration of the anni-versary of what was one of the most inspiring events in the history of Italy.
>
> The Cabinet was to attend the ceremony, and it presently became known that the King and Queen would also attend. The conviction spread through-out Italy that the occasion would be availed of to announce Italy's decision to take her place with the Forces of Liberty battling in France and declare war. All Italy was on the *qui vive*. Then, suddenly, two days before the event was to take place, the an-nouncement came that, after all, owing to the grav-ity of the moment, neither the King nor the Cabinet would attend the unveiling. . . .
>
> The absence of the King and the Cabinet from the celebration at Quarto may have given it a some-what different trend, but certainly not one less vio-lent. The orator of the occasion, Gabriel d'Annunzio, the poet and novelist, who had come from France for the purpose, delivered with telling effect an

address which was rather a lyrical rhapsody on Italian liberty and aspiration than an historical address. It fell on ears attuned to receive it, and was, in fact, a firebrand stuck into a magazine charged and ready for the explosion. That night the streets of Genoa were choked with the crowds that apotheosized Garibaldi and the orator, d'Annunzio, and clamoured for war. After this it was a continued progression— nothing could stop it. . . .

The orator of Quarto came to Rome in a sort of triumphal procession, and for days spoke in a species of lyric frenzy, from hotel balconies or in theatres to excited crowds who followed him into a state of exaltation. On the 14th he spoke in the Constanza Opera House, which was heavily guarded, all approaches being picketed, by a strong force of police and soldiers, including an extra force of cavalry to preserve order and prevent demonstrations before the Government offices and the Embassies of the Central Empires. The overflow demonstrants, left outside of the auditorium, resisted all efforts to disperse them, building barricades and tearing down a rear wall around an open lot adjoining the Opera House to use as missiles against the soldiers should the latter be too firm in attempting to clear the streets.[29]

When the state of neutral sentiment seems to be ebbing steadily away from the belligerent toward whom it is hoped to direct it, the propagandist may retire to certain last lines of defence. The Germans in the United States did what they could to encourage pacifist sentiment. The American League to Limit Armaments had been organized in 1914, by sincere pacifists who hoped to keep America out of the European maelstrom. This later developed into the American Union against Militarism, one of whose offshoots subsequently became the National Civil Liberties Bureau. The American

Union Against Militarism organized the Collegiate Anti-Militarism League, and co-operated with numerous Peace Unions and Christian Socialist Fellowship organizations. The American Neutral Conference Committee was an emergency group which had the objective indicated by its name. The Emergency Peace Federation came to an early end, as did the Conference Committee. The Germans, of course, got such aid and comfort as they could from the existence of such societies and played the peace theme heavily as 1917 approached.

A dangerous idea—from the standpoint of the Allies—which the Germans propagated in America was that the Allies were the stumbling block to peace. The British were genuinely exercised by the progress of the peace drive of the Germans and Sir Edward Grey confesses that the German effort to cast the onus of continuing the War upon the Entente, was one of the most effective moves which they made.[30]

It may be possible to stir up trouble between two neutrals and thus tie the hands of the neutral. Such a purpose appears in the rather amusing story of a German feature film named "Patria." This was a serial photoplay which was released weekly in two-reel episodes for a span of ten weeks. It was made under the direction of Whartons, in upper New York, for the International Film Service Corporation, a Hearst-owned film distributing company, later reincorporated as the International Film Service Company (Incorporated). It was made in 1916, and cost about $90,000. Mrs. Vernon Castle was the star. When it began to appear, it purported to emphasize the necessity for preparedness. By the time the first episodes were ready, the country was already launched upon a preparedness programme, leaving its anti-Japanese and anti-Mexican features as the only live ones. The picture shows the great effort of Japan to conquer America with the aid of the Mexicans. A Japanese noble, at the head of the secret service of the Emperor of Japan, was the chief villain. Japanese troops invaded California, committing horrible atrocities. The picture was first shown in New York on the 9th January, 1917. The New York *American* and other Hearst papers ran the story serially from week to week. When the anti-Japanese element had to be suppressed, the Japanese names and characters were supplanted by Mexican names and inscriptions. But in the film, they were still wearing Japanese uniforms.[31] At the last moment, it was thus converted into an effort to inflame two neutrals.

The Chicago *Tribune* once cited an admission in the *Neueste Nachrichten* of Leipzig, that Germany could look with complacency upon strained relations between the United States and Mexico, because, while digesting this hard nut, Jonathan must cease to be John Bull's willing servant.

The *Tribune* properly observed that

> If the United States had to devote all its energies to an enterprise such as the subjugation of Mexico, there would be less American ammunition going abroad.[32]

The famous Henry Ford pamphlets on *The War Record of the Chicago Tribune* reproduce this editorial side by side with an editorial on the twenty-first of the same month, in which the *Tribune* said that it preferred a campaign in Mexico to a campaign in Europe.

> If we win in a war against Mexico, we know what we get out of it—a secure continent. And it is practically impossible for us to lose.
>
> If we finally win in a war against Germany, what do we win? Blessed if we know. "The overthrow of German militarism" will be the glib answer. Yes, and the substitution of some other—Russia's, perhaps, or Japan's.
>
> However, though Fate offers us a golden apple in Mexico and bitter fruit in Flanders, Mr. Wilson, being for "Humanity" rather than for America, wishes us to taste the bitter one. He probably will have his wish.

The outcome of such policy as that proposed by the *Tribune* would have been so favourable to the Central Powers, that statements of this kind were very properly circulated by the agents and friends of Germany in America. This does not, of course, imply that those who made such assertions were themselves pro-German.

When a belligerent country has a larger contingency of its former nationals in a neutral land, it may, in an emergency, seek to draw or drive these elements into active work in its behalf. Von der Goltz, a captured German agent, wrote a book on *My Adventures as a German Secret Agent* in 1917, which credits the German propagandists with an exceedingly ingenious scheme.

> It was planned so to discredit the German-Americans that the hostility of their fellow-citizens would force them back into the arms of the German Government.
>
> I happen to know that during the first two years of the war many of the stories about German attempts upon Canada, about German-American complicity in various plots, *emanated* from the offices of Captain von Papen and his military associates ... Germany wanted to give the world convincing proof that all peoples of German descent were solidly supporting her. It was for this reason that reports of impossible German activities were set afloat— rumours of Germans massing in the Maine woods, of aeroplane flights over Canada. And since many anti-German papers had been indiscreet enough to attack the German-Americans as disloyal, the German agents used and fomented these attacks for their own purposes.
>
> But Germany overreached herself. Emboldened by the apparent success of their schemes, her principal agents, von Papen, Boy-Ed, and von Rintelen (who had begun his work in January, 1915), became careless, so far as secrecy was concerned, and so

audacious in their plans that they betrayed themselves, perhaps intentionally, as a final demonstration of their power. The results you know. In so far
as the disclosure of their activities tended further to
implicate the German-Americans, they did harm.
But by these very disclosures the eyes of many German-Americans were opened to the true nature of
the influences to which they had been subjected, and
through that fact the worst element of the German
propaganda in America received its death blow.[33]

The statement which von der Goltz made is not corroborated
by any other evidence, and the testimony of a professional spy is
always subject to the most justifiable suspicion. There is some reason to believe that this may have been fabricated for the purpose
of instigating the German-Americans against a German Government which had so cynically attempted to betray them (to this purpose the last paragraph quoted seems to be directed). But there is
no denying the fact that there are circumstances in which just such
strategy as that imputed by von der Goltz to his superiors could be
successful.

The control of inter-Ally sentiment is partly a problem of maintaining a reciprocal cordiality, and the problem of stimulating
friendly relations between a belligerent and a neutral has its biva-
lent aspects. What is said about the neutrals and about the war in
a belligerent country tends to be translated or read in a neutral
country. Thus Italian susceptibilities were wounded during the
critical days of 1915 by the statement of a French public man that
Italy was waiting "to fly to the succour of the victor." Belligerent
opinion must be supervised and managed in the interest of neutral friendship.

Ambassador W. H. Page notes that

The Cabinet has directed the Censor to suppress, as
far as he can with prudence, comment which is
unfavourable to the United States. He has taken this

action because the public feeling against the administration is constantly increasing.[34]

Bismarck flew into a rage when a communiqué was put out by
the German military authorities in 1871 saying that some shells
had struck the famous Luxembourg Gardens in Paris. He demanded
to have all the subsequent communiqués submitted to him, so that
the material which might be turned against Germany abroad could
be deleted.[35] Bismarck put the damper on editorial criticism in
Germany of the purveying of coal to the French fleet by the British, on the theory that such railing would merely handicap diplomatic arrangements.[36] His chief was a level-headed old gentleman
who felt the importance of neutral opinion, and Bismarck often
had his way, even against the military people.[37]

Our discussion so far has had to do principally with the themes
which bear upon the preservation of friendship. Let us now review
in summary from some of the methods which were employed by
the chief competitors for the favour of America. The German methods have become public knowledge through the Senatorial inquiry
conducted in 1918-1919, and writings of Ambassador Bernstorff and
others. The title of the hearings is itself a triumph of insinuation.
It was "Brewing and Liquor Interests and German Bolshevik Propaganda," and was reported in three husky volumes. The hearings
did not begin until September 27th, 1918, and did not figure heavily
in the War propaganda. A hearing which was conducted in February and April of 1918, dealt with the National German-American
Alliance.[38] Three birds were killed at one stone by these hearings:
the brewers, the Germans, and the Bolsheviks. The Anti-Saloon
League, the Department of Justice, the Military Intelligence and
the Naval Intelligence were active in pressing the investigations.

Dr. Dernburg, former Secretary of State for the Colonies, was
sent to this country at the outbreak of the War to float a German
loan. The American Government warned against lending money to
either side, and it was impossible to produce satisfactory results.
Dr. Dernburg was also an agent for the German Red Cross and
began to collect funds for this work. He also undertook to explain

the German version of the War to the American public, and set up a Press Bureau in New York. Opinions differ as to whether he came over here to do this, or whether he found that it was difficult to return to Germany and evolved this to keep him occupied. He had the assistance at the New York Bureau of M. B. Claussen of the Hamburg-Amerika line, and after the entry of Japan into the War the interpreter of the Consulate-General in Yokohama joined the staff. Daily bulletins of the German Information Service were issued, and then the activity of the bureau was extended to the preparation of pamphlets. For these efforts the services of William Bayard Hale were secured. War-pictures and film-propaganda were later added. Dr. Mechlenburg and Herr Plage were held up in America on their way from Japan and placed their services at the disposal of Dr. Dernburg. Dr. Dernburg had the assistance of a committee which he selected, consisting of Albert, Gerhardt, Fuehr and a few American journalists and business men. They conferred once or twice a month on propaganda policy. Dr. Dernburg stayed in this country until after the *Lusitania* incident, when he made a public speech at Cleveland, justifying the sinking of the boat on the theory that it carried arms. Public indignation ran so high that a sacrifice was demanded, and Dernburg was the sacrificial ram. He went home. Ambassador Bernstorff tried thereafter to keep the Germans from agitating too openly in the country, preferring to work through American citizens.

The Germans had the warm co-operation of the German-American Alliance, which was well organized in the German strongholds over the nation—St. Louis, Chicago, Cincinnati, Milwaukee. There were numberless German social clubs and societies. The Kriegsbund was composed of those who had served in the German army. There were several veterans' posts of the War of 1870. The Geneva Society was a peculiar organization of German waiters. The Turner Societies and all sorts of benevolent organizations were thriving in every German district.

The Lutheran Church was a strong asset of the Germans, for there were 6,000 congregations in the United States, whose communicants numbered some three million. Often their services were kept up in German, and many of their preachers had received training in Germany.

The Germans appealed to all nationalities with a grievance against the Allies. The American Truth Society was a vehicle for stirring up the Irish. The Jews had an ineradicable antipathy toward the Tsaristic system, and many of them sided with the Germans. Their Press frequently had such items as the following:

> It is impossible to be a comrade of Nicholas and not be a hooligan. In the days of Beaconsfield, when England was far from Russia, no massacres of Jews were made, not on the poor, and not on the rich. Today, when England is an ally of Nicholas, she must do as Nicholas does, she must make massacres, she must preach against the Jews.

> When the war broke out, I immediately enlisted (in the French army), but I was astonished on my arrival at the camp at Lyons to see that I, together with many other Jews, was placed in a legion which was composed of criminals only. From all sides we were insulted. We were given cold black coffee and dry bread, and when we protested we were told that we were dirty Jews, and we came only to eat and nothing else. I refused to eat and got sick. When I applied to the sergeant to send me to the hospital, he began to beat me, etc.[39]

Concerning the efforts of the Germans to win the negroes, and to foment discord inside the country over the race question, Captain Lester testified to the committee:

> A separate department was maintained in the Albert bureau for the handling of American race problems, the principal among which was the negro question.

The bureau obtained through newspaper agencies and exchanges and from these so-called clipping bureaux records of every lynching in the United States, and every attack by coloured men upon a white person, or every news item which showed the alleged oppression of the coloured race.

These were formed into propaganda articles, and were forwarded to the editors of established newspapers, that is, white newspapers, and also to the editors of coloured newspapers.

The field work was conducted by a man by the name of Von Reiswitz, formerly a consul, I understand, at one time at Chicago.

His headquarters, if you may say that he had any headquarters, was in and about New Orleans, and all of the negro propaganda work was conducted from Mexico by Von Eckhardt. I say all of it in the sense that the directing head was in Mexico. The men used for the negro propaganda work were Mexicans and half-breeds, and men that were brought to Mexico City and instructed and sent across the border; and the wave of negro propaganda work went from the Mexican border east, and embraced the States, principally, of Texas, Louisiana, Arkansas, Mississippi, Alabama, Georgia; and States such as North and South Carolina and Tennessee were really on the outskirts of the movement.

The propaganda was directed to stir up trouble continuously between the whites and the blacks of any nature and description. That was the first item.

The attempt was also made to win the coloured race to the cause of Germany by innumerable arguments. We have information that the propaganda took this form: That the negro leaders, who were subsidized or attempted to be subsidized, in various

> local communities and by letters—I do not mean the
> big leaders of the negro race, but small men scat-
> tered here and there—told the negroes that in Ger-
> many the blacks were equal to the whites; that in
> Europe they had no colour line. They exhibited state-
> ments, presumed to be authentic, to this effect, and
> argued with them that, if Germany won the war, the
> rights of the coloured people in the South would be
> equal to those of the whites. That was the principal
> argument. They played continuously upon lynch-
> ings.[40]

The Germans sought to touch every foreign language group
which might be suborned by controlling the American Association
of Foreign Language Newspapers.

The German University League was started in 1915, to unite all
who had attended a German university. The purpose was "to co-
operate with every effort, to strengthen the regard for the Germans
and for their aims and ideals and to secure for them fair play and
proper appreciation." Among those who were officers or trustees
are to be found the names of von Klenze, William R. Shepherd (Columbia), Carl L. Schurz, von Mach, and many other distinguished
academic and public men. Meetings were held and papers read and
distributed. The co-operation of visiting professors, such as Moritz
J. Bonn, was secured. This was a direct channel of communication
between the intellectuals of Germany and America.[41]

The Germans were active in trying to reach the professionally
trained people in the country. Nagel's pamphlet on American neutrality was circulated to 50,000 lawyers through the American
Truth Society.[42]

The women were appealed to through the League of American
Women for Strict Neutrality, which was founded in Baltimore. The
wage-earners received special attention through the Labour's National Peace Council (1915). They were often very close to the brewing interests, for the latter were very much alarmed at the impending movement for Prohibition, and German propaganda agents

sometimes took advantage of the anxiety of the brewers to make propaganda by offering to organize such a movement and turning it into a pro-German drive.

All manner of appeals to the public at large were made through all available channels. Books upon every phase of the War were put out under the auspices of the Dernburg-Albert Bureau, and the circulation of every book, beneficial to the German cause, was facilitated. A short selection of these books follows:

> *England or Germany*, Frank Harris.
> *Hindenburg's March into London*, L. G. Redmond-Howard, author of the *Life of John Redmond*.
> *Peace and America*, Hugo Münsterberg, Harvard University.
> *America's Relations to the Great War*, John W. Burgess, Columbia University.
> *The Making of Modern Germany*, Ferdinand Schevill, The University of Chicago.
> *England*, Eduard Meyer, The University of Berlin.
> *Belgium and Germany, A Dutch View*, Dr. J. H. Labberton.
> *Justice in War Time*, Bertrand Russell.
> *Behind the Scenes of Warring Germany*, Edward Lyell Fox.[43]

The New York *Mail* was purchased for the sake of reaching a metropolitan audience, and supplying a newspaper which could be quoted. Cartoons, pamphlets and photographs without number were employed, and distributed through steamship company offices.[44]

Moving pictures were sent to America in which German soldiers were shown busily feeding Belgian and French children. There were such captions as "Barbs feeding the hungry," "Do Barbarians look like this?"

The head of the British propaganda in America has conveniently summarized his methods.[45]

Practically since the day war broke out between England and the Central Powers I became responsible for American publicity. I need hardly say that the scope of my department was very extensive, and its activities widely ranged. Among the activities was a weekly report to the British Cabinet on the state of American opinion, and constant touch with the permanent correspondents of American newspapers in England. I also frequently arranged for important public men in England to act for us by interviews in American newspapers; and among these distinguished people were Mr. Lloyd George (the present Prime Minister), Viscount Grey, Mr. Balfour, Mr. Bonar Law, the Archbishop of Canterbury, Sir Edward Carson, Lord Robert Cecil, Mr. Walter Runciman (the Lord Chancellor), Mr. Austen Chamberlain, Lord Cromer, Will Crooks, Lord Curzon, Lord Gladstone, Lord Haldane, Mr. Henry James, Mr. John Redmond, Mr. Selfridge, Mr. Zangwill, Mrs. Humphrey Ward, and fully a hundred others.

Among other things we supplied three hundred and sixty newspapers in the smaller states of the United States with an English newspaper, which gives weekly reviews and comment on the affairs of the war. We established connection with the man in the street through cinema pictures of the Army and Navy, as well as through interviews, articles, pamphlets, etc.; and by letters in reply to individual American critics, which were printed in the chief newspaper of the State in which they lived, and were copied in newspapers of other and neighbouring States. We advertised and stimulated many people to write articles. We utilised the friendly services and assistance of confidential friends; we had reports from important Americans constantly, and established association by personal correspondence with influential and eminent people of every profession in the United States, beginning with the university and college presidents, professors, and scientific men, and running through all the ranges of population. We asked our friends and correspondents to arrange for speeches, debates and lectures by American citizens, but we did not encourage Britishers to go to America and preach the doctrine of entrance into the war. Besides an immense private correspondence with individuals, we had our documents and literature sent to great numbers of public libraries, Y.M.C.A. societies, universities, colleges, historical societies, clubs and newspapers.

It is hardly necessary to say that the work was one of extreme difficulty and delicacy, but I was fortunate in having a wide acquaintance in the United States, and in knowing that a great many people had read my books and were not prejudiced against me. . . .

. . . it should be remembered that the Society of Pilgrims, whose work of international unity cannot be overestimated, has played a part in promoting understanding between the two peoples, and the establishment of the American Officers' Club in Lord Leconfield's house in London, with H.R.H. the Duke of Connaught as President, has done, and is doing, immense good. It should also be remembered that it was the Pilgrims' Society, under the fine chairmanship of Mr. Harry Brittain, which took charge of the Hon. James M. Beck when he visited England in 1916, and gave him so good a chance to do great work for the cause of unity between the two nations. I am glad and proud to think that I had something to do with these arrangements, which resulted in the Pilgrims taking Mr. Beck into their charge.[46]

The chief emphasis in Sir Gilbert Parker's succinct account of his own methods is upon the use of persons as channels of influence. Influence spread from business man to business man, from journalist to journalist, from professor to professor, from worker to worker. Behind the scenes, and behind the news and pictures and speeches, there flows a mighty stream of personal influencing. The War was more debated in private than in public. The doubters were won by friendship or flattery, logic or shame, to fuse their enthusiasm in the rising wave of Allied sentiment. A sidelight on the method is contained in a letter from Sir Edward Grey to Theodore Roosevelt, dated September 10th, 1914:

> My dear Roosevelt,—J. M. Barrie and A. E. W. Mason, some of whose books you have no doubt read, are going to the U.S. Their object is, as I understand, not to make speeches or give lectures, but to meet people, particularly those connected with Universities, and explain the British case as regards this war and our view of the issues involved.[47]

When a lance was broken in public for the British cause, it was done by an American and not by a foreigner. There were no obnoxiously evident Britishers as there were Dernburgs in America. It was the social lobby, the personal conversation, and the casual brush which forged the strongest chain between America and Britain. All countries found that an effective carrier of propaganda for their cause in America was the titled foreigner who said nothing whatever for the public prints, but who talked privately and casually of the War. The sheer radiation of aristocratic distinction was enough to warm the cockles of many a staunch Republican heart, and to evoke enthusiasm for the country which could produce such dignity, elegance and affability. The wife of an important newspaper proprietor was hostess to a Count; the wife of a Senator evened the social score by countering with a Duke. A Marquis, Earl or Baron was dealt hither and thither in this diverting social game.

All this was a standing joke among sophisticated Europeans, who subtly played upon the ambitions of numerous hostesses in New York, Philadelphia, Boston, Washington and Chicago.

The most important personality in propaganda among neutrals or allies usually is the official representative at the capital. What type of man should he be and what technique should he exploit? No more brilliant success has ever been scored than that of Benjamin Franklin at Paris during the War of Independence. A Frenchman, M. Francis P. Renaut, describes him in these words:

> (Franklin) arrived preceded by a certain reputation; he was able not only to save his admirers from disillusion, but to kindle their enthusiasm. For some he was scientist who had captured the lightning, for others the genial philosopher, for others the enemy of tyranny and the ardent defender of public liberty; for all, he was the simple man of nature, the patriarch, the father of a family who unostentatiously exemplified the common virtues. And in a time when the words of Rousseau were lodged in every cultivated mind, who could fail to be moved by the spectacle of a venerable old gentleman coming to defend his country, supported on the arm of one of his grandchildren (William Temple Franklin). The politician scarcely appeared in this life, of which the smallest details captivated the Parisians; the residence at Passy with its easy access, the visits to Court without ceremony, the philosophical conversations, the relations with Voltaire and the physiocrats.[48]

The key to Franklin was expressed by implication in the last sentence: he was a non-political personality, and the lustre of his person spread to all his affiliations.

An example of a dubious selection is that of the Hon. Elihu Root as head of the American Mission to Russia. There was no question about his technical eminence as a student and administrator of international affairs, but the situation was such that he was open to attack in revolutionary Russia. As Colonel Robins testified:

> You may know that he had attacked at one time in this country a very important public person, and you may know that, as a result of that attack, editorials, the most brilliant possible of their kind, had been published for successive weeks, accompanied by cartoons, speaking of Mr. Root as the jackal of privilege, as the watchdog of Wall Street, and all that sort of thing. They had been run in the public Press. Probably the German agents in America, immediately upon his appointment, gathered these up and sent them over, and they appeared in pamphlets in Russia, translated into Russian, with the cartoons and the words changed to Russian synonyms, so that even friendly papers said, How is it possible that the great democratic President should send over to Russia to help make the world safe for democracy—to revolutionary Russia—the man who has spent most of his time, according to what we hear, in trying to make America safe for plutocracy?"[49]

If this general analysis of the technique of preserving friendship is correct, it goes to show that the chief theme of inter-allied propaganda is strenuous exertion in the common cause, and that every supporting thesis of propaganda should be sustained and reinforced. The handling of the neutral boils down to the problem of leading the neutral to identify his own interests with your own in defeating the enemy. Aside from general representations of the enemy as threatening, obstructive, and despicable, and of one's own nation as protective, helpful and upright, there must be some confidence in ultimate success. The most astute means of drawing in neutral sympathy is to draw the neutral into overt co-operation in some form. When all else fails, an appeal to pacifism and an effort to instigate trouble with another neutral may avoid active hostility. Among all the means to be exploited, the use of personal influencing is peculiarly important, as is the practice that in general neutrals should be addressed by neutrals.

Notes

[1] On the Italian situation, see C. E. Merriam, "American Publicity in Italy," *American Political Science Review*, November, 1919.

[2] See Steed, *Through Thirty Years*, II: 135.

[3] André Tardieu, *The Truth About the Treaty*, p. 240.

[4] E. L. Bernays, *Crystallizing Public Opinion*, pp. 24-27.

[5] See F. W. Halsey (ed.), *Balfour, Viviani and Joffre*; *The Imperial Japanese Mission*, Washington, 1918; *America's Message to the Russian People. Addresses by the Members of the Special Diplomatic Mission of the United States to Russia in the Year 1917*, Boston, 1918; René Viviani, *La Mission Française en Amérique*, Paris, 1917.

[6] *66th Congress, 1st Sess., Sen. Doc. No. 62. 3: 775 et seq.*

[7] One of the novelties of the propaganda to keep Russia in the War was the organization of a battalion of Russian women to shame the men into fighting Germany.

[8] Palæologue, *An Ambassador's Memoirs*, I: 103.

[9] Palæologue, as cited, II: 108.

[10] Nicolai, *Nachrichtendienst, Presse, and Volksstimmung im Welktrieg*, 59.

[11] *Le Gaulois*, October 19, 1914.

[12] August 8, 1914.

[13] *Queer People*, p. 63. Should the exigencies of the international situation require it, this quotation can be used to cast aspersions on post-war reaction in England.

[14] S. Ivor Stephen (Szinnyey), *Neutrality? The Crucifixion of Public Opinion. From an American Point of View*, Chicago, 1916, p. 18. This is a repository of German propaganda themes.

[15] Cited in Stephen, as cited, p. 171.

[16] See also, H. L. Gordon, *The Peril of the United Slates*; Rudolf Cronau, *Do we need a Third War for Independence?*

[17] See André Chéradame, *The Pan-German Plot Unmasked*, New York, 1916. Mildred S. Wertheimer restored *The Pan-German League* to its proper perspective in 1924. Roland G. Usher had written a book on *Pan-Germanism* which was published in 1913, and given a renewed lease on life by the Entente sympathizers after 1914. See also his *The Winning of the War*, New York and London, 1918.

[18] Busch, *Bismarck*, I: 158. 26 September, 1870.

[19] Busch, Bismarck, I: 148. 22 September, 1871.

[20] Busch, Bismarck, I: 406. 4 February, 1871.

[21] For example, see Auswärtiges Amt., *Greueltaten russischer Truppen gegen deutsche Civil personen und deutsche Kriegsgefangene*, 1915; K. Jünger and Dr. H. Vaörting, *Die Behandlung der Deutschen in England, Frankreich und Russland*, Berlin, 1915.

[22] Translated by E. B. Sherlock, New York and London, 1916.

[23] Rear-Admiral Brownrigg says that some influence unfriendly to Great Britain caused the film to be exhibited in the United States under the title, *HOW Britain Prepared. Recollections*, p. 37. D. W. Griffith, famous director, has recently recalled the offer made to him by Bernard Shaw in 1917 to write scenarios for him. This occurred "In 1917, just after I had completed arrangements with the British Government to do some propaganda pictures." (New York *Times*, October 11th 1926.) Another of Mr. Shaw's propaganda efforts went astray when the New York *Times* divided one of his despatches and left the impression inadvertently that Shaw was dressing down the Allies. Mr. Shaw has himself related the last incident, but professes to have no recollection of the Griffith rejection.

[24] Grey, *Twenty-Five Years*, II: 150.

[25] Eric Fisher Wood, *The Note-book of an Intelligence Officer*, 1917, reprints his letter on page 15. See also James Mark Baldwin, *Between Two Wars*, 2 vols., Boston 1926.

[26] *Sen. Doc.* 62, 1395 (*Brewing and Liquor Interests, etc.*).

[27] *My Three Years in America*, p. 89.

[28] The story is told in Page's *Life and Letters*, I: 394.

[29] *Italy and the World War*, 209 *et seq.*

[30] Grey, II: 118.

[31] See the *Sen. Doc.* 62, (*Brewing and Liquor Interests, etc.*) 1675.

[32] April 4, 1916.

[33] Condensed from pages 223-233.

[34] *Life and Letters*, II: 51 (February 15, 1915).

[35] Busch, *Bismarck*, I: 341.

[36] Busch, *Bismarck*, I: 42.

[37] Kaiser Wilhelm I. made an interesting note on the margin of a document dated May 16th, 1875: "Um glückliche Kriege zu führen, muss dem Angreifenden die Sympathie aller edelgesinnten Menschen u. Länder zur Seite stehen, und dem, der ungerecht den Krieg zuträgt, die öffentliche Stimme den Stein werfen. Dies war das Geheimnis des Enthusiasmus in Deutschland 1870! Wer ungerechtfertigt zu den Waffen greift, wird die öffenliche Stimme gegen sich haben, er wird keinen Alliierten finden, keine *neutres bienveillants*, ja überhaupt wohl keine Neutralen, wohl aber Gegner finden."

[38] The hearings were before the sub-committee of the Committee on the Judiciary. The most important report is the three-volume work known as Senate Document 62, 65th Congress, 2nd Session, 1919. "And Bolshevik" propaganda does not appear in the title to volume I.

[39] Clippings from *Wahrheit* (New York). Sen. Doc. 62, 1825, *et seq.*

[40] *Sen. Doc.* 62, (*Brewing and Liquor Interests, etc.*) 1785.

[41] For documents, see *Sen. Doc.* 62, 1372 *et seq.*

[42] *Sen. Doc.* 62, 1424.

[43] A fuller list is given in *Sen. Doc.* 62, 1410 *et seq.*

[44] Additional information about the German system appears in Lewis Melville, "German Propaganda Societies," *Quarterly Review*, 230 (1918): 70-88.

[45] Sir Gilbert Parker, "The United States and the War," *Harper's Magazine*, 136 (1918): 521-531. Extract.

[46] The British have not publicly estimated the amount of money which they spent on American as distinguished from other types of propaganda. They spent one hundred and fifty thousand dollars (£31,360 4s.) in the last four months of the War to break the German morale and to accomplish other propaganda objects.

[47] Grey, *Twenty-Five Years*, II: 143.

[48] *La politique de propaganda des Américains durant la Guerre d'Independance*, I: 52.

[49] *Sen. Doc. 62, (Brewing and Liquor Interests, etc.)* 3: 819.

DEMORALIZING THE ENEMY

It is possible to employ propaganda as a weapon of direct attack against the moral of the enemy by seeking to break up or divert the hatred of the enemy from a belligerent.

To a certain degree this can be accomplished by a campaign of simple counter-stimulation. The *Gazette des Ardennes* was published by the Germans for the consumption of the Frenchman who lived within the occupied area, and the various themes capable of employment in demoralizing the enemy were used at one time or another within its columns. The *Gazette* was exhaustively examined by Professor Marchand during the War for the purpose of establishing, if possible, a direct parallel between its attitudes and those of the *Bonnet Rouge* of Paris. His report, which was part of the evidence against the latter journal in the famous trial of 1917, has since been published as *L'offensive des Allemands, en France, pendant la guerre*. It is made up of assorted extracts from the two papers in question, and represents by far the best systematic study of one phase of War propaganda yet made. The references in this section will be to this compilation, supplemented by other material. In most cases the citations have been checked against the original.

The *Gazette* denied outright that Germany had ever plotted to attack France, and deplored the propaganda of misrepresentation against Germany. M. Léon Daudet and M. Clemenceau have the "spionnitis," when they imagine that Germany had sown France with a vast army of secret agents before or since the War.[1]

The *Gazette* defended its Kaiser and military men from the alleged calumny of the Allies. William the Second has always been recognized as a powerful influence for peace. It was he who saved Europe from war over Morocco. His pacific spirit has repeatedly been acknowledged by such men as J. Holland Rose, the eminent English historian, by Marcel Sembat, the Frenchman of letters and Socialist-patriot, and by right-thinking people everywhere. He is conscientious, peace-loving, kindly, gentle in his family relations, able in his leadership, and altogether generous in his impulses.[2]

All the stories about German barbarities are poisonous lies. The German soldiers in the army of occupation in northern France are kind to children. A picture in the *Gazette* for December 1st, 1915, shows a German soldier in the act of feeding a little French child who is perched affectionately on his knee.[3] The children cherish fond memories of "l'oncle Fritz."[4] Letters from Frenchmen in the occupied territory and from French prisoners in the hands of the Germans, were published to prove the kindly and considerate character of the German forces of occupation.[5] The irrepressible German love of music, religion and morality has manifested itself wherever German soldiers are found.

The tales of wholesale atrocity and wilful destruction are malicious generalizations from a few regrettable individual instances, which happen in every army, but less often in the disciplined German army than elsewhere. The necessities of war, as everyone knows, may require acts which are not essential in the quiet times of peace, but it is absurd to distort the facts into a wholesale denunciation of an entire nation.[6] Many of the churches which the Germans are supposed to have destroyed were never destroyed, and many of them were illegitimately used by the enemy.

The examples which have been cited so far illustrate defence by denial. Another form of defence, that of admission accompanied by justification, is illustrated by the handling of the U-Boat question. The *Gazette* explained over and over again that the submarine was nothing more nor less than a reply to the infamous and illegal British blockade.

While no form of stimulation should be neglected, and the application of counter-suggestion has a certain effect, its efficacy is by no means comparable to the influence of a skilful propaganda of diversion. To undermine the active hatred of the enemy for its present antagonist, his anger must be distracted to a new and independent object, beside which his present antagonist ceases to matter. This is a very difficult operation, and it is always advisable to carry through a work of preparation for the purpose of undermining some of the varieties of resistance which hamper the success of such a maneuver.

Patriotism is a powerful prop to belligerent ardour, and antipatriotic propaganda has some chance to succeed with those elements in the nation who begin to recover their peace time ideology after the war has worn on awhile. The *Gazette* published certain items which deplored the tendency of patriotism to lead a country into needless slaughter.[7] Patriotism which preaches hate is immoral, and the poisoning of men's minds is nothing less than criminal.[8] The war spirit should be avoided, since there is no doubt of its irreligious and unethical character.[9]

Another sustaining force against which sapping operations must be directed is the confidence of the people in their government's honesty. If a suspicion can be engendered against the propaganda of the government and the war party, a potent weapon of disintegration is created. The Germans complained that they were the victims of systematic vilification by ignorant pedagogues, irresponsible politicians, and lying newsmongers.

But the keynote in the preliminary spade work is the unceasing refrain: Your cause is hopeless. Your blood is spilt in vain. Now the heads of the French propaganda very properly criticised the early English propaganda for boasting of the size of the Allied armies during the early stages of the War, when the Germans occupied Belgium and northern France. It was only when things settled down to a stalemate or worse, and when disappointment was general, that such propaganda became effective. When the British took the offensive in 1918, in a military sense, they simultaneously sowed the German trenches with maps upon which their gains were plainly marked. They recalled the false hopes which the German leaders had held out to the people and the army. They circulated an alleged statement in a German newspaper which lamented that

> A few weeks ago it appeared as if our armies were very near their goal, the defeat of the enemy force, and peace. But what a change!

Forebodings were disseminated. A card was spread over the German trenches with the legend:

> To-day we are in retreat. Next year we shall be destroyed.

When the German generals gave public evidence of their alarm at the incursions of Allied propaganda in 1918, the Allied pamphleteers interpreted this to the Germans as a sign that their leaders wanted to keep the truth from them. A rumour that the German Government was at last disposed to make peace was circulated as another evidence of weakness.

The Americans, who entered the field of direct propaganda against Germany, and especially the German army, spent most of their energy advertising the news of America's strength. Little leaflets with a row of soldiers, whose size varied with the monthly increase in the number of American soldiers, were distributed over the German lines. 1,900,000 Americans are now in France, said the card, and more than ten times as many stand ready in America. The extent of German casualties and tonnage losses was emphasized. That they were short of food and raw materials was insinuated by such means as circulating the report that another smuggler had been arrested in a German city.

Tracts with such questions as these were distributed far and wide:

> Will you ever again be as strong as you were in July,
>   1918?
> Will your opponents grow daily stronger or weaker?
> Have your grievous losses suffered in 1918 brought
>   you the victorious peace which your leaders
>   promised you?
> Have you still a final hope of victory?
> Do you want to give up your life in a hopeless
>   cause?[10]

Another theme of first-rate importance when it is in juxtaposition to the foregoing is the privations to which the soldier and his family at home are subjected. Stories of want and misery at home were featured in a special French propaganda sheet, which was prepared for use among German soldiers, the *Briefe aus Deutschland.* In the brilliant attack upon Italian morale, which preceded the disaster of Caporetto in 1917, the Italian soldiers were sent appeals, ostensibly from home, beseeching them to lay down their arms and return to their families.

The joys of home were subtly suggested by the French editors of *Die Feldpost* (another sheet for the German troops). They celebrated the Christmas season of 1915 by recalling all the simple pleasures of Christmas at home with the family in peace.[11] The amusements of civilian life were featured in the propaganda literature for the sake of intensifying war weariness.

Another means of stressing want and privation is to circulate, as the Americans did, something which suggests the relative affluence and luxury of the enemy. A card, which was an exact reproduction of the official German field postal card, said:

> Write the address of your family upon this card, and
> if you are captured by the Americans, give it to the
> first officer who questions you. He will make it his
> business to forward it in order that your family may
> be reassured concerning your situation.

(On the reverse):

Do not worry about me. The war is over for me. I
have good food. The American Army gives its prisoners the same food as its own soldiers: Beef, white
bread, potatoes, beans, prunes, coffee, butter, tobacco, etc.[12]

This was no new wrinkle in propaganda technique, for it is recorded that handbills were circulated among the British troops on
Bunker Hill, offering them seven dollars a month, fresh provisions
in plenty, health, freedom, ease, affluence, and a good farm, should
they desert and join the American Army.[13]

All the preparatory or auxiliary themes outlined so far are supposed to facilitate the task of substituting new hates for old. The
next step is to concentrate upon the particular object of animosity
about which it is hoped to polarize the sentiment of the enemy.
One of the possible alternatives is to transfer suspicion and hatred
to an ally.

The German propaganda did what it could to disinter the an-
cient animosity of the French for the English. France, they said, is
the cat's-paw of the English. The English have been exceedingly
backward in their war preparations, as Winston Churchill has recently acknowledged.[14] Their game is to let France bleed for them.
Indeed, they are taking pains to establish themselves in permanent buildings at Calais, and any student of history knows how long
it took to dislodge England the last time she had her clutches on
Calais.

The truth, declared the Germans, is that, far from threatening
you, we are willing to join you in a common crusade against England, who has conspired with some of your meanest politicians to
use your blood to crush our trade competition. We will gladly free
you from the machinations of England, and help you to expand
your colonial domain at the British expense. Between us we can
dominate Europe, and to dominate Europe is to dominate the
world. At the same time, we can emancipate you from Russia,
whose Tsar is using France to enable him to grab Constantinople.[15]

The Allies, in their turn, strained every muscle to drive a wedge between Austria-Hungary and Germany. Rumours that the Dual Monarchy was negotiating a separate peace, were circulated among the German soldiers on the Western Front, for the purpose of stirring up hatred against Austria, and of demonstrating the hopelessness of the cause for which they had suffered so much. The report that the Austrians and Hungarians had plenty of food provoked considerable animosity in Germany, where the food restrictions were severe. The Austrians, for their part, were taunted as the slaves of Prussia, and wheedled by the possibility of territorial compensations at the expense of Germany, should they change sides.

An ally is not the only possible object of diversion. The government and the governing caste may serve just as well. If the ruling person, clique or class can be made sufficiently obnoxious, Revolution comes, and in Revolution there is little remaining capacity for active hatred of the external enemy.

During the last war every belligerent took a hand in the perilous business of fomenting dissension and revolution abroad, reckless of the possible repercussions of a successful revolt. There is reason to believe that, as early as 1915, the Germans were attempting to foster the collapse of Russia, by placing revolutionary reading matter in the hands of those Russian prisoners who might eventually return to Russia through exchange or release.[16] The famous episode of the sealed car, which contained Lenin and forty men, happened in 1917.

The Allies set about quite consciously to uproot the Kaiser and the Imperial system in Germany. One of the leaflets which the French scattered over Germany contained a picture of the Kaiser and his husky sons, unscathed by war; on the opposite side stood many rows of wooden crosses, to mark the final resting places of his loyal German subjects.[17] Another leaflet showed the Kaiser and his general staff, sitting about a table, conversing genially and drinking beer; the reverse pictures an explosion in a front-line trench, where many bodies are being ripped to pieces.[18]

German Republicans who lived abroad were drafted or volunteered to discuss the responsibility of the Kaiser for the War. After the collapse of the great offensive in the spring of 1918 the Wilsonian propaganda in Germany reached its apex. His speeches were strewn far and wide, and they were successful in creating the impression that a Republican Germany would receive a soft peace from the western democracies. Care was taken to print all the passages of Wilson's speeches which had been suppressed in Germany in red ink.[19]

The British tried to suggest the imminence of revolutionary disturbances in Germany by means of news items, which told about secret precautions recently taken in Berlin, where a G.H.Q. order had just directed certain measures to be taken for the suppression of strikes. Every Socialist meeting which was suppressed received considerable publicity on the Western Front. The following item is a particularly subtle effort to carry the idea of revolution. It is in the form of a despatch from Stockholm:

> The German Minister in Stockholm has requested the Swedish Foreign Office to seize the copy of the *New York Herald Magazine of the War* of the 14th of July because it publishes on the front page a photograph of the German Emperor, underneath which are the words:—"What shall we do with the Kaiser after the War?" The Minister of Justice is said to have ordered the copies in question to be seized.[20]

Although the Germans were finally bested in the game, they tried strenuously to demoralize the Allies through Revolution. Through the *Gazette* and every other channel open to them they endeavoured to hang the responsibility of the War upon Poincaré and his clique. This was the group, they said, whose insane lust for revenge led them to carry on illicit negotiations with military and diplomatic circles in Belgium, to finance strategic railways in Russia, when they ought to have been providing for social welfare at home, to refuse to thwart the propaganda for Pan-Slavism, and to violate Belgian neutrality before Germany entered the War.

The Germans came into possession of a crushing reply to the professions of international idealism with which the Allies filled the air. They gave as much publicity as their limited resources would permit to the secret treaties which the Allied powers had made. The idealistic Allies had carved up the world among themselves. Russia was promised Constantinople. Great Britain got the neutral zone north of its sphere of influence in Persia. The Italians got the Trentino and Trieste, plus the Slavic territories of Gorizi, Gradisca, Istria, Dalmatia and Valona. They were promised 200,000 Germans who lived in the Brenner Pass region and who had been Austrian subjects since the fourteenth century. The important ports of the Adriatic (except Flume) fell into their hands outright, or were neutralized. They secured the Greek Dodekanese Islands, some provinces in Asia Minor, and promises of colonies in Africa. Rumania was given territories inhabited by Serbs, Hungarians, Ruthenians and other Slavic nationalities. France gave Russia a free hand in Poland in return for a free hand on the western front in reference to Alsace-Lorraine, the Saar, and the left bank of the Rhine. Besides all this, the Turkish Empire and the colonies of Germany were sliced up and parcelled out.

The revelation of these treaties not only created inter-Allied troubles, because the secret treaties revealed that the Allies had made contradictory promises to some of the weaker powers, but it had an immediate influence on the morale of Labour. The revelation of Allied duplicity produced the repercussions which have been referred to before.[21]

The Germans carried their attack upon national unity very far. They sought to arouse the wives at home by calling attention to the alarming extent to which prostitution was practised at the front. Dr. Graux records that, as early as July 1915, anonymous pamphlets were distributed in France, elaborating this theme.[22]

No effort was spared to arouse the soldiers at the front against the supposed excesses of politicians, profiteers and officers behind the lines. The *Gazette* for November 5th, 1916, alluded to the wives of soldiers left at home who find duty too burdensome to bear. The

French Government was known to be responsible for importing the black inhabitants of Morocco into the War, and the *Gazette* took occasion to publish a letter which contained the remark that

> Those dirty Moroccans have left offsprings right and
> left, like the Annamite.[23]

The French reproduced and circulated a cartoon from *Simplicissimus*, in which a German schoolmaster asked an emaciated pupil why anyone is called a poor sinner, who is condemned to severe punishment. The reply was:

> "Because a rich sinner is never punished severely."[24]

The authorities encouraged fraternization between the Austrian and the Italian troops before the Caporetto affair, carefully using for that purpose some Austrian Communists, who had been infected by Communism or Socialism on the Russian front. Sometimes German pacifists were permitted to travel abroad, although the most rigorous limitations were placed on their agitation at home.

The Germans appealed to every possible cleavage in the French nation, seeking to instigate party versus party, farmers versus urbanites, provincials versus Parisians, workers versus employers, the army versus the nation, the army versus the government, and the legislature versus the executive.[25]

We have spoken of anti-Ally and anti-Government propaganda, but some attention must be given to a third important possibility, anti-State propaganda. The late War proved how effective the instigation of secession may be, when the belligerent is a heterogeneous State. The Allies began to talk about self-determination early in the War. The Tsar announced that he proposed to grant autonomy to a united Poland on the 16th of August, 1914. By the spring of 1916 the astronomer-aviator, Stefanik, offered to drop Czech proclamations by Masaryk over the lines of the Austrian Army, opposite the Italians.[26]

The Russians had dropped some gold coins with the Czechish national castle minted on one side inside the lines by aeroplane, but it was not until after the Declaration of Corfu in July, 1917, that the propaganda offensive against the Dual Monarchy began to inflict its greatest damage. According to this declaration, Pashitch and Trumbitch, "the authorized representatives of the Serbs, Croats and Slovenes," recognized the desire of our people "to constitute itself in an independent national state"; adopted as its name "the Kingdom of the Serbs, Croats and Slovenes"; provided for the unification of its flag and Crown, but also for the free use of special Serb, Croat and Slovene flags and emblems; for the freedom of the Orthodox, Roman Catholic and Mussulman creed; declared that the Adriatic must be "a free and open sea," and that "the Kingdom will include all territory compactly inhabited by our people and cannot be mutilated without attaint to the vital interests of the community."

The policy of partitioning Austria-Hungary was opposed, even at this comparatively late date, by numerous elements among the Allies. The New Europe, which was launched in October 19th, 1916, by Seton-Watson, Masaryk, Steed and certain others, tried to overcome the reluctance of the British Government to come out boldly for the policy of partition. The Allied governments were embarrassed by the deal into which they had entered to bring Italy into the War in 1915, at which time the aspirations of the Southern Slavs were not definitely formulated. The Italians had been offered guarantees which were utterly incompatible with the unity of the Southern Slavs, and the Italians were disposed to hang fast to the advantages of the treaties. They preferred annexations to the problematical friendship of an aggrandized Serbia, and they feared that a dismembered Austria would join Germany. Wickham Steed, of the London *Times*, an active member of the pro-Serbian propaganda group, credits the Jewish financial houses with wishing to maintain the German-Jewish financial system, which had formed the economic framework of Pan-Germanism, and with wishing to strengthen every element of opposition to the break-up of Austria-Hungary. The Roman Catholic hierarchy was likewise against the total submergence of the largest remaining Roman policy in Europe. British society cherished a soft spot for the Austrians because their homes were so well kept, their shooting so good, and their urbanity so unruffled.[27]

Indeed, it was not until after the disaster of Caporetto in October, 1917, that the Slavs and the Italians were able to agree, and to enable the Allied propaganda to assume its final proportions. Even then, it was not until the "Pact of Rome" of March, 1918, that the way was entirely cleared for one of the greatest propaganda feats of the War, the Congress of Oppressed Hapsburg Nationalities, which met at Rome in April. On October 26th, 1918, there was a convention in Philadelphia of twelve nationalities, who were determined upon securing liberty from their former rulers. The presiding officer was Professor Masaryk, who was the president of the Czecho-Slovak National Council, which had been recognized by the Allied governments. Most of the Press spoke of the gathering in Independence Hall as a Czecho-Slovak Convention because of Masaryk's prominence and the tremendous impression which had been made upon the public mind by the Czecho-Slovak Legion in Russia, and the Division of Czecho-Slovak troops in France. All the delegates to the Convention solemnly signed a Declaration of Independence, and the event was widely heralded in America and Europe.[28]

Another brilliant stroke on the part of Allied propaganda was the encouragement of Zionism. In November, 1917, Mr. Balfour, then Foreign Secretary of Great Britain, committed the British government to the establishment of a Jewish National Home in Palestine. This gave the material for an able appeal to the Jews in Germany and, incidentally, increased the interest of American Jewry in the War. General Ludendorff regarded the Balfour Declaration as the cleverest thing done by the Allies in the nature of war propaganda, and lamented the fact that Germany had not thought of it first.

The efforts made by the Central Powers to instigate secession fell flat. As early as the spring of 1915 the Austrians tried to dissolve Russia. The French Ambassador was told by Goremykin, President of the Council, on the 10th of April, 1915, that

> Austria is making great efforts to create a national
> movement among the Ukrainians. Surely you know
> that there is a society for the Liberation of the
> Ukraine in Vienna? It publishes pamphlets and maps
> in Switzerland. I get them, and they certainly reveal
> very intense propaganda activity.[29]

Germany tried to stir up the Irish against the English and to precipitate trouble in Northern Africa, Egypt and India. They tried to split Belgium by encouraging the "Walloon movement," but to little avail.

Several movements which were, in effect, a *reductio ad absurdum* of the principle of self-determination were begun during the War. One of them grew in the fertile brain of a member of the Austrian Press service. He chanced to be in occupied Italian territory and overheard a conversation which he could not quite make out. He discovered that it was a local speech known as Friul, spoken in a few villages in Udine Province. He wrote an article demanding self-determination for the users of Friul, and precipitated quite an angry Press campaign in Italy.

A large element in propaganda against the enemy is the invention of ways and means for the transmission of suggestions to the enemy. It is proposed to deal with some of the more specialized appliances which were used for this purpose in the last War rather than to touch upon them in the section which is devoted to the general consideration of tactical matters.

Efforts were first made by the belligerents to penetrate behind the lines of their opponents by means of insertions in the neutral Press. Newspapers were purchased in Switzerland and other neutral countries for this purpose. Almost simultaneously the belligerents began to invent ways and means of direct transmission.

The French began to publish a regular periodical in October, 1915, for dissemination among the soldiers of their opponents. The periodical was variously known as *Die Feldpost*, *Kriegsblätter für das deutsche Volk*, and *Das freie deutsche Wort*. Books and occasional pamphlets were copiously employed. A tiny edition of

J'accuse was sent far and wide, for the purpose of preaching German responsibility for the War. By the same method various books were published from the pens of Dr. Herman Fernau, Dr. Muehlen, Prince Lichnowsky and others. Several fervent brochures, prepared by Dr. Hermann Rosemeier, who until his flight in September, 1914, had edited the *Morgenpost* of Berlin, were distributed.[30]

Die Kriegsfackel was put out occasionally for the sole purpose of discussing the question of war guilt.[31] *Briefe aus Deutschland* and *Grüsse an die Heimat* were also published irregularly. The former was devoted to letters and news items upon internal conditions in Germany, and the latter was made up of letters from German prisoners who testified about their excellent treatment in France. The French forged a number of the *Strassburger Post*, a famous organ of Germanization, on the 29th of August, 1916, and on the 16th October, 1917. This was principally intended to encourage the pro-French elements inside Alsace and Lorraine, and was full of sparkling satire upon German administration. The famous yarn about the British intention to occupy Calais was dealt with as follows:

> We are able to confirm this almost incredible news (that the French have leased Calais to the English for 99 years). Our correspondent has interviewed a French officer of high rank (adjutant) in Switzerland, originally from the vicinity of Beaucaire, who, in tears, and with every mark of dejection, confessed that he had himself seen the city of Calais and the English government conclude the contract. The rental was fixed at 255,000 pounds sterling per month; it is payable in advance on the first of each month. Upon receiving this amount, the Mayor of Calais divides it among the inhabitants of the city. All expenses for light and street cleaning, together with an obligation to sprinkle sand on the sidewalks in case of a freeze are assumed by the renter; the owner pays for repairs. Either party may terminate

the contract at will upon nine months' notice.—Behold the depths to which France has fallen in humiliating herself before the perfidious Albion! If the citizens of Calais imagine that the intrepid German Michel intends to deliver them from the clutches of the English, that nation of shopkeepers, they are deluding themselves. . . . We have already tried it once, and we will most assuredly not undertake it again.[32]

The French also forged a number of the *Frankfurter Zeitung* in July, 1917. They copied and parodied the leaflets which were used for war loan propaganda in Germany. Republican propaganda which was written by Siegfried Balder and a troupe of others was sent over the lines. Special pamphlets were devoted to justifying the French claim to Alsace and Lorraine.

In addition to these efforts, the French published *La Voix du Pays* for distribution among the occupants of the invaded territories and of Alsace and Lorraine. Special appeals were addressed to the Bavarians in the hope of stirring up the South against the North. The French tried to send as much of their propaganda as possible through the Swiss postal service into Germany. They used a Swiss publishing house to prepare material which they smuggled over the border. One clever agent sold preserves to Germany and stuffed the cartons with Allied propaganda stuff.

In 1916 the British War Office[33] created a branch of the Directorate of Military Intelligence known as M.I.7.b., the new staff establishing *Le Courrier de l'Air* for the purpose of reassuring the inhabitants of the invaded territory that the cause was not lost. Copies of the paper even reached the interior of Germany, where they aroused the fury of the German authorities. This paper was published uninterruptedly from April 6th, 1917, until January 25th, 1918. Its publication was suspended for a time, as a result of an order issued by the German military command to try the occupants of any aeroplane which carried "seditious literature" by court-martial, and to inflict severe penalties upon them. This threat was followed by an example of its execution, and the *Courrier* was suspended until a new mode of dissemination could be perfected. Publication was resumed March 7th, 1918.

The development of better methods of distribution is traced by Major Street in these pages:

> There is no intrinsic difficulty in scattering pieces of paper any more than there is in scattering pieces of steel, but the desired destination of the two forms of missile varies, as does the effect they are intended to produce. A shell, to secure its maximum effect, should burst in the centre of a group of men; propaganda leaflets, on the contrary, should be dispersed as widely as possible, and then should avoid the highly disciplined group, and should arrive within the grasp of the lonely sentry, free from the influence of his compatriots, and with nothing else to divert his thoughts. The group would probably treat a leaflet as a joke, the isolated man would read it through sheer boredom, and would possibly be induced to believe that there was something in its argument. And once propaganda has secured even the vaguest mistrust of the doctrines that it combats, its task is more than half accomplished.
>
> Both the Allied Powers and the Central Empires experimented with propaganda projectiles, using the trench mortar as their means of projection. The idea was, in most cases, to construct a bomb with a small bursting charge, which should, upon its arrival over the opposing lines, release a shower of pamphlets upon the heads of an astonished enemy. But the system had its obvious drawbacks. A trench mortar has always been an unpopular weapon, credited with the effect of incurring retaliation more than outweighing the damage it may possibly produce. Further, the most susceptible might well be expected to resent a

shower of words hurled at him by so direct a method or, if not to resent it, at all events to ridicule it as rather too obvious a *ruse de guerre*. There is something inconsistent about an army that makes life unbearable with "flying pigs" one moment, and the next sends out, through the mouths of the very same weapons, a flood of literature proclaiming that all men are brothers, or some other pacific doctrine. It was not long before the trench mortar, as a projector of propaganda, was abandoned in favour of the aeroplane.

This later weapon seemed at first to have every qualification for the purpose. It could scatter innumerable leaflets from any convenient height, and, owing to the length of time taken by them in falling, their arrival had no visible connection with its flight. Far more effect would naturally be produced by a leaflet blowing into a trench from nowhere in particular than from one obviously hurled by a lethal engine. Further, the aeroplane had a far greater penetration, could scatter its propaganda over rest-billets and railheads as well as over the trenches themselves. The advantages of this were twofold the leaflets could be found and picked up over a far greater area, and men some way back from the line had more leisure and inclination to ponder their contents. But, on the other hand there were many other calls upon the aeroplanes available. It was argued with a considerable show of reason that if a plane could be sent upon a flight over hostile territory it would be better employed dropping bombs than propaganda. Some went so far as to say that the best propaganda that could be dropped over the enemy were bombs and plenty of them, a contention that was correct as regards the Rhine towns and incorrect as regards London. At all events, it was felt that the aeroplane was too valuable a fighting machine proper to be employed as a disseminator of leaflets.

The next idea was the employment of observation balloons, which were to carry a supply of pamphlets to be thrown overboard when the wind was blowing towards the enemy lines. Apart from the fact that the occupants of the balloon were usually too busy with their proper function of observation to worry much about casting packets of paper into space, the observation balloon had many disadvantages. A more ingenious and elaborate development of the observation balloon scheme was a revival of the man-lifting kite. When the wind was favourable, the kite was flown from some suitable spot, and a "follower," carrying a bundle of leaflets, caused to travel up the taut string of the kite. The "follower" was fitted with an automatic release, which functioned at a predetermined height, allowed the leaflets to fly away, and the "follower" to fall to the ground again ready for recharging. When the contrivance did not jamb, it was a very entertaining toy to play with.

It was not until late in 1916 that the free balloon was seriously considered as a vehicle of propaganda. The idea had always been obvious; load a balloon with the leaflets it was intended to distribute, send it up with a favourable wind, and there you were. The difficulty lay in predicting within a thousand miles or so where the balloon would come down. It was not until the science of meteorology, urgently impelled by the needs of the Artillery, made its marvellous war-time developments, that balloons could be used scientifically. "Meteor," in the shape of the various meteorological experts attached to the forces, eventually became able to gauge the velocity and direction of the wind at practically any height in any given locality. The rest was simple, so soon as a simple and reliable release had been evolved. You took your balloon to a given spot, say, ten miles behind the lines, you knew your balloon would rise to, say, six thousand feet, and travel at that height until its burden was released. "Meteor" gave the velocity of the wind at twenty miles an hour, south-west, at that height and place. Forty miles from the balloon position, and bearing north-east, was an enemy concentration camp. Load your balloon with the required type of propaganda leaflet, set your release to act in rather less than two hours, to allow of drift of the leaflets when falling, and there you were.

. . . The balloons were made of paper, "doped" with a preparation to render them hydrogen tight.

As equipped for service in France, a propaganda balloon section consisted of a couple of three-ton lorries for the conveyance of the hydrogen cylinders, balloons, and leaflets, with the necessary personnel of officer and a few men. Certain stations were selected, such that some desirable target could be reached with any direction of wind from north round by west to south. . . .

The means of attachment was the solution of the whole problem of the use of balloons, and was as simple as it was ingenious. A length of the orange-coloured woven tinder, sold at every tobacconist's for use in pipe-lighters, was taken, and one end of it fixed to the balloon. The sheaves of leaflets were strung on cotton tags, as used for binding papers in Government offices. The end of each tag was driven through the length of tinder at calculated distances from the free end. The rate of burning of the tinder was ascertained by experiment, and found to be, say, one inch in five minutes. If the target were twenty miles an hour, the balloon would be over the target

in forty minutes. The tags would then be inserted at
close intervals from six to ten inches from the end
of the tinder.

Just as the balloon was released, the end of the
tinder was held against a lighted cigarette, and commenced to burn.

The Allies had the wind at their backs during most of the summer and autumn of 1918, when their propaganda attained its greatest proportions, and material was distributed over a zone, 150 miles
deep, behind the German lines. By August they had achieved a distribution of 100,000 leaflets a day, which meant that between four
and five million leaflets were sent over monthly.

The Allies solved the problem of distribution much better than
the Germans were able to do. One of the finest strokes of German
propaganda was the publication of the captured list in the *Gazette
des Ardennes*. This made it possible for the people in the occupied
territory to have a valid excuse to read a paper which was obviously pro-German.

A clandestine Press service was built up to supply the Belgians
with news of the Entente world, and was an important influence
alike in the stimulation of their own morale, and in permeating
the nearest German populations.[34]

This review of the problem of demoralizing the enemy seems
to show that the principal theme is the impossibility of victory,
and that a discouraged nation may turn against an ally, or its own
governing class, and lose by the secession of minority nationalities.

Notes

[1] *Gazette*, July 2, 1917, citing an item from the *Frankfurter Zeitung*
   Marchand, p. 97.

[2] *Gazette*, 17 November, 1917. Marchand, p. 143.

[3] Reproduced opposite page 145 in Hansi and Tonnelet, *A Travers
   les Lignes Ennemies*.

[4] *Gazette*, 13 August, 1916. Marchand, p. 25.

[5] *Gazette*, Same.

[6] *Gazette*, 7 June, 1916. Marchand, p. 190.

[7] 23 September, 1916. Marchand, p. 85.

[8] *Gazette*, 9 January, 1916. Marchand, p. 15.

[9] *Gazette*, 3 July, 1917. Marchand, p. 27.

[10] Heber Blankenhorn describes the American campaign in *My Adventures in Propaganda*.

[11] Hansi and Tonnelet, Figure 4, opposite p. 24.

[12] Reproduced in Blankenhorn, p. 78.

[13] C. K. Bolton, *The Private Soldier under Washington*, p. 90. Cited by Salmon, *The Newspaper and the Historian*, 340.

[14] *Gazette*, 7 September, 1916. Marchand, p. 49.

[15] *Gazette*, 26 April, 1917. Marchand, p. 47.

[16] A Russian who was permitted to visit some of these prison camps through the Red Cross arrangements made this the subject of a complaint.

[17] Reproduced in Hansi and Tonnelet, p. 136.

[18] Reproduced in Hansi and Tonnelet, p. 160.

[19] See Hansi and Tonnelet, p. 152.

[20] This and similar examples are given in Campbell, *Secrets of Crewe House*.

[21] Page 62.

[22] Graux, *Les Fausses Nouvelles*, II: 151.

[23] *Gazette*, April 29, 1917.

[24] See Hansi and Tonnelet, P. 23.

[25] Marchand, Section II.

[26] Steed, *Through Thirty Years*, II: 102.

[27] Steed, II: 129.

[28] For an account of the proceedings, see the agitation journals. The *Czecho-Slovak Review* for November, 1918, summarizes it briefly.

[29] Palæologue, *An Ambassador's Memoirs*, I : 327.

[30] *Die Vorgeschichte des Krieges; Deutsches Volk, wach' auf!* See Hansi and Tonnelet, opposite p. 56.

[31] See Hansi and Tonnelet, opposite p. 38.

[32] Hansi and Tonnelet, p. 60.

[33] Major C. J. C. Street, "Propaganda Behind the Lines," *Cornhill Magazine*, 3rd Series, 47 (1919): 488-499.

[34] See, for the story of *La libre Belgique*, Jean Massart, *The Secret Press of Belgium*.

8

CONDITIONS AND METHODS OF PROPAGANDA: A SUMMARY

Successful propaganda depends upon the adroit use of means under favourable conditions. A means is anything which the propagandist can manipulate; a condition is anything to which he must adapt. A propagandist can alter the organization of his activities, modify the streams of suggestion which he releases, and substitute one device of communication for another, but he must adjust himself to traditional prejudices, to certain objective facts of international life, and to the general tension level of the community. Both the conditions and the methods of propaganda have been mentioned explicitly or by implication in the course of the present study, and the time has come to draw them together in more systematic form.

The achievements of propaganda are affected by the traditional prejudices of the nation and of each constituent group. The French had the advantage of a great historic friendship with America, a heritage of the gratitude which the struggling colonists felt for aid of the French in the Revolution. The Germans counted upon the sympathy of their former nationals, and of the Irish-Jewish blocs. The British could rely upon a very deep and pervasive community of feeling, which was so general that it was frequently ignored in the presence of more spectacular and less profound attitudes.

Propagandists are always likely to run foul of some deeply imbedded prejudice. Thus the Germans seized upon the alleged franctireur excesses of the Belgian people to justify their own acts to the world and to the German public. But when the Prussians began to circulate tales of Catholic priests who urged their parishioners to kill the invader with every means in their command, a cross-current was set up at home. The Catholics arose to contradict the rumours. The Catholics had organized a *Zentralauskunftstelle der katholischen Presse* in 1900. This was revamped into the *Rechtschutzstelle für die katholische Geistlichkeit* at Frankfurt in 1913. In 1906 another service was set up at Cologne, bearing the name *Priesterverein Paz für das katholische Deutschland*. Both services began to cast insinuations and contradictions upon the Prussian versions of Catholic atrocities in Belgium, and these were snapped up abroad and used by the Allies to discredit the German tales about Belgium.[1]

Such prejudices continually circumscribed the propagandist. His freedom is further restricted by the network of connections between nations. The British held the cable communications between America and Europe in the hollow of their hands, and this had far-reaching results. The Germans tried in vain to offset such a handicap by exploiting the wireless, but with mediocre success. Anyone who knew the history of American foreign attitudes could have predicted in 1914 that the British viewpoint stood an excellent chance of infecting America, for American public opinion has often been a cockle-shell, floating helplessly and unconsciously in the wake of the British man-of-war. After the Civil War the American nation was a warm friend of Russia and bought "Seward's ice box" as a gift of gratitude for the Tsar's moral support during the conflict. In the supervening years, America had few direct contacts with Russia, but American friendship passed over into active hostility. The explanation is very simple: America was fed on the British Press and Britain was in conflict with Russia.

There are objective similarities and differences in social customs and institutions between two nations, and these cannot be waved aside. After all is said and done, it was true that Britain, France and Belgium were more democratic than Germany in their basic political institutions, and that Americans spoke English and read English, and not German. Americans knew Shakespeare and not Goethe, and they thought the Battle of Waterloo was won by the Duke of Wellington, and not by Blücher. The basic patterns of American life were more English than German.[2]

There are often interpenetrations of population which make it difficult to control sentiment at will. The customs and habits and competitive power of various immigrant groups in America influenced the American attitude and the attitude of their countries of origin. Many of the Russians who returned home when the Revolution came, carried back tales of reeking tenements and twelve-hour shifts in the steel mills. When the American propagandists undertook to extol the virtues of American democracy, some embarrassing questions were always forthcoming from the audience.

One form of population interpenetration, which is particularly important in war, is the quartering of invaders upon the inhabitants of a conquered territory. A foreign military occupation produces all sorts of friction between the authorities and the inhabitants, and the distressing incidents which abound in war are particularly common then. The Germans occupied Belgium and were embarrassed by compromising collisions with the civilians. The Allies were able to make tremendous play with everything that happened and a great deal that did not; the Germans could only retort by repeating the horrors of the Russian occupation of Eastern Prussia, which was too far away to arouse the sympathy and pity of the Americans.

There may be important connecting links of an economic character between two countries. It is generally recognized as a principle of international politics that when a country has loaned money to another it is likely to come to the aid of its debtor, should a third party threaten its ability to pay. The Americans who loaned their money to the Allies during the period of American neutrality may have advanced it out of sentimental preference for the Allied cause (the House of Morgan was English in origin and affiliation), but once tied to the Allies, the cords of sympathy were strengthened by bonds of gold. The sequel confirms the axiom that the creditor is bound to the debtor.

During the war-time the relative military strength of the contesting parties is a decisive point. Great movements of retreat cannot be concealed for long, and prolonged humiliation spreads the seeds of discord and defeatism. The German propagandists could invent no new hope to replace the disillusionment of mid-summer, 1918; the appeal to arms had exhausted their credit, and destroyed the simple faith of the masses. Lord Grey has written some sage words about how easy it is to exaggerate the role of diplomacy in war-time, and what he says applies to propaganda, which is one of the tools of diplomacy. The pivotal front is the military front.

> Even the battle of the Marne was, to outside opinion, rather the saving of Paris than a great victory, an arrest of the German advance rather than a turning of the tide in favour of the latter. Then followed the first battle of Ypres, in which the Franco-British line was brought near to another catastrophe. In 1915 there were no Allied successes of magnitude sufficient to counteract the deplorable impression made by the huge Russian disasters. In 1916 the Germans failed at Verdun, but the French suffered heavily, and the year was rather one of German failure than of Allied success, except the Brusiloff offensive. This brought the Rumanians in. Even the gaps in the Austrian line made by Brusiloff were completely stopped in a short time. The task of Allied diplomacy in Europe during the war was indeed uphill and thankless work.[3]

The preceding paragraphs have enumerated some of the connecting links which bind nations together and which condition the success of propaganda. These are, for the most part, quite tangible things which anyone can see on close inspection: the communication network, similarities and differences in customs and institutions, interpenetration of population, economic ties, relative military power. We now come to a limiting factor which is unquestionably present, but which is neither simple to describe nor to explain: the tension level.

By the tension level is meant that condition of adaption or mal-adaption, which is variously described as public anxiety, nervous-ness, irritability, unrest, discontent or strain. The propagandist who deals with a community when its tension level is high, finds that a reservoir of explosive energy can be touched off by the same small match which would normally ignite a bonfire.

Some day it will undoubtedly be possible to connect the funda-mental biological and psychological processes with this phenom-enon, but to-day the field is a battleground of rival conjectures. Every school of psychological thought seems to agree, however, that war is a type of influence, which has vast capacities for re-leasing repressed impulses, and for allowing their external mani-festations in direct form. There is thus a general consensus that the propagandist is able to count upon very primitive and power-ful allies in mobilizing his subjects for war-time hatred of the enemy. The possibility also exists that there are physiological or psychological types which respond more readily than others to the bellicose stimuli circulated by the propagandist.[4]

It may be that further research will confirm the hypothesis of Clark Wissler, that there are special situations in the cultural life of a group in which definite psychological dispositions lead toward expansion. This anthropologist writes:

> when a group comes into a new solution to one of its important culture problems, it becomes zealous to spread that idea abroad, and is moved to embark upon an era of conquest to force the recognition of its merits.[5]

He also says that the extension of the material culture zone beyond the zone of political control, is likely to produce irritations which lead to an attempt to enlarge the political zone to coincide.[6]

Certainly, there is reason for believing that the propagandist who works upon an industrialized people, is dealing with a more tense and mobile population than that which inhabits an agrarian state. Industrialism has apparently increased the danger from

those secret mines which are laid by repression, for it has introduced both the monotony of machine tending, and the excitement
of much secondary stimulation. The rhythm and clang of exacting
machinery is no less characteristic of the industrial way of life, than
the blazing array of billboards, window displays, movies,
vaudevilles, and newspapers, which convey abundant and baffling
possibilities of personal realization. The stage is set, and

> a coarse patriotism, fed by the wildest rumours and
> the most violent appeals to hate and the animal lust
> of blood, passes by quick contagion through the
> crowded life of the cities, and recommends itself
> everywhere by the satisfaction it affords to the sen-
> sational cravings. It is less the savage yearning for
> personal participation in the fray than the feeling of
> a neurotic imagination that marks Jingoism.[7]

Both literacy and the Press are offspring of the machine age.
The Press lives by advertising; advertising follows circulation, and
circulation depends on excitement. "What sells a newspaper?" A
former associate of Lord Northcliffe answers:

> The first answer is "war." War not only creates a
> supply of news but a demand for it. So deep-rooted
> is the fascination in war and all things appertaining
> to it that a paper has only to be able to put up on its
> placard "A Great Battle" for its sales to mount up.[8]

This is the key to the proclivity of the Press to aggravate public
anxiety in moments of crises.

So much for the general factors which condition the success of
propaganda. Success depends upon traditional prejudices, objective
connections between nations, and the changing level of popular irritability. No matter how skilful the propagandist may be in organizing his staff, selecting suggestions, and exploiting instruments

of transmission, his manipulative skill will go for nought if there is no favourable juxtaposition of social forces to aid him.

The degree to which the propagandist is master of his fate depends in part upon the method of organization which he adopts. A number of agencies always engage in greater or less measure in war propaganda work; the Foreign Office, the Diplomatic and Consular staffs; the War Department, the General Staff and Field Headquarters and the principal service departments of internal administration. Since propaganda is, by its nature, incapable of complete segregation in the hands of one staff, unity must be achieved by the devious path of co-ordination, rather than by the simple act of exclusive delegation. During the last War the nations sought to minimize the dangers of contradiction, malproportion and duplication by resorting to one of three main types of co-ordination: the Press conference (Germany); the committee of executives, each responsible for a principal branch of propaganda work (Great Britain) and the single propaganda executive, operating in the name of the principal departments (the United States). The Germans got no further than common Press conferences and sporadic efforts at co-ordination because of the excessive friction between their civil and military authorities. Except for special commissioners who were sent to certain of the most important foreign countries, the French relied upon their existing agencies of government. The British were finally constrained to set up a committee of executives of approximately ministerial importance, each one of whom was charged with some such important branch of propaganda as enemy, home, allied or neutral. By securing a man of prestige to head each important service, policy was itself occasionally modified for the better. Northcliffe brought the Cabinet to straighten out its policy toward the Italians and the Jugo-Slavs, and the results vindicated the maxim that policy and propaganda should go hand in hand. The United States solved its problem by creating an ex-officio committee of the heads of principal departments (State, War and Navy) and one earnest and aggressive man who did the effectual work. Integration in Creel's hands was justifiable because of the comparative simplicity of America's propaganda both at home and abroad. The British had to deal with such a complex of foreign problems that extreme integration might have stifled ready adjustment.

The war experience seems to warrant the belief that the directors of each important propaganda service should be men whose prestige equals that of the policy determining officers, and that the staff should be selected from newspapermen—rather than proprietors—from popular writers, and from the members of the new propaganda profession.

The War abundantly demonstrated that the relation between the propaganda services and the legislature is a thorny problem. The executive arm of a democratic government may pervert a propaganda bureau to partisan, personal or class ends, and it may bind the legislature in advance, by stimulating public opinion, to favour its own policy. The executive may use the bureau to popularize an erroneous picture of the facts, and the legislature, conscious of all this, may assail the executive in unmeasured terms and undermine public confidence in its leaders. The best adjustment here does not depend upon statutes or ordinances, but upon the cultivation of informal channels of acquaintance and communication through which legislators may be brought into closer contact with the facts of the service. If matters go badly, they can, and should, protest. But their remarks should be grounded upon something more tangible than mere mistrust. It was the failure to close the gap between the legislator and the administrator, which led to the undignified and unjust criticism of the Committee of Public Information in the American Congress. There is no doubt, of course, that democratic governments must assume the task, regardless of all complicating difficulties, of mobilizing minds as well as men and money in war.

The general form of propaganda organization is a variable one, which the propagandist may adapt to his purposes. His problem, however, consists principally in selecting the social suggestions best calculated to evoke the desired responses. In this he is governed, in the first instance, by the broad strategic aims of propaganda. There are four major objectives:

(1) To mobilize hatred against the enemy;
(2) To preserve the friendship of allies;
(3) To preserve the friendship and, if possible, to procure the co-operation of neutrals;
(4) To demoralize the enemy.

The general theory of the appeals to be employed to achieve each aim has been developed in the previous chapters of this inquiry, and may be summarized rather briefly at this point.

To mobilize the hatred of the people against the enemy, represent the opposing nation as a menacing, murderous aggressor. Represent the enemy as an obstacle to the realization of the cherished ideals and dreams of the nation as a whole, and of each constituent unit. It is through the elaboration of war aims that the obstructive role of the enemy becomes particularly evident. Represent opposing nation as satanic; it violates all the moral standards (mores) of the group, and insults its self-esteem. The maintenance of hatred depends upon supplementing the direct representations of the menacing, obstructive, satanic enemy by assurances of ultimate victory.

To preserve friendly relations with an ally, the cardinal themes are our strenuous exertion in the prosecution of the war, and our hearty assent to the cherished war aims of the ally. This may be supported by demonstrations of respect and esteem and by all the themes of domestic propaganda.

To win the friendship of a neutral, lead the neutral to identify his own interests with the defeat of our enemy. In addition to the ordinary devices, seek to draw the neutral into active co-operation in some non-military capacity. If all else fails, re-enforce pacifism, by portraying the horrors of war, and the unwillingness of the enemy to make peace, and stir up trouble between two neutrals.

To demoralize the enemy, substitute new hates for old. The edge of animosity may be somewhat blunted by direct counterstimulation, but diversion depends mainly upon spreading discouragement and instigating defeatism. The way is then paved for violent campaigns against allies, against the governing class, and among national minorities, against the unity of the state.

These themes were present in each war propaganda during the last War, but some of them were more effectively utilized by one belligerent than another. The British were amazingly successful in the development of humanitarian war aims. The Germans aroused much resentment and suspicion abroad by talking about a war of German Kultur, and by underplaying the humanitarian ideal. The British talked about a war to protect international law and to guarantee the sanctity of treaties, and they fought against a monster, known as autocratic militarism, in the name of democracy. British public men began to talk about a war to end war long before the German statesmen learned this vocabulary. Indeed, the colourless and halting pronouncements of Bethmann-Hollweg seemed more like concessions wrested from an unimaginative soul than programmes promulgated by a determined leader. Wilsonian phraseology touched the imagination of powerful elements throughout the world. In the duel of words the Germans fought with pasteboard against steel.

The Germans were never able to efface the initial impression that they were aggressors. This was due in part to the stupidity of their own appeals. They continued to talk about "Einkreisung" in America, where the danger of encirclement is a theoretical conjecture for which there is no counterpart in recent American tradition. They never dramatized the aggressiveness of their enemies as did the Allies, who invented the myth of the "Potsdam Council." They never succeeded in getting over the idea of a war hatched by a vain and dissolute uncle (Edward VII.) in a fit of pique at the success of his nephew (William II.); they failed to humanize and dramatize the diplomatic game, and held fast to diplomatic jargon and German catchwords, which lacked fire and fury in America.

Much of the German propaganda proved to be a boomerang. It is appalling that responsible directors of propaganda should have done everything in their power to circulate the charge that the Belgians were sniping. The Kaiser went so far as to make a public protest to President Wilson. The truth is that the report that the Belgians were sniping aroused admiration in America. It seemed to show how plucky these little Belgians really were, for the American public was a civilian public, and it knew that Belgium was little and that Germany was big, and it cheered whenever the underdog bit.

The explanation of the maladroitness of the German propaganda is partly the influence which the military mind had upon it. To the soldier it is utterly inexcusable for a civilian to shoot a man in uniform. He has a strict code of ethics, which is dictated by consideration for his own skin, and he distinguishes sharply between what is permitted a man in uniform, and what is permitted a man out of uniform. These elementary distinctions are vague, and nearly meaningless to the public mind in such a country as the United States, where military training is the exception and not the rule. The American cartoonists reflected the civilian mind when they lampooned the big, coarse German, who howled to heaven that the little fellow whom he was beating had stung him with a pebble from a sling shot. The failure of the Germans to neutralize the Cavell incident has already been alluded to, and it typifies a military mind which is opaque to the civilian point of view.

Instead of complaining about the snipers in Belgium the Germans would have been better advised to have appointed a distinguished jury of neutrals to investigate the Welfare of the Belgian people, and to have broadcasted its report all over the world. As it was, they never neutralized the effect of the Bryce report.

The Germans cast no anchors to windward during the opening weeks of the War. They talked about the invincible German army, and predicted victory on a definite date.[9] They did not advertise the invasions in East Prussia, and their march through Belgium and northern France seemed to belie any theory of unpreparedness.

The French propaganda was lucid and simple. Her retiring armies told a *prima facie* story of who had been prepared for the War (after the early cloud of false news had blown aside), and her chief propaganda was that of simple satanism. The Germans were never able to popularize so striking an epithet as "Hun" or "Boche" and their clumsy exhortations to hate or their sneering references to the "All-lies," were much less powerful and invidious. The French vocabulary had powerful words like humanity and democracy, which reverberated with a tremendous clang abroad.

Little attention has been paid here to that aspect of influencing, which is often called "propaganda of the deed." By this is usually meant some isolated act of violence, which is intended to produce a powerful impression. The dropping of bombs upon enemy
cities was less for immediate military and strategic purposes, than
for propaganda purposes. It was supposed that civilian morale
would crack under the strain of perpetual fear. This, besides the
propaganda of frightfulness and other acts of frightfulness, was
supposed to produce discouragement and defeatism.

Since much of the talk about frightfulness during the last War
was sheer propaganda against the enemy, the effect of overt acts
of this kind can be judged by the influence of such propaganda.
On the whole, its chief result was to stiffen the determination of
the people to defend themselves.

It may be unreliable, but there is a story with a flash of insight
which tells about the German aviator who objected to dropping
any more bombs on London, because he had not entered the War
to be a recruiting officer for the British army. Civilians become
habituated to raids, as Londoners did to the Zeppelin raids, and
humour and ridicule soften the trial. The London stores advertised
all sorts of accessories for "Zeppelin parties," and one is even supposed to have offered a special line of "Zepp nighties."

The Allied propaganda of discouragement made little impression on the Germans until 1918. Indeed, the British wasted some
of their early effort on vain boastings, when the German army was
actually in victorious march against them. The American propaganda against the Germans was essentially a propaganda of discouragement and revolution. It was the British who did most of
the propaganda of dissolution against Austro-Hungarian armies,
and they scored notable successes. Success in propaganda of this
kind depends much more upon the existence of strains and stresses
in an enemy state than does success in propaganda among neutrals.

The preceding paragraphs have contrasted the strategy of some
of the principal War propagandas, and rehearsed the general theory
of how to select powerful appeals for the achievement of the four
propaganda aims. There are humbler criteria of tactical nature,

which the working propagandist applies to each suggestion. The tactical objectives may be summarized thus:

1. To arouse the interest of specific groups;
2. To nullify inconvenient ideas;
3. To avoid untruth which is likely to be contradicted before the achievement of the strategic purpose.

Effective propaganda is catholic in its appeal. It ignores no loyalty inside a nation. Protestants, Catholics, Jews, workers, financiers, farmers, merchants, city dwellers, and ruralites, sportsmen and philosophers, men of affairs and academicians, women and men, old and young; every possible line of cleavage in the nation is appealed to by some direct or indirect device.[10]

R. J. R. S. Wreford exactly described this process when he said that the expert propagandist

> must decide as to the public which is most likely to be, or to become, sympathetically disposed toward the interests which he represents; he must then select the aspects of those interests best calculated to appeal to the predilections of this public; and he must then present these aspects in an attractive manner.[11]

Propaganda material must reach the meanest as well as the keenest intelligence. In the case of the crude prophecies of victory which were made during the War, it was safe to predict that they would carry reassurance to the most superstitious and credulous strata of the population, but that the sophisticated would pass them contemptuously by. It is perfectly safe to launch the crude and sophisticated together, for the people capable of reacting to the latter will not be estranged by the former; they will merely remain indifferent and condescending. A cock-and-bull story about the Kaiser's lust for war, as revealed by his habit of spitting three times whenever the Union Jack was displayed, would probably not win

Belgravia, no matter how popular it might be in Poplar. But a learned tome, prepared with all the dexterity of the trained academician, could defend the same general theme to the satisfaction of an intelligent public. Part of the superiority of British propaganda during the War was due to its amazing suppleness. In 1917 the journalist Arthur Bullard commented on this fact and wrote,

> The appeal which brought the first wave of volunteers was "Bleeding Belgium," the duty of the strong as good sportsmen to defend the weak. Then the attempt was made to stir national pride by posters quoting the Kaiser's alleged insulting reference to "the contemptible little English Army." An effort was made to frighten the people by the supposed danger of invasion. Somewhat later, pictures were displayed of the famous treaty which had been called a "scrap of paper." Every note was sounded from rage against "the baby killers" to fidelity to the pledged words as the basis of international relations. But by far the greatest response came on the appeal to democratic idealism, the issue between popular rule and military despotism.[12]

Every suggestion must have an interesting appeal to a definite group, but some suggestions must be expressly designed to nullify inconvenient ideas. This brings us to the second tactical standard of good propaganda, which appears in the conduct of war influencing. When a government undertakes to influence the people within its own boundaries, it is usually able to control the cable, telegraph, telephone, Press, postal and wireless services, while war lasts. But psychological frontiers never coincide with geographical frontiers, and summary suppression is never a complete success. Governments learn to nullify rather than to conceal undesirable ideas.

Part of this technique is the control of emphasis. Underemphasis may be procured in the Press by relegating an item to an obscure column with an inconspicuous headline, by incorporating in another story, by omitting detail, by contradiction on the part of the writer or "witness," by quotations which cast doubt upon the assertion and related devices. Conversely, favourable ideas may be given prominent columns, striking headlines, independent treatment, circumstantial detail, impressive corroboration and ceaseless repetition.

In practice, the simplest mode of nullifying important reports is by the device of compensation. It is ridiculous to pretend that the enemy never wins a point. The depressing news of an enemy gain should, however, be counterbalanced by a simultaneous gain. This was what Winston Churchill used to do at the Admiralty, for

> he would hold on to a bit of bad news for a time on the chance of getting a bit of good news to publish as an offset, and I must say that it not infrequently came off.[13]

When American preparations began to assume disquieting proportions, the German Press played up the collapse of Russia.

Compensation sometimes takes the form of pointing out that the enemy is as badly off as the home public. At one time during the War, the food administration in Berlin announced that 50 grammes of fresh lard would be distributed on a certain day, but circumstances intervened and it became impossible to make good. The disappointment of the people was somewhat appeased by the publication of impressive statistics of the huge losses of lard, to which the enemy had been subjected by the U-Boat campaign.

The most convenient mine of counter-propaganda material, is the opposition Press inside a foreign country. The German Press greeted the appointment of Foch to the supreme command by reprinting some articles in the French radical Press, which interpreted the appointment as a last straw, admitting that bad leadership had brought about the present plight at the front.

Unfavourable intelligence may be nullified by a flat denial, but defence by denial is not of itself efficacious when alarming news is abroad. Defence by admission and justification usually accomplishes more, especially when placed in the form of a counterattack. Certain losses at the front may be covered by ostentatious hints at a great plan to draw the enemy from his base of supplies and snare him. Poison gas may be justified by assaulting the cruel, inhuman and illegal methods of warfare to which the enemy has resorted.

The public should be prepared in advance for the occurrence of an event, which might otherwise produce an undesirable repercussion. Thus precautions should be taken to discredit an authority which is to render an ultimate verdict, and which is almost certain to be unfriendly. The Germans looked with open contempt upon the panel selected to inquire into the Belgian atrocities, and they blackguarded both its integrity and its technique before publishing its results.

The public may have bad news "broken" to it gently by publishing a disquieting question, followed by a few facts, and then by the worst. Panic is thus circumvented, since the processes of discounting the future have produced a certain stability of response in the public mind.

When it is proposed to inaugurate a policy to which there may be some objection, it is possible to instigate a demand for the very policy which it is intended to introduce. This is the indirect initiative, or, as a Belgian student of propaganda[14] has christened it, the *initiative éventée* (the fanned initiative). He observed its operations at the time of the Brest Litovsk negotiations between Germany and Russia. There was a great deal of objection in Germany among the parties of the Left to a downright policy of annexation, so the Government proceeded cautiously. The *Kölnische Volkszeitung* published a report that the English were negotiating with Russia for the right to occupy the Riga Islands. Instantly there were spontaneous editorials throughout Germany, demanding prompt action by the Imperial Government to forestall the accursed British. The Government took the islands.

Bad news and unwanted criticism may be nullified by distracting the attention of the public from them. A distraction is managed by springing a sensation which is unrelated to the inconvenient focal point of attention. The arrival of the *Deutschland* served this purpose in Germany at a dull moment during the War.

Yet a third general tactical standard has emerged in the course of our analysis. It is concerned with the relation of propaganda to truth. To what extent is it necessary for the suggestions employed in propaganda to conform to the canons of critical veracity?

Actual propaganda, wherever studied, has a large element of the fake in it. This varies from putting a false date line on a despatch, through the printing of unverified rumours, the printing of denials in order to convey an insinuation, to the "staging" of events. One of the world war fakes was the use of pictures of the Jewish pogrom of 1905, somewhat retouched, as fresh enemy atrocities. Of a similar type was the following: the London *Daily Mirror* of August 20th, 1915, published a picture of three German officers, who held various vessels in their hands. The sub-title was, "Three German Cavalrymen loaded with gold and silver loot," which they had taken in Poland. This was, in fact, a defaced reproduction of a picture, which had originally appeared in the *Berliner Lokalanzeiger* for the 9th of June, 1914, and which had shown the winners of the cavalry competition in the Grünewald. The officers had cups and trophies in their hands. The sub-title read:

> Vom Armee-Jagdrennen in Grünewald. Von links: Lt. Prieger, Zweiter: Lt. v. Egan-Krieger. Dritter: Lt., v. Herder. Sieger.[15]

Sir Campbell Stuart, looking back upon the British propaganda from the vantage ground of a victorious peace, has written that "only truthful statements" should be used in propaganda. This seems, in the light of practice, an impracticable maxim. It was not unusual during the War to invent a great deal of material out of whole cloth. One of the best examples of this sort of thing was the famous cadaver story. Two captured photographs chanced to come to the desk of the Chief of the British Army Intelligence, Brigadier General J. V. Charters. One of them showed dead German soldiers being hauled away for burial behind the lines, and the other showed dead horses on the way to the soap factory. Knowing the reverence of the Chinese for their ancestors and the uncertainty of Chinese opinion toward the Germans, he thoughtfully interchanged the titles of the two pictures, and sent the edited material to Shanghai for release. "German cadavers on way to the soap factory," soon found its way to Europe and America and spread distaste and contempt of all things German.[16]

This was, of course, a plain lie. But it was plausible, and it was incapable of complete refutation during the War. During war, plenty of horrors are sure to occur. They grow dank and rank on every hand, and a mustard seed of truth may blossom and bloom. Indeed, a very sophisticated British soldier, a literary man, who was not one to be taken in by this sort of thing, related something in his own experience which might have given rise to a story of this kind. Shortly after having heard this tale for the first time, he was engaged in active fighting in Bellicourt. A British shell squashed a German field kitchen, and what he saw when he went to inspect the ruins, gave the clue to the "corpse factory."

> A quite simple case. Shells had gone into cookhouses
> of ours, long before then, and had messed the cooks
> with the stew.[17]

The truth about the relation of truth to propaganda seems to be that it is never wise to use material which is likely to be contradicted by certain unconcealable events before the political objective of propaganda is attained. It is foolish to promise victory on a definite date in the imminent future, because the prediction may be falsified by the event and lead to a certain backwash of discouragement and suspicion. It is perfectly permissible to assert that ultimate success is sure, even though no critically-trained intelligence could accept such a statement as proved, because it is impossible to disprove this proposition before the attainment or the total eclipse of all hope of attaining the political objective.

It is evident that propaganda must avoid self-contradiction in the same context addressed to the same group or to groups in intimate contact with one another. There is comparatively little danger in telling the Protestants through their official organs that the war is a great Protestant crusade, and in encouraging the Catholics to regard it as a great Catholic movement; but it would be absurd to mix the appeals to the same audience. Every special group tends to make the war over in its own image, and the task of the propagandist is usually to facilitate, rather than to fabricate.

The three tactical principles which have just been recapitulated, may be stated in these words:

1. Suggestions should be circulated which promise to arouse the interest of specific groups.
2. Suggestions should be chosen to nullify inconvenient ideas which cannot be suppressed.
3. Suggestions should be used which are likely to pass uncontradicted until the propaganda aim is realized, and this implies, in particular, that self-contradiction in the same context to the same public must be avoided.

The successful choice of propaganda material according to these standards presupposes accurate prediction, not only of the immediate results of its circulation, but of the countercurrents which may be instigated. If methods of prior testing can be devised, the propagandist will approximate somewhat closer to the omniscience once imputed to him by a New York newspaper, which wrote,

the public mind to the trained propagandist is a pool into which phrases and thoughts are dropped like acids, with a foreknowledge of the reactions that will take place, just as Professor Loeb at the Rockefeller Institute can make a thousand crustaceans stop

swimming aimlessly about in the bowl and rush with
one headlong impulse to the side where the light
comes from, merely by introducing into the water a
little drop of a chemical.[18]

Thus far, our survey of the means of propaganda has covered
the methods of organizing and the criteria for selecting suggestions for strategic or tactical reasons. There remains the problem
of choosing from among the numerous instruments of transmission which are available. Suggestions may be spoken, written, pictorial[19] or musical, and the possible variations in the form of the
stimulus-carrier are infinite. The soundest method for the propagandist to follow is to cultivate the habit of identifying himself
imaginatively with the subjects to be influenced, and to explore all
the possible avenues of approach to their attention. Consider, from
this point of view, a group of people who are riding in a street car.
They may be influenced by placards posted inside the car, by posters on the billboards along the track, by newspapers which they
read, by conversations which they overhear, by leaflets which are
openly or surreptitiously slipped into their hands, by street demonstrations at halting places, and possibly by yet other carriers of
suggestions.

Of possible occasions for suggestion there is no end. People
walk along the streets or ride in automobiles, trams, subways,
elevated trains, boats, electrical or steam railways; people congre-
gate in theatres, churches, lecture halls, eating places, athletic
parks, concerts, barber shops and beauty parlours, coffee-houses
and drug stores; people work in offices, warehouses, mills, factories and conveyances. An inspection of the habit patterns of each
community reveals a web of mobility routes and congregating cen-
tres, which may be taken advantage of for the dissemination of
interested fact and opinion.

No *obiter dicta* about the comparative values of a given system
of transmitting stimuli can have the same importance as the habit
of mind which enables the propagandist to test each given situation for its inherent possibilities. The forms of suggestions are few

and elemental, but the possible occasions and carriers are infinite. The technical literature on advertising is full of the most precise information on the effect of different colours, sizes, shapes and elevations of outdoor posters on suggestion. All this is indispensable to the working propagandist, but it is distinctly ancillary to the problem of achieving and preserving a perspective on the problem of control, which uses broad and rather flexible categories of analysis. These are the leading questions: What are the proposed subjects of stimulation doing? How many separate occasions can be isolated? How many spoken, written, pictorial, musical or demonstrative suggestions can be interposed? What are carriers by which they may be transmitted into the experience-world of the subjects?

For the sake of suggesting the more common instruments of propaganda, Mr. Creel's summary of the work of the Committee on Public Information may be quoted:[20]

> Thirty odd booklets were printed in several languages. Seventy-five million copies were circulated in America, and many million copies were circulated abroad. Tours were arranged for the Blue Devils (French soldiers), Pershing's Veterans, and the Belgians, and mass meetings were arranged in many communities. Forty-five war conferences were held. The Four Minute Men commanded the volunteer services of 75,000 speakers, operating in 5,200 communities, and making a total of 755,190 speeches.

> With the aid of a volunteer staff of several hundred translators, the Committee supplied the foreign language Press of America with selected articles. It planned war exhibits for the state fairs of the United States, a series of inter-Allied war expositions, and secured millions of dollars worth of free advertising space from the Press, periodical, car and outdoor advertising forces of the country.

> It used 1,438 drawings prepared by volunteers for the production of posters, window cards and

similar material. It issued a daily newspaper with a 100,000 circulation for official use. It ran an information service and syndicated feature articles for the Press. Plate-matter for the country Press, and specialized material for the labour, religious and women's Press was supplied. Moving pictures were commercially successful in America and effective abroad, such as "Pershing's Crusaders," "America's Answer," and "Under Four Flags."

Over two hundred thousand stereopticon slides were distributed. Still photographs were prepared, and a stream of 700 pictures per day of military activities were censored. Cable, telegraph and wireless were employed by an official news service. A special mail and photograph service was also built up for the foreign Press. Reading-rooms were opened abroad, schools and libraries were fitted out, photographs were displayed prominently.

Missions were sent to the important districts of the world to look after American propaganda on the spot.

The service cost the taxpayers $4,912,553, and earned $2,825,67023 to be applied on expenses.

As we have seen, the problem of penetrating the enemy's country with propaganda material was solved during the last War by an ingenious device, the free balloon. After employing the Press of adjacent neutral countries, stationary balloons and aeroplanes, this mode of transmission was finally perfected and substituted. The Allies had the benefit of the prevailing westerly winds, and they laid down a barrage of print over the German lines.

One of the lessons to be drawn from the success of British propaganda in the United States is the cardinal importance of persons as means of carrying suggestion. No avenue of approach can safely be ignored, but the powers behind the impersonal agencies must be reached, and this is best managed by personal contact.

The British were astute enough to work chiefly through Americans, and none of their agents came to the premature disgrace and humiliation that befell Dr. Dernburg.

This completes our brief summary of the conditions and methods of propaganda. Success, it may be reiterated, depends upon the astute use of propaganda means (organizations, suggestions, devices) under favourable conditions.

Notes

1 See Albert Hellwig, "Zur Psychologie des Belgischen Franktireurkrieges," *Preuss. Jahrb.*, Bd. 174: 361-388.

2 For an able exposition of these points see the booklet by Professor Moritz Bonn, *Amerika als Feind*.

3 Lord Grey, *Twenty-Five Years*, II: 165.

4 For the concept of the tension level in individual psychology, see the masterly essay by Pierre Janet in the *Traité de psychologie* (edited by Dumas), Tome I. Applications of the notion of liberated repressions to war will be found in the books of such widely separated psychologists as Ernest Jones and George Patrick (*Essays in Psycho-analysis* and *The Psychology of Relaxation*).

5 *Man and Culture*, p.339.

6 Same, p. 174.

7 John A. Hobson, *The Psychology of Jingoism*, chapter 1, London, 1900.

8 Kennedy Jones, *Fleet Street and Downing Street*, p. 108.

9 The reason their propaganda began rather late and lost many openings was that they expected an early military victory.

10 For an example, see the description of Lithuanian propaganda on page 118.

11 "Propaganda Good and Evil," 19*th Century and After*, 93 (1923): 514-524. He patly defined propaganda as "the dissemination of interested fact and opinion."

12 *Mobilizing America*, p. 44.

13 Brownrigg. *Indiscretions of a Naval Censor*, p. 13.

14 He occupies an official position at present.

[15] Ferdinand Avenarius exposed several of these falsifications during the War in the booklet, *Bild als Verleumder*, the enlarged,
post-war edition of which is named *Die Mächte im Weltwahn*.
A French rejoinder was named *L'imposture par l'image*.

[16] See the N.Y. *Times*, 20 October, 1925. Will Irwin, the able journalist who took the trouble to try to verify the atrocity tales of
the War, has described several versions of the story that German soldiers cut off the hands of Belgian babies and carried
them along as souvenirs. He found them all unproved and
wildly improbable. Admiral Sims has categorically declared that
the reports of the terrible inhumanity of submarine command-
ers was, with a single exception, pure fabrication.

[17] C. E. Montague, *Disenchantment*, p. 93.

[18] New York *Tribune*, July 12th, 1918. Cited in Military Intelligence
booklet on *Propaganda in its Military and Legal Aspects*, p. 93.
Stern-Rubarth has named the "*Prüfung der möglicher Rück-
wirkung*" among his five principles. See his *Propaganda als
politisches Instrument*.

[19] The literature of caricature, cartoon and illustration during the
War is reviewed in L. M. Salmon, *The Newspaper and the Historian*. See especially p. 381 and after. Karl Demeter dealt with
the film propaganda of the Entente in the *Archiv f. Politik u.
Geschichte*, 4 (1925): 214-231.

[20] Adapted from George Creel, *How We Advertised America*.

THE RESULTS OF PROPAGANDA

After this rapid review of the means and conditions of war propaganda we are in a position to undertake an appraisal of its results. The history of the late War shows that modern war must be fought on three fronts: the military front, the economic front, and the propaganda front. The economic blockade strangles, the propaganda confuses, and the armed force delivers the coup de grace. Employed in conjunction with the other arms of offence, propaganda saps the stamina of the armed and civilian forces of the enemy, and smoothes the path for the mailed fist of men and metal. The economic blockade slowly squeezes the vitality out of a nation, and depends for its maximum effect upon a prolonged struggle. Propaganda is likewise a passive and contributory weapon, whose chief function is to demolish the enemy's will to fight by intensifying depression, disillusionment and disagreement.

As the U.S. Military Intelligence described the function of propaganda, it

> attacks the whole army at its base; threatens to cut it off from its base, to stop the flow of reinforcements, supplies, ammunition, equipment, food, comforts, and above all, to weaken the moral support that sustains the troops in the hardships and cruelties of war far from home.
>
> "Armies fight as the people think" was the wise epigram of the British General Applin. It might be

extended to say that armies fight as armies think,
for, as George William Curtis said: "Thoughts are
Bullets."[1]

Notable successes in which propaganda had an important and
perhaps a decisive part were scored in the last War. In common
with every other weapon of attack, propaganda has a surprise value,
which the Central Powers realized to the full, in the ingenious propaganda offensive, which preceded their attack upon the Italians
in 1917 at Caporetto. The spirit of the Italian armies was dissipated,
and their lines cracked and broken. In reply, the Allies won a striking success in 1918, when they forced the postponement of the
Austro-Hungarian offensive against Italy, from April until June,
by sowing demoralization among the troops of the subject nationalities. Mutinous troops blew up ammunition dumps behind the
lines, and sabotaged the whole military plan.

One of the gravest triumphs of the War was won when the Germans put the Russians out of the running. They strained every
muscle to complete the disintegration which culminated in the second Revolution. They permitted the famous "sealed car" to convey
Lenin and forty associates from Switzerland, across Germany on
their way to Russia. The ruthless Bolshevists accepted aid from
any quarter and completed the job, in spite of all the frantic work
of the American Red Cross and the special propaganda services of
the Entente group.

But the crowning victory of the War was at the expense of the
Germans. German morale depended upon the hope that the victory which had been so many times within their grasp, was just
over the horizon. Strained to the breaking point by the inexorable
clutch of the economic blockade, their great hopes of the spring
and summer of 1918 crumpled into rubbish, the German army and
the German people were ready to lend an ear to the seductive voice
of Mr. Wilson.

If the great generalissimo on the military front was Foch, the
great generalissimo on the propaganda front was Wilson. His
monumental rhetoric, epitomizing the aspirations of all humanity

in periods at once lucid and persuasive, was scattered far and wide over Germany. He declared war upon autocracies everywhere, and solemnly adhered to his distinction between the German people and the German rulers. His speeches were one prolonged instigation to revolt. He and Lenin were the champion revolutionists of the age. Throughout the entire War his pronouncements had won a substantial measure of confidence and respect in the minds of that minority of democratically-minded men, who longed to transform the pre-war Germany of class discrimination and special privilege. And when the clouds of adversity darkened the sky in 1918, they were joined by immense numbers of their compatriots, pinched by privation and despair, anxiously searching the heavens for portents of a soft peace. They turned, not to Clemenceau—hard, relentless vulture, poised like an avenging conscience, to tear at the vitals of a fallen adversary, nor to Lloyd George—nimble, unstable and uncertain, but to this mysterious figure in the White House, aloof from the ordinary passions of petty men, who spoke in elegiac prose of a better world, when wars should be no more and a brotherhood of democratic peoples should bury their heritage of ancestral rancour, and march toward a world of fellowship and reconciliation. It was to this man, mercilessly ridiculed and caricatured from one end of Germany to another through long years of hesitation and then of belligerency, that the Germans turned in their extremity.

Could it be that at last a statesman had arisen to lead the peoples of the world in the path of friendship and peace? Had a great prophet at last soared above vindictiveness and animosity to bring understanding to a harassed universe? This butt of ribald jest was transformed at a stroke in those closing months of hunger, insecurity, foreboding and hallucination into a saviour. The people grasped at straws and saw deliverers where they had seen but pedantic fools before.

Such matchless skill as Wilson showed in propaganda has never been equalled in the world's history. He spoke to the heart of the people as no statesman has ever done. For a few brief months he embodied the faith of the idealists in a better world, and the last desperate hope of the defeated peoples for a soft peace. He was raised to a matchless pinnacle of prestige and power, and his name was spoken with reverence in varied accents in the remotest corners of the earth.

Just how much of Wilsonism was rhetorical exhibitionism and how much was the sound fruit of sober reflection will be in debate until the World War is a feeble memory. From a propaganda point of view it was a matchless performance, for Wilson brewed the subtle poison, which industrious men injected into the veins of a staggering people, until the smashing powers of the Allied armies knocked them into submission. While he fomented discord abroad, Wilson fostered unity at home. A nation of one hundred million people, sprung from many alien and antagonistic stocks, was welded into a fighting whole, "to make the world safe for democracy." And the magic of his eloquence soothed the suspicions which Central and South America cherished toward the mighty colossus of the North, and brought most of them into the War on the Allied side.

The propaganda of disintegration which was directed against the tottering realm of the Hapsburgs bore fruit in disaffection and ultimate secession among the Czechs, Slovaks, Rumanians, Croats, Poles and Italians. The Balfour Declaration hastened the reversal of Jewish sympathies in 1917.

Some of the triumphs of propaganda were in the field of recruiting. In the race for Allies, the Germans won in Bulgaria and Turkey, but the honours went to the Allies in the United States, Italy, Rumania, Greece and in a wide array of lesser countries, and Germany stood isolated in sympathy, except for Spain and Sweden. The hand of the whole world was raised against the Teuton. The great tug of war in America was only won by the British and the French after a desperate struggle against the German propaganda. The French were admirable in the very simplicity of their appeal. They invoked the sacred name of Lafayette, implored the gods of democracy, blackguarded the Germans and advertised the Americans who had enlisted on the side of the French. The British had less traditional affection to draw upon, and much more to explain away, but they had the powerful asset of the cables and the good sense to work, not secretly, but just outside the glare of publicity. And neither the British nor the French were severely handicapped by a military-diplomatic programme, which hurled all their fine pretensions in their teeth.[2]

Now a formidable list could be drawn up of the propaganda drives which failed or which accomplished their objective after a long period of waiting. Not all the propagandas to instigate defeat, Revolution, or secession and to preserve friendship succeeded. After all, India, Egypt, Ireland and Morocco did not respond to the proddings of German agents to rise up as one man to cast off the yoke of the Englishman and the Frenchman; Austria-Hungary, Germany, Bulgaria and Turkey did hold out for four long years. France, Great Britain, and most of the Allies persisted through all discouragement to victory, in spite of the dangerous German peace offensive of 1916-17. But before regarding these negative results as a defeat for propaganda, it must be remembered that propaganda was not only an offensive weapon; it was a powerful means of defence as well. Unity could be preserved just as it could be demolished by propaganda. Indeed, propaganda was present on both sides of every hotly-contested sector, and though it is one of those weapons whose precise effect is largely a matter of surmise, it is one which it would be foolhardy to neglect.

A defeated country naturally exaggerates the influence of propaganda. The Italians sought to save their faces after the Caporetto disaster[3] by complaining of the terrible and insidious German propaganda, and Ludendorff devotes a great many pages to explaining just how it was that he did not lose the War, and how the Alien and Radical riff-raff in the population collapsed behind the lines, leaving a sort of vacuum, in which the German troops fell, victorious to the end.

It is especially difficult to extricate the strands of propaganda influence from the means of control which are closely allied to it. When the Nivelle offensive drowned in a sea of blood in 1917, no less than twelve army corps were tainted by mutinous demonstrations. Soldiers began to start home, infuriated by the insensate

butchery of their comrades. It was the remarkable work of General Pétain which restored orderly enthusiasm to the front and
thwarted the ominous diversion of hatred which threatened to turn
the French soldiery against their own leaders and away from the
enemy. He relied by no means exclusively upon propaganda.[4]

But when all allowances have been made, and all extravagant
estimates pared to the bone, the fact remains that propaganda is
one of the most powerful instrumentalities in the modern world.[5]
It has arisen to its present eminence in response to a complex of
changed circumstances which have altered the nature of society.
Small, primitive tribes can weld their heterogeneous members into
a fighting whole by the beat of the tom-tom and the tempestuous
rhythm of the dance. It is in orgies of physical exuberance that
young men are brought to the boiling point of war, and that old
and young, men and women, are caught in the suction of tribal
purpose.

In the Great Society it is no longer possible to fuse the way-
wardness of individuals in the furnace of the war dance; a new and
subtler instrument must weld thousands and even millions of
human beings into one amalgamated mass of hate and will and
hope. A new flame must burn out the canker of dissent and temper
the steel of bellicose enthusiasm. The name of this new hammer
and anvil of social solidarity is propaganda. Talk must take the
place of drill; print must supplant the dance. War dances live in
literature and at the fringes of the modern earth; war propaganda
breathes and fumes in the capitals and provinces of the world

Propaganda is a concession to the rationality of the modern
world. A literate world, a reading world, a schooled world prefers
to thrive on argument and news. It is sophisticated to the extent of
using print; and he that takes to print shall live or perish by the
Press. All the apparatus of diffused erudition popularizes the symbols and forms of pseudo-rational appeal; the wolf of propaganda
does not hesitate to masquerade in the sheepskin. All the voluble
men of the day—writers, reporters, editors, preachers, lecturers,
teachers, politicians—are drawn into the service of propaganda to
amplify a master voice. All is conducted with the decorum and the

trappery of intelligence, for this is a rational epoch, and demands its raw meat cooked and garnished by adroit and skilful chefs.

Propaganda is a concession to the wilfulness of the age. The bonds of personal loyalty and affection which bound a man to his chief have long since dissolved. Monarchy and class privilege have gone the way of all flesh, and the idolatry of the individual passes for the official religion of democracy. It is an atomized world, in which individual whims have wider play than ever before, and it requires more strenuous exertions to co-ordinate and unify than formerly. The new antidote to wilfulness is propaganda. If the mass will be free of chains of iron, it must accept its chains of silver. If it will not love, honour and obey, it must not expect to escape seduction.

Propaganda is a reflex to the immensity, the rationality and wilfulness of the modern world. It is the new dynamic of society, for power is subdivided and diffused, and more can be won by illusion than by coercion. It has all the prestige of the new and provokes all the animosity of the baffled. To illuminate the mechanisms of propaganda is to reveal the secret springs of social action, and to expose to the most searching criticism our prevailing dogmas of sovereignty, of democracy, of honesty, and of the sanctity of individual opinion. The study of propaganda will bring into the open much that is obscure, until, indeed, it may no longer be possible for an Anatole France to observe with truth that "Democracy (and, indeed, all society) is run by an unseen engineer."

Notes

[1] *Propaganda in its Military and Legal Aspects*, Introduction.

[2] The importance of propaganda in neutral countries has been illustrated, of course, in many other wars before the last one. President Lincoln tried every expedient to stimulate the pro-North sentiment in England's industrial wage earners during the Civil War. He sent Henry Ward Beecher and perhaps a hundred other agents to England to plead the cause of the anti-slavery side. One of the most effective and original stunts was

to send a ship loaded with foodstuffs, to relieve the suffering
in the cities.

3 The report of the special commission of inquiry into the Caporetto
disaster which was appointed by the Italian Government is not
now available, and complete judgment cannot be made upon
the whole affair.

4 For a description of his methods, see Mayer, *La psychologie du
commandement*, and, in general, the reference in the section
upon morale and military psychology in the bibliography.

5 Sir Thomas More foreshadows the extensive use of propaganda
in Utopia. He records how the Utopians spread distrust among
their enemies by offering a reward for the capture or the voluntary surrender of prominent enemy leaders, and how they
seek to divide the enemy by fostering the ambition of a rival to
the reigning prince.

BIBLIOGRAPHY

It is scarcely profitable in a study of this kind to rehearse the long list of printed materials which have been cited. Instead, a list that bears upon some of the main features of the general problem will be appended.

I. The Technique of Influencing International
Attitudes, During and Since the War.

Angoff, Charles, "The Higher Learning goes to War," *American Mercury*, June, 1927, XI: 177-191.

Baudrillart, Mgr. Alfred, *Notre Propaganda*, Paris, 1916.

—. *Une campagne française*, Paris, 1917.

Baschwitz, Kurt, *Der Massenwahn*, München, 1924.

Bernstorff, Count, *My Three Years in America*, New York, 1920.

Blankenhorn, Heber, *Adventures in Propaganda*, Boston, 1919.

Brownrigg, Rear-Admiral Sir Douglas, *Indiscretions of the Naval Censor*, London, 1920.

Busch, Moritz, *Bismarck*, New York, 1898.

"Cincinnatus," *Der Krieg der Worte*. Stuttgart, Berlin, 1916.

Cook, Sir Edward Tyas, *The Press in War-time, with some account of the Official Press Bureau*. London, 1920.

Creel, George, *How We Advertised America*, New York, 1920.

Démartial, Georges, *La guerre de 1914. Comment on mobilisa les consciences*. Paris, 1922.

Demeter, Karl, "Die Filmspropaganda der Entente im Weltkriege," *Archiv f. Politik und Geschichte*, 4 (1925): 214-231.

Drouilly, J. Germain et Guérinon, E., *Les chefs-d'œuvre de la propagande allemande*. Nancy, Paris, Strasbourg, 1919.

Got, A., "La littérature pangermaniste d'après-guerre," *Mercure de France*, 167; 403-21, October 15th, 1923.

Graux, Dr. L., *Les fausses nouvelles de la grande guerre*. Paris, 1919. 5 tomes.

Hallays, André, *L'opinion allemande pendant la guerre*, 1914-18, Paris, 1919.

Haas, Albert, *Die Propaganda im Ausland*. Weimar, 1916.

Hansi (Johann Jacob Waitz) et E. Tonnelet, *À travers les lignes ennemies. Trois années d'offensive contre le moral allemand*. Paris, 1922.

Hartmann, Peter, *Französische Kulturarbeit am Rhein*. Leipzig, 1921.

Kerkhof, Karl, *Der Krieg gegen die deutsche Wissenschaft*. Charlottenburg, 1922.

Lasswell, Harold D., "The Status of Research on International Propaganda and Opinion," *Proceedings of the American Sociological Society*. Chicago, 1926.

Ludendorff, General, *Meine Erinnerungen*. Berlin, 1919.

Marchand, Louis, *L'offensive morale des Allemands en France pendant la guerre*. Paris, 1920.

Melville, Lewis, "German Propaganda Societies," *Quarterly Review*, 230 (1918): 70-88.

Merriam, Charles E., "American Publicity in Italy," *American Political Science Review*. November, 1919.

Military Intelligence Branch, Executive Division, General Staff, U.S.A., *Propaganda in its Military and Legal Aspects*. Washington, 1919.

Mühsam, Kurt, *Wie wir belogen wurden. Die amtliche Irreführung im Weltkrieg*. Berlin, 1920.

Parker, Sir Gilbert, "The United States and the War," *Harper's Magazine*, 136 (1918): 521-531.

Prezzolini, Guiseppe, *Dopo Caporetto*, Roma, 1919.

Rivaud, A., "La propagande allemande," *Revue des sciences politiques*, July-September, 1922.

Ruhlmann, Paul M., *Kulturpropaganda*. Charlottenburg, 1919.

Schönemann, F., Die *Kunst der Massenbeeinflussung in den Vereinigten Staaten von Amerika*. Stuttgart, 1924.

Steed, Henry Wickham, *Through Thirty Years*. New York, 1924. 2 vols.

Street, Major C. J. C., "Propaganda Behind the Lines," *Cornhill Magazine*, 3d. Series, 47 (1919): 488-499.

Stuart, Campbell, *Secrets of Crewe House. The Story of a Famous Campaign*. London, 1920.

Stuelpnagal, Otto v., *Die Nachkriegs-Propaganda der Alliierten gegen Deutschland*. Berlin, 1922.

Whitehouse, Vira B., *A Year as a Government Agent*. New York, 1920.

Wiehler, *Deutsche Wirtschaftspropaganda im Weltkrieg*. Berlin, 1922.

Daily Extracts from the Foreign Press (June, 1915—).

Daily Digest of the Foreign Press (March 20th, 1916—).

Daily Review of the Foreign Press (March 23rd, 1916—).

Brewing and Liquor Interests and German (and Bolshevist) Propaganda. Hearings before a sub-committee on the Judiciary of the U.S. Senate, 65th Congress, 2nd Sess., Washington, 1919. 3 vols.

The National German-American Alliance. Hearings before a sub-committee of the committee on the Judiciary. U.S. Senate, 65th Congress, 2nd Sess., Washington, 1918.

II. General Studies of Public Opinion and Propaganda.

Adler, Georg, *Die Bedeutung der Illusionen für Politik und soziales Leben*, Jena, 1904.

Allport, F. H., and Hartman, D. A., "The Measurement and Motivation of a typical Opinion in a Certain Group," *American Political Science Review*, XIX, No. 4, November, 1925, 735-760.

Angell, Norman (Lane), *The Public Mind*, New York, 1927.

Bauer, Wilhelm, *Die öffentliche Meinung und ihre geschichtlichen Grundlagen*. Tübingen, 1914.

Bernays, E. L., *Crystallizing Public Opinion*. New York, 1923.

Birnbaum, Alfred, *Das Wesen der Propaganda. Eine Psychol. Studie*, Berlin, 1920.

Bogardus, E. S., "Analysing Changes in Public Opinion," *Journal of Applied Sociology*, IX, 5, May-June, 1925, 372-381; also *Proceedings of the American Sociological Society*, 1926.

Chassieriaud, R., *La formation de l'opinion publique*. Paris, 1914.

Christensen, A., *Politics and Crowd-Morality*, New York, 1915.

Conway, M., *The Crowd in Peace and War*. New York, 1915.

Deherme, Georges, *Les forces à régler. Le nombre et l'opinion publique*. Paris, 1919.

Dodge, R., "Psychology of Propaganda," *Religious Education*, 15: 241-52, October, 1920.

Eltzbacher, *Die Presse als Werkzeug der auswärtigen Politik*. Jena, 1918.

Fluegge, G., "Zur Psychologie der Massen," *Preuss. Jahrb.*, 1921, 183, 345-369.

Gersdorf, Karl v., *Ueber den Begriff und das Wesen der öffentichen Meinung*. 1846.

Griffith, C. R., "A Comment upon the Psychology of the Audience," *Psychol. Monog.*, 1921, 30 (No. 136), 36-47.

Hayes, E. C., "The Formation of Public Opinion," *Journal of Applied Sociology*, 10; 6-9, September, 1925.

Hendrich, Franz Josias von, *Ueber den Geist des Zeitalters und die Gewalt der öffentlichen Meinung*, 1797.

Higham, C. F., *Looking Forward. Mass Education through Publicity*. London, 1920.

Holtzendorff, Franz v., *Wesen und Wert der öffentlichen Meinung*. München, 1880.

King, Clyde L., "Public Opinion as viewed by Eminent Political Theorists," *U. of Pennsylvania Public Lectures*, Philadelphia, 1916.

Kracauer, S., "Die Gruppe als Ideenträger," *Archiv f. Sozialw.*, 49 (1922): 594-622.

Kraus, Herbert, "Prolegomena zum Begriff der öffentlichen Meinung," *Festschrift*. Franz von Liszt, Berlin, 1911, 148-167.

Kulke, Eduard, *Zur Entwicklungsgeschichte der Meinungen*, Leipzig, 1891.

Kydd, Samuel, *A Sketch of the Growth of Public Opinion*, London, 1888.

Le Bon, *The Crowd* (12th edition). London, 1920.

—. *Les opinions et les croyances*, Paris, 1911.

Lee, Ivy L., *Publicity*, New York, 1925.

Lippmann, W., *Public Opinion*. New York, 1922.

—. *The Phantom Public*. New York, 1925.

Lipsky, Abram, *Man the Puppet*. New York, 1925.

Long, John C., *Public Relations*, New York, 1924.

Lowell, A. L., *Public Opinion in War and Peace*. Cambridge, 1923.

Lumley, F. E., "Propaganda," Chapter VIII, in *Means of Social Control*. New York, 1925.

Mackinnon, W. A., *History of Civilization and Public Opinion*, third edition, 2 vols., London, 1849.

—. *On the Rise, Progress and Present State of Public Opinion in Great Britain and other parts of the World*, London, 1828.

Martin, E. D., *The Behavior of Crowds*, New York, 1920.

Millioud, M., "La propagation des idées," *Revue Philosophique*, 69; 580-600; 70: 168-191.

Moysset, Henri, *L'opinion publique*. Lyon, 1910.

Papon, Jean Pierre, *De l'action de l'opinion sur le gouvernement*, 1788.

Park, R. E., *Masse und Publikum*, Bern, 1904.

Pieper, Karl, *Die Propaganda. Ihre Entstehung u. religiöse Bedeutung*, Aachen, 1922.

Plenge, Johann, *Deutsche Propaganda, Die Lehre von, d. Propaganda als prakt. Gesellschaft. Mit e. Nachw. von Ludwig Raselius*. Bremen, 1922.

Quiett, G. C., and Casey, R., *Principles of Publicity*, New York, 1926.

Riis, R. W., and Bonner, C. W., *Publicity*, New York, 1926.

Ross, E. A., *Social Control*, New York, 1901.

Rossi, P., *Le suggesteur et la foule, psychologie du meneur*, Paris 1904.

Sagaret, J., "L'opinion," *Revue Philosophique*, LXXXVI (1918): 19-38.

Salmon, L. M., *The Newspaper and Authority*. New York, 1923.

—. *Newspaper and the Historian*. New York, 1923.

Schultze-Pfaelzer, Gerhard, *Propaganda, Agitation, Reklame. Eine Theorie des gesammten Werbewesens*. Berlin, 1923.

Schwertfeger, Bernhard, "Propaganda," *Handbuch der Politik*, V (1922): 470-474.

Shepherd, W. J., "Public Opinion," *American Journal of Sociology*, XV (1909), 32-60.

Sighele, S., *Psychologie des Auflaufs und der Massenverbrechen*, Leipzig, 1897.

Stern-Rubarth, Edgar, *Die Propaganda als politisches Instrument*. Berlin, 1921.

Strong, E. K., "Control of Propaganda as a Psychological Problem," *Scientific Monthly*, 14: 234-252, March, 1922.

Szirtes, Artur, *Zur Psychologie der öffentlichen Meinung*. Wien and Leipzig, 1921.

Tarde, G., *L'opinion et la foule*, Paris, 1901.

Thiébault, Dieudonné, *Traité sur l'esprit public*, Paris, An VI.

Thurstone, L. L., "The Method of Paired Comparisons for Social Values," *Journal of Abnormal and Social Psychology*, XXI, 4, January-March, 1927. (First of a series of papers dealing with the technique of measuring opinions.)

Tönnies, F., *Kritik der öffentlichen Meinung*. Berlin, 1922.

Wallas, Graham, *Human Nature and Politics*. London, 1908.

—. *The Great Society*. New York, 1914.

Weeks, A. D., *Control of the Social Mind*. New York. 1923.

Wilder, R. H., and Buell, K. L., *Publicity*. New York, 1923.

III. Special Historical Studies of Opinion in International Politics.

Alzona, Encarnacion, *French Contemporary Opinion of the Russian Revolution of* 1905. Col. U. Studies, No. 228, Vol. C, 1921.

Angell, Norman (Ralph Lane), *Patriotism under Three Flags*. London, 1903.

Ebbinghaus, Therese, *Napoleon, England and die Presse* (1800-1803), München u. Berlin, 1914.

Gazley, John G., *American Opinion of German Unification*, 1848-1871. Col. U. Studies, No. 267, Vol. CXXI, New York, 1926.

Martin, B. Kingsley, *The Triumph of Lord Palmerston*. London, 1924.

Périvier, A., *Napoléon journaliste*, Paris, 1918.

Price, Maurice T., *Christian Missions and Oriental Civilization*, Shanghai, 1924.

Raymond, Dora N., *Contemporary British Opinion during the Franco-Prussian War*. Col. U. Studies, No. 227, Vol. C, 1921.

Thompson, Geo. Carslake, *Public Opinion and Lord Beaconsfield*, 1875-1880, two vols., London, 1886.

IV. Morale and Military Psychology.

Andrews, L. C., *Leadership, Military Training*. Philadelphia 1918.

—. *Military Manpower*. New York, 1920.

Campeano, M., *Essai de psychologie militaire individuelle et collective*. Paris, 1902.

Gallishaw, J., and W. Lynch, *The Man in the Ranks*. New York, 1917.

Gavet, André, *L'Art de commander*. Nancy, 1921.

Goddard, H. C., *Morale*. New York, 1918.

Gulick, L. H., *Morals and Morale*. New York, 1919.

Hall, G. S., *Morale*. New York, 1920.

Hocking, W. E., *Morale and its Enemies*. New Haven, 1918.

House, F. N., *Industrial Morale*. Chicago, 1924 (Thesis).

Mayer, Lieut., *La psychologie du commandement*. Paris, 1923.

Maxwell, W. N., *A Psychological Retrospect of the Great War*. New York, 1923.

Miller, A. H., *Leadership*. New York, 1920.

Munson, E. L., *The Management of Men*. New York, 1921.

Peterson, J., *Psychology of Handling Men in the Army*. Minneapolis, 1919.

Rohan, Henri, duc de, *Le parfait capitaine*. Paris, 1744.

Terman, L. M., "Psychology and Pedagogy of Leadership," *Peda-gogical Review*, XI: 113-51.

Ziehen, A., *Die Psychologie grosser Heerführer*. Leipzig, 1916.

SUPPLEMENTAL MATERIAL

PROPAGANDA BEHIND THE LINES
MAJOR C.J.C. STREET

It is almost to utter a platitude to say that war has lost its picturesqueness, had developed into a science, an elaborate game played
by men in mud-stained khaki, crowned with steel hats painted with
the strange discords of camouflage. The old panoply has vanished;
bright coloured tunics, shining breast-plates. The very polished
muzzles of the guns have given place to an universal neutral tint,
shared alike by weapon and man.

Yet war has still its picturesque side—I remember one September dawn seen from an Observation Post that will remain with me
as the most beautiful thing that I have seen—and, to counterbal-
ance it, the most matter-of-fact, cold-blooded, calculating side, that
very few have ever realised. For, to the actual business of physical
maiming has been added the more subtle process of insidious
slaughter of *morale*, a far more difficult, but none the less effective, method of warfare. The Germans have always preached it.
They practised it from the first, 'frightfulness' being merely the
clumsy German interpretation of the theory of the destruction of
morale. Bernhardi lays as much stress upon it as upon perfection
of manoeuvre. The Allies, keener students of psychology, substituted persuasion for brutality, and developed a system of military
propaganda that has never before been equalled.

It must be emphasised that the ultimate object of propaganda
in war is the destruction of enemy morale, and its corollary, the
strengthening of friendly *morale*. It consists of the dissemination
of ideas, designed to react in different ways upon their various

recipients. The enemy must be made to feel that his cause is hope-less from the start, has no chance of ultimate success, and is based upon delusive ideals, It is usually impossible to convince the re-sponsible organisations of the hostile nation, such as the Govern-ment or the Army Commands, though it may be feasible to hamper them in their decisions. But it is comparatively easy to influence the rank and file, civilian as well as military, and to produce an atmosphere of despondency fatal to success.

In the same way, the general public of neutral nations must be supplied with the arguments of victory and of a just cause, followed by a judicious 'booming' of every success, great or small, and by brilliant descriptions of the spirit that animates the Allied troops. The neutral, especially when weak and necessarily somewhat at the mercy of the side that eventually proves victorious, is natu-rally disposed to sit on the fence and lean towards the side that he imagines to be winning. And the importance of such neutral lean-ings can never be exaggerated after the experiences of the late war.

Finally, allied and friendly nations, even the belligerent nation itself, must be kept in good heart by emphasising the justice of their cause, the magnificent bearing of their troops, the demoralisation of the enemy. Reverses must be explained and shown to be but temporary, information of each success must be widely disseminated and its meaning made clear.

It is obvious that, so far as friendly, allied, and neutral nations are concerned, the Press must be the principal organ of propa-ganda. Press propaganda is a subject by itself, with which we need not now concern ourselves. But in the case of enemy countries, and the invaded districts on the friendly side, the Press is closed. The zone of fighting acts as a barrier behind which we cannot pen-etrate; if we are to develop propaganda behind this barrier we must seek more indirect methods. It is with some of these methods that the present article proposes to deal.

In the late war, practically the whole of Belgium and a very large and thickly populated portion of France were for four years in enemy occupation. The inhabitants of these territories had no means of communication with their friends; they were entirely subjected to enemy influences in every detail of their lives. The strictest precautions were taken to prevent news filtering through to them from other than enemy sources, while they were subjected to every possible method of sapping their nationality. One of the most obvious duties of the propaganda service was therefore to counteract this influence by the dissemination of the truth as to the Allied cause and its progress. It was a difficult problem, but a most successful solution was eventually found, and will be described later.

The main task of the Allied propagandist was, however, to produce depression and unrest in the enemy camp. It is not too much to say that the results of a well-directed propaganda preparation to an attack can be far greater than that of the most intense preliminary bombardment, given a receptive and easily influenced enemy. The most striking example of a successful propaganda preparation was shown in the Italian collapse of 1917. It must be remembered that the hostile persuasion found a ready soil in which to take root. The Italian troops were worn out with the unending struggles on the Isonzo, and were disaffected by the economic troubles of their wives and families at home. In this soil the enemy sowed promises of an early and favourable peace, intermingled with menacing stories of the invincible armaments arrayed upon the Austrian side. Their defeat was due to their impressionable nature, but in justice be it said that this same nature was wholly responsible for their magnificent recovery.

The aim of propaganda behind the enemy lines is directly and indirectly to produce discouragement, in preparation of an attack by arms. And it must be emphasised that the farther the influence can he made to extend into the hostile country the better. To produce discouragement among the troops themselves is certainly the first step towards success, but this can rarely be effective if the country behind them supports them enthusiastically. A man is always more prone to listen to the encouragement of his friend than to the threats of his enemy. But once the civilian population be discouraged the infection travels rapidly to the troops. Experience has shown that nothing is more destructive to the *morale* of an army than a stream of despondent letters from friends and relatives at home.

But it would be less than logical to consider the forms of propaganda in enemy territory before those employed in the invaded districts. And of the latter, the most far-reaching was that unique periodical, *Le Courrier de l'Air*.

Early in 1916, the War Office realised the might of the moral weapon, and cast about to find the personnel wherewith to forge it. A branch of the Directorate of Military Intelligence was created, and known as M.I.7.b. An Army Order was issued, inviting those officers and men who had previous literary experience to communicate with the new organisation. As a result, a more or less regular staff of some thousand writers was enrolled, who, as an act of grace, consented to contribute the produce of their pens during such times as they could spare from more active military duties. From these were selected two or three who were unfit for service overseas, a number subsequently raised to twenty, who were attached to the staff of M.I.7.b., and gave their whole time to the production of propaganda. By this means the War Office obtained the pick of the literary brains of the Service at no expense, for the officers devoting their whole time to this work would otherwise have been drawing their pay and kicking their heels at a Command Depot or elsewhere. It need hardly be added that their contributions, though published throughout the globe, were unpaid.

An early function of M.I.7.b. was the establishment of *Le Courrier de l'Air*. The needs of the invaded districts had long been felt, and it was realised that a newspaper of Allied tendencies, aerially distributed, was the best way to meet that need. So, after much discussion, the first number of *The Courrier,* as it came to be called, was produced, in the form of a single sheet, some eight inches by six. It was a memorable production, destined to be the first regular aerial newspaper of the world. It bears the date of April 6, 1917, and carries in its leading column an exhortation that most admirably sets out its aims and scope. A *nos Lecteurs,* it is headed, with a sub-heading MM. *les Patriotes Martyrisés!* But, perhaps, it is better translated.

'This weekly paper will be distributed every week by Allied aeroplanes among our brave Belgian and French friends living in the unhappy territory now in the occupation of the enemy. It has for its sole object the dissemination of the truth about the war. To you, who have so greatly suffered for your country, truth can only bring the assurance that the day of deliverance is at hand. Be sure, my friends, that here you will find nothing but the truth. I, who fall from the skies, have no idea of deceiving you, as the Bosche deceives his own people, with fine promises and with vain hopes, false dreams that can never come true. On the contrary, if I seem optimistic it is because at the present time every event, military or political assures me that the fortunes of Germany are on the wane. The whole world, from China to the United States, arms itself against the barbarous enemy of civilisation. Might is powerless before Right. Truth triumphs over lies. Finally, the motto of the *Courrier de l'Air* will always be: Truth, the whole Truth, and nothing but the Truth!'

This exordium is followed by translations of the weekly communiqués, by brief surveys of the military events of the week, and by miscellaneous news items of interest to the Belgians, such as *'le British Academy' vient di consacrer une séance à la glorification du poète Verhaeren*. The whole paper makes a very attractive news-sheet, bright and cheerful, and, as we now know, came as a true breath from Heaven to the inhabitants of the invaded districts. Despite the price set upon them by the Germans, copies of the *Courrier* spread like wildfire throughout Belgium and Northern France, and even reached Germany, to the mortification of various Army Commands. There was no need for the printed injunction—*Avis au lecteur:*

'You are requested not to tear up this paper, nor to destroy it when read. Rather lend it to your

neighbour, and to the neighbour of your neighbour, seeing that they too are anxious to know what is happening in the world.'

Space will not admit of the quotation of further passages from the *Courrier*, which pursued an uninterrupted existence until it reached its forty-third number on January 25, 1918. By this time it had become a very serious thorn in the side of the German *Kommandatur*, and orders were issued that the occupants of any aeroplane brought down while carrying this or other 'seditious literature' would be tried by court martial and sentenced to severe penalties. This threat was followed by an example of its execution, and instructions were given that the publication of the *Courrier* should be suspended pending the inauguration of fresh means of distribution. Experiments were set on foot immediately, and as a result of this, distribution by balloon was begun.

A description of this means of aerial dissemination of propaganda will be given later; at present we may concern ourselves with its effect upon the *Courrier*. Publication was resumed on March 7, 1918, with No.44, which bears above the title the legend 'By balloon—*Durch Luftballon*.' The foreword of this number is worth recording.

'For nearly a year, the *Courrier de l'Air* has been brought to you every week by our brave airmen. It has carried messages of truth and hope from the free world, from the peoples beyond the iron grip of German militarism. No credit must be given to the boast of the Germans, they seek to deceive you, to deceive their very selves. In respect of men, of munitions, of resolution, England is stronger than ever. France, resolute and confident, will carry on until the military force of Germany be exhausted. Italy, recovering from the unforeseen blow of last winter, is already beginning to force back the enemy. The great Republic of America has thrown all her weight into the scale of the Allies, and pours into France every day from her inexhaustible reserves a stream of men and of munitions. Be of good cheer, the end is irrevocable. The *Courrier* will come to you by balloon, but the delivery will be more regular and plentiful than ever it was by aeroplane. When the wind blows from the direction of the Allies, be on the alert. From these white balloons, floating so high in the vastness of the atmosphere that you can hardly see them, will fall a rain of *Courriers*.'

From this time the *Courrier* flourished, through the dark days of the spring of 1918 until the last issue, which is dated November 7. It is only fair to say that the summaries of the situation, viewed dispassionately after the lapse of time, give a remarkably just picture of events. There is no hiding the seriousness of the German onslaught, only, as might be expected, a sober jubilation over its failures, such as the check before Amiens, the skilful strategy of Arras, the gallant stand at Givenchy. Even when the tide turned in July, when all the world knew that the war was won, the Courrier retained its reputation for moderation. It was, to some extent, inspired, in that it had the advantage of production by the staff of the War Office, but it had no access to sources of information denied to the British press.

Of the last number, one story must be told. The officer—in civil life a distinguished scientist—who was at that time acting as editor, had secured permission to visit the fighting zone, in order to arrange certain details as to the distribution of his paper. He was a somewhat resplendent person, who had never seen active service owing to his age, and consequently regarded his mission as one involving some personal danger. Armed *cap à pie*, he left the comparative security of the War Office to face the hazard of war, much to the delight of his sub-editor, in civil life a clergyman of the Church of England, and withal an intrepid gunner and kite-balloonist, now incapacitated from further active service. The latter, his superior's back once turned, composed, under the heading of 'Tartarin s'en va-t-en guerre,' a paragraph for the *Courrier* that would be spoilt by translation.

> 'L'histoire nous vient du G.Q.G. belge. Elle est d'ailleurs tout à fait délicieuse et digne de l'esprit proverbiale des Belges. Un invité au Q.G., dont le séjour en France devait être bref, mais fort agréable, y arriva en grande tenue: canne-épée, beau casque de fer reluisant, uniforme dernier cri, muni de boutons d'or d'un éclat aveuglant, gilet qui pouvait, à la rigueur, servir de ceinture de sauvetage. Etrange mélange du Beau Brummel jadis et du guerrier moderne!'

This is probably the first and only example of an editor being lampooned in his own journal.

But we must leave the consideration of the *Courrier* for a short examination of methods of propaganda in enemy countries. Much has lately been heard of this particular activity, especially since Lord Northcliffe lent it his name, but it is as well to point out that it was in a flourishing state of existence for over a year before the brothers Harmsworth devoted their energies to propaganda. The first attempts to influence the hostile nations were the insertion of carefully worded articles in the Press of bordering neutral states. This may be called the indirect method, and was certain of a limited success, for neutral opinion, as recorded in the national Press, was eagerly sought throughout the Central Empires. The objection to it was, that it had very little chance of influencing the rank and file, at whom propaganda must chiefly be aimed. Only the more highly educated classes were likely to have access to neutral papers, and the hostile Press was certain not to reproduce articles unfavourable to its cause.

The next step, adopted almost simultaneously by all the Allies, was the production of leaflets, and other matter, written in simple German that could be understood by the least educated. These leaflets were intended for direct distribution in and behind the enemy lines, and they introduced the problem of how most effectively to scatter them. There is no intrinsic difficulty in scattering pieces of paper, any more than there is in scattering pieces of steel, but the desired destination of the two forms of missile varies, as does the effect they are intended to produce. A shell, to secure its maximum effect, should burst in the centre of a group of men; propaganda leaflets, on the contrary, should be dispersed as widely as possible, and then should avoid the highly disciplined group, and should arrive within the grasp of the lonely sentry, free from the influence of his compatriots, and with nothing else to divert his thoughts. The group would probably treat a leaflet as a joke, the isolated man would read it through sheer boredom, and would possibly be induced to believe that there was something in its argument. And once propaganda has secured even the vaguest mistrust of the doctrines that it combats, its task is more than half accomplished.

Both the Allied Powers and the Central Empires experimented with propaganda projectiles, using the trench mortar as their means of projection. The idea was, in most cases, to construct a bomb with a small bursting charge, which should, upon its arrival over the opposing lines, release a shower of pamphlets upon the heads of an astonished enemy. But this system had its obvious drawbacks. A trench mortar has always been an unpopular weapon, credited with the effect of incurring retaliation more than outweighing the damage it may possibly produce. Further, the most susceptible might well be expected to resent a shower of words hurled at him by so direct a method, or if not to resent it, at all events to ridicule it as rather too obvious a ruse de guerre. There is something inconsistent about an army that makes life unbearable with 'flying pigs' one moment, and the next sends out, through the mouths of the very same weapons, a flood of literature proclaiming that all men are brothers, or some such other pacific doctrine. It was not long before the trench mortar, as a projector of propaganda, was abandoned in favour of the aeroplane.

This latter weapon seemed at first to have every qualification for the purpose. It could scatter innumerable leaflets from any convenient height, and, owing to the length of time taken by them in falling, their arrival had no visible connection with its flight. Far more effect would naturally be produced by a leaflet blowing into a trench from nowhere in particular than from one obviously hurled by a lethal engine. Further, the aeroplane had a far greater penetration, could scatter its propaganda over rest-billets and rail-heads as well as over the trenches themselves. The advantages of this were twofold: the leaflets could be found and picked up over a far greater area, and men some way back from the line had more leisure and inclination to ponder their contents. But, on the other hand, there were many other calls upon the aeroplanes available. It was argued with a considerable show of reason that if a plane were to be sent upon a flight over hostile territory, it would be better employed dropping bombs than propaganda. Some went so far as to say that the best propaganda that could be dropped over the enemy were bombs and plenty of them, a contention that was correct as regards the Rhine towns and incorrect as regards London. At all events, it was felt that the aeroplane was too valuable a fighting machine proper to be employed as a disseminator of leaflets.

The next idea was the employment of observation balloons, which were to carry a supply of pamphlets to be thrown overboard when the wind was blowing towards the enemy lines. Apart from the fact that the occupants of the balloon were usually too busy with their proper function of observation to worry much about casting packets of paper into space, the observation balloon had many disadvantages. A more ingenious and elaborate development of the observation balloon scheme was a revival of the man-lifting kite. When the wind was favourable, the kite was flown from some suitable spot, and a 'follower,' carrying a bundle of leaflets, caused to travel up the taut string of the kite. The 'follower' was fitted with an automatic release, which functioned at a predetermined height, allowed the leaflets to fly away, and the 'follower' to fall to the ground again ready for recharging. When the contrivance did not jamb, it was a very entertaining toy to play with.

It was not until late in 1916 that the free balloon was seriously considered as a vehicle of propaganda. The idea had always been obvious; load a balloon with the leaflets it was intended to distribute, send it up with a favourable wind, and there you were. The difficulty lay in predicting within a thousand miles or so where the balloon would come down. It was not until the science of meteorology, urgently impelled by the needs of the Artillery, made its marvellous war-time developments, that balloons could be used scientifically. 'Meteor,' in the shape of the various meteorological experts attached to the forces, eventually became able to gauge the velocity and direction of the wind at practically any height in any given locality. The rest was simple, so soon as a simple and reliable release had been evolved. You took your balloon to a given spot, say ten miles behind the lines, you knew your balloon would rise to say six thousand feet, and travel at that height until its burden was released. 'Meteor' gave the velocity of the wind at twenty miles an hour, south-west, at that height and place. Forty miles from the balloon position, and bearing north-east, was an enemy concentration camp. Load your balloon with the required type of propaganda leaflet, set your release to act in rather less than two hours, to allow of drift of the leaflets when falling, and there you were.

The results obtained from early experiments at home were deeply interesting, especially on the occasion when the dummy leaflets were plain pieces of paper, which fell from the sky upon the astonished population of Salisbury Plain. When it had struck those in authority to inscribe the pieces of paper with instructions for those who picked them up to write on them when and where, and to return them to the experimental station, the results showed that surprising accuracy could be obtained, and that the balloons would travel for a considerable distance without excessive loss of gas. In one case, balloons released on the east coast of England dropped their burdens in northern Italy. The balloons were made of paper, 'doped' with a preparation to render them hydrogen tight.

As equipped for service in France, a propaganda balloon section consisted of a couple of three-ton lorries for the conveyance of the hydrogen cylinders, balloons, and leaflets with the necessary personnel of an officer and a few men. Certain stations were selected such that some desirable target could be reached with any direction of wind from north round by west to south. The section proceeded to one or other of these stations, which were usually in proximity to a kite balloon post to ensure the necessary telephone communication with 'Meteor' (and also to be able to borrow hydrogen in emergency), and proceeded to fill, load, and release balloons as long as the wind held.

During the summer of 1918, one of the most useful of these stations was near Lozinghem, roughly speaking half-way between Béthune and Choques, and a convenient point in a bold salient of the British line. The scene there during a favourable wind was a most interesting one. The lorries were drawn up back to back, with canvas screens stretched between them, to form a shelter within which the balloons could be inflated. The balloons were unpacked, a pipe led from the hydrogen cylinders into the neck of each, and then the balloons blown out. When full, they each had a lifting capacity of ten or twelve pounds. The force and direction of the wind having been ascertained from 'Meteor,' the target was determined, and the appropriate bundle of leaflets selected. If the wind was blowing in such a way as to carry the balloons well over Belgium, the opportunity would be taken of delivering the weekly issue of the *Courrier*. If it were blowing from the west, the load was made up of pamphlets appealing to the German troops in some billeting area. In any case, the most suitable matter for the selected target was attached to the balloon after inflation.

The means of attachment was the solution of the whole problem of the use of balloons, and was as simple as it was ingenious. A length of the orange-coloured woven tinder, sold at every tobacconist's for use in pipe-lighters, was taken, and one end of it fixed to the balloon. The sheaves of leaflets were strung on cotton tags, as used for binding papers in Government offices. The end of each tag was driven through the length of tinder at calculated distances from the free end. The rate of burning of the tinder was ascertained by experiment, and found to be, say, one inch in five minutes. If the target were twenty miles away, and the wind were blowing at thirty miles an hour, the balloon would be over the target in forty minutes. The tags would then be inserted at close intervals from six to ten inches from the end of the tinder.

Just as the balloon was released, the end of the tinder was held against a lighted cigarette, and commenced to burn. The balloon soared up into the sky, carried rapidly out of sight by the wind. In thirty minutes the first tag burnt through, and the papers fluttered separately to the ground, closely followed by those held by the next tag. By this means it was found possible to ensure a large percentage of the leaflets falling in or around a given target.

We have already seen that the actual matter distributed varied according to the destination for which it was intended. The invaded districts were served with such fare as the *Courrier*, or with pamphlets containing such special news as it was guessed that the Germans would suppress. Enemy troops and enemy territory were flooded with leaflets of an entirely different kind, the motive of which was invariably discouragement, it being axiomatic that the chief function of military propaganda is encouragement of one's friends and discouragement of the enemy. The principal line of argument was the necessity of the ultimate defeat of Germany, both politically through the blockade, and militarily, by the ever-increasing pressure of the forces brought against her.

Various means were employed to bring these facts home to the German people, and no less an authority than Ludendorff, in the extracts from his Memoirs recently quoted in *The Times,* bears testimony to their efficacy. Two examples may be given. The first was a cartoon, consisting of two sketches. One of these was inscribed '1914,' and depicts Germania, proud and flourishing, driving a donkey cart, the donkey symbolising the German people, fat and prosperous, the cart vaguely resembling the chariot of Boadicea. In front of the donkey, Germania dangles from the end of his whip a magnificent carrot, labelled Sieg. The other sketch was inscribed '1918,' and shows the same equipage after four years of war. Germania is now almost a skeleton; seated by her are two bloated figures, the profiteer and a gentleman suspiciously like Hindenburg, weighing down the now patched and rickety cart. The donkey, thinner and more weary than Germania herself, still holds

along, with bent knees and staring eyes, fixed now on an attenu-
ated vegetable held out before it, labelled Ersatz Sieg. That this
cartoon was appreciated is proved by the statements of prisoners,
who affirmed that copies of it changed hands in the German lines
for five marks apiece. And for every man who displayed it as a curiosity, at least ten must have pondered on the truth of its lesson.

Another leaflet that achieved notoriety was the 'Comparative
Menus.' *The Berliner Tageblatt* was sufficiently injudicious one
morning to bewail the high cost of living in Germany, and, by way
of enforcing the moral, published the menus and corresponding
prices of various restaurants in Berlin. Our propagandist seized
upon the opportunity, and promptly issued a leaflet, showing in
parallel columns the German menus and prices, as divulged by the
Tageblatt, and the menus and prices of various representative London restaurants from the Ritz to those taverns that display a sign
proclaiming them 'A good Pull-up for Carmen.' The result was star-
tling, even to the sceptic, and must have produced a profound impression in Germany.

Space will not permit of reference to other forms of propaganda,
of which the daily repartee exchanged by the various wireless stations was perhaps the most amusing. One incident of wireless propaganda, however, deserves to be quoted, even at the risk of spin-
ning out an already over-long story. In the early days of the Bolshevist revolution, Tchitcherin devoted himself unstintingly to the
production of grandiloquent appeals. His rhetoric was always addressed impartially 'To All,' which gave it a peculiar sonorousness.
But once he addressed it 'To all Cossacks!' under which preface he
gave vent to an impassioned appeal, 'Rise, mighty defenders of
Russia! Cast out the enemies of our beloved country! Slay and fear
not! To arms, Don! To arms, Kuban!' and much more to the same
effect. The Cossacks took him at his word—and promptly massa-
cred every Bolshevist envoy they could lay their hands upon!

From: *The Cornhill Magazine*,
vol. 47 (November 1919), pp. 488-499.

CONTROL OF PROPAGANDA AS A PSYCHOLOGICAL PROBLEM
PROFESSOR EDWARD K. STRONG, JR.

Retiring vice-presidential address before Section I,
Psychology, American Association for the Advancement
of Science, at Toronto, December 30, 1921.

An interesting phenomenon of the last few years has been the una-
nimity with which millions of men and women have conformed in
their thinking and in their actions to what certain leaders wanted.
Vast sums of money have been raised for liberty and victory loans,
for the Red Gross and for many other agencies. Citizens of the
United States consented to universal conscription, cut down their
daily use of sugar, closed down their factories on certain days, and
went without gasoline for their autos voluntarily and enthusiastically. To an extraordinary degree men and women in nearly all the
countries of the world have cooperated in carrying out programs
necessitating radical changes in their every-day life; and they have
done so not because they were ordered to do so, and so were forced
to it, but because they freely responded to suggestions presented
in skillfully conducted propaganda.

Because of the surprising success of all this propaganda, the
innumerable times it has been employed and the ease with which
it has been carried out, people generally have become conscious of
propaganda as a great tool or method for influencing others. Propaganda has, of course, existed for ages. But it has not been comprehended so clearly by the mass of people as it is to-day. And certainly it has never before been employed on such great numbers of

229

men and women. To-day it is a clearly recognized method of social control.

If propaganda were a means of influencing others along lines only of benefit to society, it could be hailed with great acclaim. But unfortunately it can also be employed for dishonest and socially vicious programs, just as well as for honest and worthwhile movements. At the present time the advertising of patent medicines that can not possibly cure, and of stock in companies formed for no other purpose than to defraud the public, appears in altogether too many of our publications. Federal authorities estimated that in five years, 1910-15, the 2,861 swindlers that were arrested had defrauded the public of $351,000,000, averaging a dishonest gain of $123,000. All authorities are agreed that such swindling increased very greatly during the war, and possibly reached its climax some time after the armistice. If so, it is now on the decline. Let us hope so!

The drive, a new form of propaganda, has now become a regular business. According to James H. Collins, somewhere between a billion and a billion-and-a-half dollars have been raised in one year for various causes other than governmental. Many of these have been worthwhile, but unfortunately many have been the reverse. A bureau that makes a business of investigating national and interstate money-raising activities, reported that by April, 1920, the number of drives had risen to 1,021, of which the bureau approved only 124. The district attorney of New York County investigated 534 money-raising activities in 1918 and put 384 of them out of business. One gang of ex-convicts had obtained $500,000 in eight months.

But we are less concerned here with swindling propaganda than with those forms not so palpably dishonest. It is important that our citizens be protected from pecuniary loss, but it is far more important that the United States, for example, deals with Russia, Mexico and the Irish question in the right way. And it is just such problems that furnish us with propaganda very difficult to handle.

As a case in point, consider the Russian situation. Those opposed to the Bolsheviki have attempted to destroy the movement by linking it up in our minds with the fact that the Bolsheviki were under German influence, that they were anarchists, that they were guilty of murder and atrocities, that they persecuted the Church, that they had nationalized women and were deliberately corrupting the morals of children, and now, recently, that their government is so unstable that we can not do business with them. The friends of this political and social revolution have told us entirely different stories. And so-called unbiased persons have often made statements which do not agree with what any one else has set forth.

Consequently to-day the average citizen confesses he really does not know what the facts are in this and many other important issues. He has been deluged with facts, near-facts and falsifications put forth by interested parties, so that he has a mass of un-digested and conflicting ideas on these subjects, or else has become frankly partisan to one view.

President Butler, of Columbia University, recently called attention to the dangers to society of this sort of thing. "Liberty," he said, "which once was endangered by monarchs and by ruling classes, has long since ceased to fear either of these; it is now chiefly endangered by tyrannous and fanatical minorities which seize control for a longer or shorter time of the agencies and instruments of government through ability and skill in playing upon the fears, the credulity and the selfishness of men."

The question naturally arises, is there no way of controlling propaganda? Certainly there are ways and they are enforced more or less in the case of certain types of propaganda. But there are other types which are not so easily evaluated and consequently not so easily handled.

A perusal of literature on this subject gives one the impression that very few to-day are sincerely interested in the matter, except those apparently who desire to control or eliminate propaganda directed at their own. It is still viewed as highly ethical for us to sort and reject and trim in the name of our own view of truth, justice, democracy and loyalty to our group. But it is anti-social for the other fellow to do so. If we are Republicans we want the editor of our newspaper to give us good Republican views and to damn the Democrats. If we are Democrats, we want the reverse. We really want "facts" that support our views. It is too uncomfortable to be confronted with many counter "facts."

Naturally as a psychologist, I view this matter as an interesting psychological problem. It is my purpose in this place to discuss certain psychological aspects of the subject and to point out some of the ways in which propaganda may be controlled. It is also my purpose to call attention to certain types of propaganda which at present I see no way of controlling, in the hope that others may become interested in the subject and labor to work out some adequate methods.

First of all let us clarify the use of certain terms which are employed in discussing the subject and at the same time come to an understanding of the psychological elements which are involved.

The word "propaganda" means essentially the spread of a particular doctrine or a system of principles, especially when there is an organization or general plan back of the movement. Propaganda differs from "education" with which it is purposely confused, in that in the case of the former the aim is to spread one doctrine, whereas in the case of the latter the aim is to extend a knowledge of the facts as far as known. Advertising men have never been able to agree on a definition of "advertising" and I should not want to attempt here what they have failed to do. But I think we can distinguish between advertising and propaganda by saying that advertising is usually concerned with making known and desirable a definite commodity or service with the definite aim of leading many individuals, as such, to acquire the commodity or service. Propaganda includes many types of advertising, but it is mainly concerned with the subtle presentation to the public of information so chosen and so focussed that among many individuals there develops a general "point of view" which is favorable to the aim of the propagandist and leads to action in that general direction. A further distinction between these two methods of influencing people pertains to the methods employed rather than the object. The advertiser buys space upon which appears his message, and the reader knows it a paid advertisement. The propagandist may advertise, but he especially aims to employ space he did not buy, at least directly, and not to permit the reader to know that the material is propaganda. He believes his material will have greater effect when its source is unknown.

It is clear that both advertising and propaganda make use of argument and suggestion. And much has been written and said as to these two methods of influencing others. We have no quarrel in this paper with argumentative or "reason-why" appeals to the public. But we are very much concerned with appeals involving suggestion.

The term "suggestion" has been employed in a great variety of ways, sometimes in a narrow sense, but usually in a rather broad and indefinite way. Frequently it is used to cover all the means of imparting information and exerting influence other than through reasoning. Without going into the subject here, let us recognize three phases of non-rational influencing of others. In the simplest form one or more ideas are presented which are known to be associated in the minds of the audience with another idea not mentioned. The audience thinks the non-mentioned idea because of their established habits of thought. In this way a speaker may denounce most viciously and unfairly a prominent man without giving his name, by skillfully referring to one or more of his known characteristics. The desired effect is accomplished and without making it possible for the prominent man to reply. Then there is the more complicated phase of suggestion where an action is brought into the mind of the audience—the action being a familiar one and also one that will be desired as soon as mentioned. Thus a school boy at recess says, "Let's get a drink." The other boys might not have gotten a drink if they had not been reminded of the action. But as soon as it is called to mind, they feel the desire and so go. So also a nation like Germany, all primed for war, as in 1914— I don't refer here to her military preparations, but to the state of mind of her citizens—was ready to act immediately when her leaders said "Let's fight." It was the absence of just such a mental state in the United States that kept us out of war. Later on the attitude was developed—almost over-developed before it had a chance to function—and we were eager to act when the word was given.

In both these phases of suggestion the effect is produced because there exists within the mind of the person being influenced certain habits of thinking and action and when the proper stimulus or cue is given the associated thinking and acting immediately follow. There is still a third phase of suggestion, which I prefer to call motivation, in which a person is led to do something which is unfamiliar or which he would not do if it were merely mentioned. It is because of this third method of influencing others that the control of propaganda is so difficult. Let us see what this process of motivation is.

Consider an example: An electric light and power company launched a newspaper campaign some time ago in order to sell vacuum cleaners. The appeals were made to women to buy the cleaners in order to save labor and to make their homes cleaner and healthier. Many cleaners were sold. But the stock on hand was far from exhausted. Some time later the company launched another campaign, in which they directed their appeals to husbands, not wives. In these advertisements they depicted, for example, a successful business man in his office surrounded with filing cases, typewriters, dictaphones, and the like, and in another cut, showed the wife at home with a dust-cap on her head, sweeping the dining room, with the dust flying all about. The caption underneath read something like this: "Why not equip your wife's office like your own?" This second campaign sold more vacuum cleaners than the first one. Why? Because the man's love for his wife was aroused and this strong force was coupled to the idea of vacuum cleaners. Buying a vacuum cleaner then became a most satisfactory manner of expressing love. In advertising to the wives, on the other hand, no such fundamental motive was aroused. The vacuum cleaner would save labor, it is true, but it would not give to the wife as much satisfaction for the money as a new rug to be seen by every one coming into the home, or as new clothes for the children.

In this case we have men led into doing something they had no intention of doing, of buying something that little concerned them, and that they probably knew very little about. They were so led because love for their wives was aroused and they were shown how this love could be very adequately expressed. With minor changes, the advertisement could have sold them an electric washing machine, or any useful household device. They were not sold, then vacuum cleaners so much as they were the satisfaction of pleasing their wives.

Motivation involves two elements—first, the arousal of a strong desire, and, second, the presentation of a certain action which appears to be a satisfactory way of expressing the aroused desire. Moreover the action in such cases is not one that the individual would perform if it were merely suggested.

The question has often been discussed: Could the United States have declared war in 1914? I think there is no doubt that there was insufficient war sentiment at that time to have permitted mere suggestions from the President to be effective. But I think there is also equally no doubt that proper propaganda would have motivated the country into war. The years 1914 to 1917 may be looked upon as a period in which such sentiment developed and was finally put into action in a calmer and far less emotional manner than usually prevails at such a time.

Recent work in psychology has emphasized the distinction between an "idea" and a "sentiment." The sentiment, according to Rivers, is an idea emotionally toned. "House" is thus an idea, whereas "home" is a sentiment, for home always includes an emotional consciousness of mother and father, brothers and sisters, old familiar associations and the like. When the sentiment becomes suppressed and lost to consciousness it is called a "complex." Sentiments and complexes, we are coming to see more and more are extremely important in explaining behavior; much of abnormal conduct being traceable to the existence of complexes.

Motivation is thus the process of deliberately developing a sentiment, of deliberately associating an idea with an emotion, of tying together in the mind of another the love for wife and the idea of buying a vacuum cleaner, or of sympathy for the Belgians and hatred of the Germans, and the idea of war.

The aim of propaganda is to develop sentiment and then precipitate action through mere suggestion. Let us consider some implications which are involved in all this.

First of all let us note that theoretically any emotional element can be associated with any specific line of action. Practically, certain combinations are difficult to accomplish, but theoretically they are possible. Thus, the correspondence school arouses the boy's love for his mother and challenges him to make her proud of him and "funnels" the aroused emotional desire into taking a correspondence course. The same appeal could be utilized to get young men to go to church, to quit gambling, to work harder for their employer, to enlist when war is declared, to do anything the boy could be made to believe his mother would approve of.

In the last political campaign for President of the United States, the maternal instinct was appealed to by both sides. A Democratic editorial appealed as follows:

"Mother of America! Mother of Pennsylvania! Mother of Pittsburgh! Do you want your boy to go to war? Is the roll of battle drums sweeter in your ears than the song of his voice in the home? Would you rather have his hands in fierce grip on gun in battle's rack than have his arms in love about your neck? That is the question you must answer to your God and your fellow-man when you go into the voting booth on November 2. Do not let demagogs confuse you. The issue is plain: A vote for the league is a vote for peace; a vote against the league is a vote for war. . . . Mother of an American boy! The munition makers of the world are arrayed against American participation in the League of Nations. They are snatching at your vote, because with it they may claim the body of your first-born. Mother of a Pittsburgh boy! The question comes home to you! Your boy was not born to be food for guns."

A Republican advertisement stated in part:

"Women! For your own good vote the Republican ticket. . . . The American woman asks of her country: That it be a secure place for her home and for her children and that it be security with honor. That it give her children opportunity to lead their lives even better than she and her husband led theirs. That it be just in its relations with other nations, and merit the pride which the best of its citizens have in it, in its history and its ideals. A policy which has these purposes will have the support of American womanhood and American motherhood. That is the Republican policy and has been Republican policy from the days of Abraham Lincoln. The Republican policy is to protect the security of the United States by preserving its right to make decisions regarding its actions in the future as events in the future demand. The Republican party is unwilling to pledge now that it will protect European boundary lines and to deprive Congress of the power to say in each case what the action of the United States will be. . . ."

Here we have the same instinctive emotional element aroused and then associated with two diametrically opposite lines of action. Both of these articles are intended to arouse a mother's love for her boy and consequent horror of war, and then show that her desire could be best obtained by voting the Democratic ticket in one case and the Republican ticket in the other.

A second fact can be considered regarding motivation. It is that no logical connection needs to exist between the emotion which is aroused and the program which is outlined. And further still, there need be no logical establishment of the fact that the program is really the best one to be pursued or even that it is honestly conceived.

Consider the propaganda for the Red Cross, an organization for which we are all enthusiastic. The Red Cross has rendered inestimable service. And because its work has touched our hearts a real sentiment has been built up about its name. So strong is this sentiment that one now finds himself unable to resist the request for annual dues. But my friends—I have asked several—and I do not know whether all the money that is now raised is really needed, nor how it is spent, nor whether the organization is efficiently administered or not. I am not saying this in the way of criticism: I am only pointing out that when one's emotions have been properly

aroused one acts as directed and without intellectually considering the matter.

Take the recent "Clean-up and paint-up" campaign as another
illustration of what most would call a worthy propaganda. A trade
journal, *The American Paint and Oil Dealer*, started it off with an
editorial in May, 1912, in which it was pointed out that for many
years there had been special campaigns inciting people to clean-
up their towns and their neighborhoods for some specific gala occasion. It was now time "to back the idea that you clean up and
paint up and keep cleaned and painted up, not just once a year,
but the whole year through." "The idea was to inculcate into the
minds of people pride in home and city, and in thrift and cleanli-
ness, and to appeal to that pride to the end that it might be organized and wisely directed for the benefit not only of the paint industry, but of the whole United States of America. Enlisted in this
campaign were various types of people. Material was prepared that
appealed to every one of these types in a most specific manner."

E. F. Soule writing in Associated Advertising tells us how Chambers of Commerce were the principal bodies that helped put the
campaign over. He describes how fire departments were aroused
to the need to prevent fires as well as to put them out; how police
departments became much more interested in enforcing sanitary
ordinances along with the street-cleaning departments; how
women's clubs helped the good work along; etc. In 1920 there were
7,000 towns and cities engaged in this campaign. And illustrative
of the work accomplished it is reported that in Cincinnati 384
buildings were torn down that were a fire menace and the city so
cleaned up as to lessen the annual premiums for fire protection by
$850,000.

According to Soule not over $25,000 was spent in any one year
by the organization back of this campaign, although a great deal of
publicity was given in newspaper editorials and in the advertising
of many companies in connection with their own products.

Now note: This campaign is characterized as having been un-
selfish. The big idea was not to sell merchandise, it is claimed, but
"to sell the people of this country citizenship, pride of home and

ownership, and a desire to be of greater service to the community of which they were a part."

These were the motives, desires or wants that were aroused and then hundreds of business men saw to it that they were expressed by way of buying their goods, whether it was paint, oil, lawn mowers, flower seeds, or even safety razors. Clearly any emotional desire can be coupled up with any line of action and there needs to be no real logical connection between them.

Propaganda depends upon this psychological process of motivation for its success. And motivation, as we have seen, is the deliberate process of arousing one's emotions and desires and then suggesting a line of action by which these desires may be expressed. And we have seen further that any emotional element can be associated with any specific action; and that when one is well motivated he ignores intellectual considerations touching upon the honesty of the statements or the efficacy of the program.

So much for our analysis of motivation—the principal psychological process in propaganda. Now let us consider how propaganda may be controlled by society so that dishonest and pernicious campaigns may be prevented without interference to worth while propaganda.

The most convenient method of considering the many angles of the subject will be through discussing propaganda in terms of the following three aspects: First, propaganda considered with regard to the truth or falsity of the statements in which it is presented; second, with regard to the action suggested as the means of satisfying the aroused desire; and third, with regard to the emotional element, the desire that is aroused. The matter of control can accordingly be discussed in terms of these three question: First, how far can propaganda be controlled in terms of the validity of the statements which are made? Second, to what extent can propaganda be controlled in terms of the action which is proposed? And third, to what extent can propaganda be controlled in terms of the emotional elements that are involved!

First of all, then, how far can propaganda be controlled in terms of the validity of the statements which are made?

Society has long dealt with false statements and already has postal regulations, laws against slander, libel and the like. To protect politicians the English law provides a fine not to exceed £100 if the name and address of the printer and publisher is omitted from a poster relating to the candidature of any person for Parliament and other offices. The Association of Advertising Clubs of the World carries on a steady campaign against dishonest advertising and has accomplished a great deal of good against this type of propaganda. At this time, thirty-six states have passed the Printers' Ink Statute or a modification of it, thereby facilitating convictions in such cases. And the Association of Advertising Clubs of the World is spending money and effort in enforcing it. Control of propaganda publicly making dishonest statements can clearly be taken care of.

But unfortunately many undesirable propaganda will not fall under the class of propaganda publicly making dishonest statements. One very undesirable sort is spread by word of mouth. No one knows from whence it comes, and exactly what is back of it. We had many stories thus circulated against the Germans during the war, and we have the same sort of thing carried on against prominent men almost all the time. Stories of Roosevelt's excessive drinking were thus circulated. And it was not until they were publicly expressed that he had an opportunity of disposing of them through law suit. Such word of mouth propaganda is fostered in times of emotional stress and particularly wherever people believe they are not being told all the facts. The best possible cure for it is publicity of the sort that makes people believe they are getting all sides to the question.

But in addition to this sneaking underhand propaganda there are all sorts of campaigns which are very undesirable, but which adhere technically to the truth. They cannot accordingly be prosecuted for dishonesty. Some of them, however, give false impressions just the same. This is so because the human brain does not necessarily think in a logical manner. For example, the statement, "No watchman here between 6 P. M. and 6 A. M." means just that and no more, but actually the effect is as though the statement had gone on to say that a watchman was on duty in the day time. For a distributor of a food product to advertise that his goods contain no arsenic is to give the impression that the goods of at least one of his competitors do contain that poison. And the lurid page description of two successful gushers between which the advertising company's property is located gives the impression one is surely buying stock in a gusher-to-be, even though the company's property may be several miles from either of the described oil wells.

Then there are other kinds of propaganda which deal with this subject in such a general way that no one can challenge their statement. One of the packing companies ran an advertisement some time ago which came no nearer to stating facts than this: "Possibly, we are partially to blame for the lack of understanding which exists in regard to our business. In the past, knowing that attacks upon us have been based on tissues of half-truths, adroitly handled innuendo and misinformation, we may have forgotten that the public were not in full possession of the facts." The statement is a very clever one, undermining criticism without giving a single fact in reply except the company's own belief that all attacks have been based on half-truths.

To require that propaganda contain truths and not falsehoods is a desirable regulation, but it will not stop undesirable campaigns.

Let us consider second to what extent propaganda can be controlled in terms of the action which is proposed.

If the proposed action is that of buying, it is not difficult to evaluate the propaganda, or advertising as it would usually be in this case, upon the grounds that the individual did or did not get value received. But if the proposed action is that of giving money for some cause or charity, justification upon such grounds is far more difficult. If a woman, very fond of cats, wants to endow a hospital for them, run by thoroughly incompetent people whom she likes, isn't that sufficient to justify her action and the propaganda, as far as she is concerned? It is hard to attack such action in terms of the rights of individuals, but it is being more and more attacked upon the grounds of social welfare. Business men through their Chambers of Commerce in sheer defense are increasingly investigating such propositions and in many places list the charities that they will countenance. Out of the war has come the Community Chest movement whereby all social agencies in a district make up their budgets in advance and after they have been gone over by both disinterested and interested parties, a single united effort is made to raise the total amount in one campaign for the year. Such plans help the worthy cause and interfere with the unworthy one. But they do not eliminate the unworthy campaigns.

The establishment of bureaus, whose business it is to investigate all organizations asking for funds—organizations like the National Information Bureau—renders it easier to determine whether any organization is desirable or not. Can society go farther here? Can society not only positively help the worthy cause, but put the unworthy, inefficient or unnecessarily duplicating agency out of business? There is no question but that many individuals are being fooled every year and much money squandered through such non-worthwhile causes. But at the same time, we must remember that most new uplift movements have encountered great opposition at the start, and to increase this opposition still more through the establishment of legal regulations may do society in the long run more harm than good.

In addition to campaigns to sell a commodity or service or to obtain gifts, there are other campaigns devoted to accomplishing specific actions of a sort much more difficult to estimate fairly. Political campaigns aim to secure votes for certain men; propaganda appears from time to time to influence citizens to vote for or against certain measures; propaganda appeared in many forms a short time ago, appealing to citizens of the United States to intervene in Mexico; lobbies are familiar accompaniments to our legislatures, each one aiming to accomplish a specific program; unions appeal to public opinion to aid them in winning a strike and companies appeal to the same public to help them prevent or break the strike, etc. We are so accustomed to our political machinery that we do not often stop and ask ourselves whether it is geared up so as to serve society in the best way. Only when some enthusiastic social uplifter boasts that she and four others alone put a measure through a state legislature by the use of skillful lobbying, or a secretary of a business man's organization calmly announces months in advance that Congress will do away with a bureau because his organization is demanding such action, and his prophecy comes true, does one wonder whether some sort of control of propaganda would not be worthwhile even here. And one waxes quite indignant, as did a former Secretary of War, when he comes to realize that much of the propaganda for bringing back the bodies of our dead soldiers was instigated by the journal of the undertakers and casket makers.

To control such propaganda we must have facts and we must have a body to review the facts. This we do not have in many cases. A political campaign on a clean-cut issue is supposed to be a trial as to the merits of the two sides before all the citizens who through their votes decide the issue. This is the theory of democracy. It works pretty well in many cases, surprisingly well in some. But in most campaigns the issue is not clean-cut and in nearly all campaigns the political strategist endeavors to confuse the issue, so that many a time a citizen votes against what he really wants. And then there are many measures coming up in our fearfully complex life of to-day upon which the average man is not at all competent to pass judgment. Except in a few instances, society has not yet organized itself so as properly to handle such matters. In the case of struggles between capital and labor, we are steadily advancing toward the insistence upon both sides that they shall present the facts as they see them and also toward the establishment of tribunals which shall weigh all the facts and decide the issue. The impartial chairmanship program maintained by the clothing industry in Chicago and other cities has worked very satisfactorily and seems to be the ideal machinery for controlling propaganda in that field. Its greatest merit lies, it seems to me, in the fact that complaints are studied and evaluated very shortly after they arise, thus eliminating the getting under headway of extensive propaganda with all the arousal of emotions that propaganda assures.

But there are many issues to-day, strongly supported by a minority, regarding which it is difficult to obtain facts. And as long as one side is insistent and the other side largely indifferent, society cannot expect that the minority will present facts regarding their claims. For it is not facts that will sell the program, but emotion and the emotion which is aroused needs not be logically connected with the issue. So a few harrowing tales of deserted mothers and their poverty stricken children bring us a mother's pension program because a few people believe this is the best solution. Possibly it is. I am not here arguing the case. But how much real thinking has entered into the matter by disinterested parties before a legislature has voted!

We have briefly considered the possibilities of controlling propaganda in terms of the action which is proposed—when the action is that of buying, giving money, or gaining support for definite political or other issues. But there is an entirely different type of response which some propaganda aims to accomplish. It is that where no definite act is suggested, at least directly, but where public opinion is to be changed. Pro-German propaganda before and during the war, or pro-Irish propaganda to-day, or the New Era Movement of the Presbyterian Church, or the International Typographical Union advertising in the newspapers do not aim at getting any one to do a specific act. What is aimed at is the development of a broad sentiment with the perfectly clear understanding that when this sentiment is established the individual will do something to forward the cause. To evaluate the propaganda in such cases, the entire program must be considered. And as individual members of a big movement emphasize different aspects it is very difficult to determine just what the movement stands for. For example, legal action was instigated some time ago against a union because in its constitution, if I remember correctly, it stood for a soviet type of government. But no progress could be made because no specific action had been taken by the union, openly against the laws of the United States. Now possibly the constitution as far as this point was concerned was and had always been a dead letter. But possibly the point was the very heart and center of the union 's life. Still, how can its propaganda be limited until it has resulted in definite action? But if it cannot be controlled until anti-legal action commences, then there can be no control of such situations until most of the harm (or good) has been accomplished. For if the propaganda has accomplished the establishment of a certain sentiment without interference and then specific action has been suddenly advocated, no legal machinery in existence can stop the action. The existence of a sentiment in Great Britain, that treaties to which they were a party must be observed, was one of the factors that forced that nation into war with Germany when the latter violated the neutrality of Belgium. As Sir Edward Gray said, "My God, what else could we do!"

There is another very vexatious phase of this point. When a sentiment has been established the individual may do almost anything which he feels will advance the cause in which he is interested. Can a propagandist be held responsible for the actions of his followers because he stirred them up originally. A newspaper publisher's propaganda against McKinley may have caused that president's assassination, as some have felt. But is the publisher responsible for an act he did not specifically advocate, even though, for the sake of argument here let us say, he did stir the assassin emotionally and against the President? The newspapers report the non-cooperation propaganda of Mahatma Gandhi of India and how this leader is fasting one day a week in protest against the rioting which his followers are indulging in. To maintain that the publicist is responsible for what his followers do seems very unfair: to hold that he is entirely unaccountable opens the way for most subtle and dangerous attacks on society.

This leads us squarely up to the issue: shall propaganda be evaluated only on the basis of the actions that result or on the basis of the motives back of the propaganda?

Our law basically concerns itself with man 's behavior and takes little account of motives. But a distinction is made between wilful murder and unintentional manslaughter. And a man can be convicted of murder if a person's death results within a year from his shooting at a chicken with intent to steal it. The intention to steal makes the accidental death murder. Here man is held responsible for the final results of his criminal intention in just about as far reaching a manner as if he had inflamed another who then went out and murdered a complete stranger. Responsibility for the actions of another under certain circumstances, has been established. The Court of Appeals of New York State has recently awarded damages to an employee who when reprimanded by his foreman for negligence called the foreman a liar, and was struck and knocked down by the foreman. His glasses were shattered and vision in one eye destroyed. It was held that the employer should be held responsible for an excitable and violent foreman in the prosecution of his duties as such, at least until there is sufficient interruption in the performance of such duties as to justify the conclusion that the foreman had abandoned his employment and that the assault was an independent and individual act, as distinguished from acts within the terms of his employment.

In connection with the Espionage Act the Attorney General's Department opposed the proviso that "anti-war utterances or propaganda would not be punishable if made with good motives and for justifiable ends" on the grounds that it would make it difficult to prosecute and convict. Regulation according to this view must be in terms of actions, and motives can not be considered. Twenty-two states have adopted the Printers' Ink Statute regulating dishonest advertising in which no reference to motive or intention is made. Sixteen other states have, however, inserted the word "knowingly" or its equivalent, thus making it necessary to prove that the dishonest advertising was intentional. Legal action in these sixteen states is based primarily then upon the motive, not the act.

The 1918 Report of the Attorney General states the policy of that department regarding the enforcement of the Espionage Act. It is of significance here. One paragraph reads as follows:

"The Department throughout the war has proceeded upon the general principle that the constitutional rights of free speech, free assembly and petition exist in war time or in peace time, and that the right of discussion of governmental policy and the right of political agitation are most fundamental rights in a democracy. It has endeavored to adhere to the principle that neither the Government nor any group or class of citizens should be permitted to take advantage of the war situation to suppress discussion and agitation of domestic problems, whether political, social, economic, or moral. At the same time, however, it has held to the view that neither under the guise of political theory, social conviction, or religious creed should any man or group of men be permitted to indulge in propaganda which has the deliberate purpose of disintegrating our strength in the war or which is of an essential nature necessarily producing that effect."

In other words, the policy outlined here maintains that the welfare of the nation is paramount and that any propaganda which can be classified as injuring the national war program will be condemned regardless as to how this propaganda could be classified in terms of rights of free speech, free assembly and the like. And further that motive is of little consideration in comparison with an overt act.

So far we have considered the possibilities of controlling propaganda from the two aspects: first, as to whether the statements in it were true or false; and second, as to whether the proposed action was socially worth while or not. This discussion has seemingly emphasized the necessity of taking motives into account. Now let us consider the third aspect of the subject—the element of aroused desire, the emotional background and psychologically true cause of the action.

"We have seen that theoretically any emotion may be aroused as the basis for stirring one to act and that there needs be little or no rational connection between the two. The detailed suffering of a little girl and her kitten can motivate our hatred against the Germans, arouse our sympathy for the Armenians, make us enthusiastic for the Red Cross, or lead us to give money for support of a home for cats. The story may be true or concocted for the purpose; the inferences against the Germans or for the home for cats may be also true or false; the organization carrying on the propaganda may be efficiently administered or not—all these considerations little concern us. We feel the emotion, we want to do something because by acting we will feel better, and away we go regardless of mere intellectual considerations.

Here is the real psychological problem concerning propaganda. Take away the emotional element and society need have no fear of propaganda. For man is always very slow to act in terms of ideas alone. Witness his indifference when he really knows the political organization in control of his municipality is flagrantly dishonest. He does nothing until his emotions are aroused by a whirlwind speaker, or by personal injury. So long as a radical writes or speaks in a philosophical manner society can rightly be indifferent. But when he discards the intellectual aspects of his views, seizes upon some slogan and fills his writings or speeches with concrete tales of human suffering and the arrogance of the rich, society rightly becomes alarmed. For now the radical is setting fire to dynamite and neither he nor any one else can tell what may result.

At the present time the prospects do not appear over bright of controlling propaganda through regulation. There is, however, a method of weakening its influence, and that is by fighting one propaganda by another, or by general publicity. The trouble, however, with fighting bad propaganda by good propaganda, aside from the very practical consideration that the former is usually better equipped financially, is that seldom is the public supplied with facts upon which a real conclusion can be thought out. Instead it is inflamed to take sides and a deadlock results, or the matter is settled by some sort of resort to force. Just in this way arose the turmoil about the League of Nations program. Instead of thinking it through and arriving rationally at a real conclusion, Wilsonites and anti-Wilsonites became emotionally aroused and it was voted down because the latter group had the greater force measured in votes. Both sides know the real issue is not dead, and the Republicans who defeated Wilson's program are now attempting at Washington to find the conclusions we should have reached months ago. Fighting propaganda with propaganda is not likely, then, to give us satisfactory results.

Can propaganda be controlled through publicity? Yes, if we had perfect publicity. But that, apparently, we cannot have. Hence, we can only hope to have partial control by this means.

It has been suggested that propaganda could be controlled by national control of all publicity. Would such regulated and censored publicity help here?

The two extremes of publicity are no freedom of speech and complete freedom to say whatever one wants to. The Anglo-Saxons have decided that freedom is better than no freedom. The French lean quite strongly to centralized control of all publicity. Observers both from within and without that country testify that such censorship deadens public interest in the news of the world. And it certainly makes possible all manner of mouth-to-mouth whisperings—the most insidious and undermining of all propaganda. An editorial in the New York Times only the other day called attention to the marked difference in behavior of radicals in this country and abroad concerning Sacco and Vanzitti, who have been condemned to the electric chair for murder. Abroad the Reds have inspired the rank and file of their group with rage over the so-called persecution by the American Government of those radical leaders and several assassinations have been attempted as a result. In this country no such disturbance has resulted because, as the Times points out, everyone is familiar with all the facts of the case and so even the Reds can not be stirred up over the affair.

Possibly publicity is the one best cure we have to-day for handling those forms of propaganda which are not readily controlled by other means. But if this is the case it means that more of our newspapers and magazines will have to convince the public that what they print is not controlled by certain interests. At the present time I should judge that great numbers of citizens believe most newspapers, if not their own, distort the facts to fit their purposes. And again, if publicity is to cure the evils of propaganda, it means that society must work out some more satisfactory method than now exists of providing the groups of poor people with adequate publicity to offset the enormous advantage that groups composed of wealthy people have in commanding the printed page. Too few newspapers print to-day, and too few can ever afford to print, the detailed testimony in a labor controversy, yet unless the laboring man feels his side is presented, he will have supplied to him and will read wild denunciations of capital instead of the sworn testimony of his leaders as given before a board of arbitration.

Another means of controlling propaganda lies in educating the public to an understanding of the methods employed in propaganda. It is thought that man likes to feel he is being appealed to on logical grounds: that he resents being "'soft-soaped." And that he does not want to be "worked," or to have something "put over on him." Possibly, it is contended, articles such as have appeared recently in our magazines recounting the methods by which propagandists have fooled men and women may educate the public to see through a publicity campaign. Personally, I do not believe that very much can be accomplished in this way, for, as Barnum claimed, the public likes to be fooled; and secondly, clever appeals to the emotions will nearly always win when pitted against intellectually held convictions.

In closing, I want to emphasize one point. It is possible to-day for a group to carry on a very subtle propaganda with the immediate aim of developing some sentiment. There is no machinery to stop them, whether the sentiment is socially good or bad. For sentiment is an emotional state of mind and as long as no action results, society to-day has no way to handle it. So France mourned at the Strasbourg statue in Paris each year and kept alive the sentiment to retake Alsace-Lorraine. Of course, we completely sympathize with her. But it made Germany prepare all the more for war. And the world sat back and looked on while Germany established the sentiment in the minds and hearts of her citizens that they lived only for the fatherland and that war was the truest expression of their country's life. The Grand Army of the Republic and the Confederate Veterans have perpetuated northern and southern antipathies and the American Legion must of necessity keep us antagonistic toward Germany. For these organizations are surcharged with emotion. General O'Ryan is quoted in the papers as follows:

"Ten years from now the battlefields of Europe will not look as they appear to-day. They will bear monuments of men on horseback and the young men will grow up thinking of war in terms of medals, glory and men on horseback rather than in terms used by the young men of to-day who were in the war. Delay in solving this problem will mean that those who profit by war will get control of the kids and that's what they want. The youngsters will be hypnotized to believe anything in the name of patriotism and they will want to get medals and glory of their own."

If war is to be eliminated, it will be necessary to control the sentiments that are developed in each and every country. Similarly if peace is to be attained between capital and labor, the right sentiment will have to be developed. Many an employer has been smarting under conditions now past when labor had the whip hand. He is now getting even, as he says. He is reacting to a sentiment of revenge and at the same time building up a similar one in the minds of his employees. This is the sure road to worse conditions.

As far as I can see, society has reached the point in its development when it must take motives into account, because man has now learned how to arouse motives to action in an economical and wholesale way. And in regulating motives society must come to evaluate the sentiments that propaganda is aimed to create, and to regulate in some way the use of phrases arousing emotions, as distinguished from phrases appealing to rational consideration. Without control in some way of the emotional element in propaganda, legal action will never stop the most dangerous of propaganda which arouses a sentiment first of all and then at the proper moment in one fell swoop precipitates that sentiment into action.

From: *The Scientific Monthly*, vol. 14, no. 3 (March 1922), pp. 234-252.

PSYCHOLOGICAL WARFARE

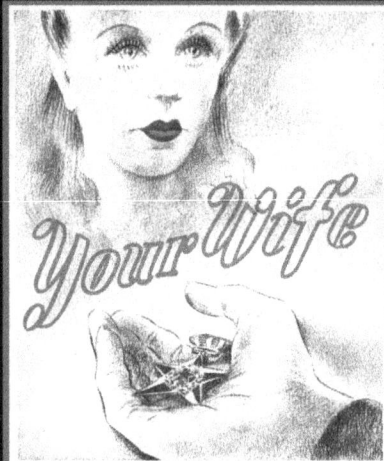

Your Wife

••• SHE WOULD PREFER YOUR SAFE RETURN

PAUL M. A. LINEBARGER

ISBN 1-61646-055-5

COACHWHIP PUBLICATIONS

COACHWHIPBOOKS.COM

DOWN RAMP!

THE STORY OF THE
ARMY AMPHIBIAN ENGINEERS

BRIGADIER GENERAL
WILLIAM F. HEAVEY

ISBN 1-61646-057-1

ISBN 1-61646-138-1

COACHWHIP PUBLICATIONS

COACHWHIPBOOKS.COM

YORKTOWN

THE STRATEGY, PEOPLE, AND EVENTS
SURROUNDING THE FINAL BATTLE IN THE
AMERICAN WAR OF INDEPENDENCE

ISBN 1-61646-101-2

COACHWHIP PUBLICATIONS

COACHWHIPBOOKS.COM

BASTOGNE

The Story of the First Eight Days
In Which the 101st Airborne Division Was
Closed Within the Ring of German Forces

COLONEL S. L. A. MARSHALL

ISBN 1-61646-062-8

www.ingramcontent.com/pod-product-compliance
Lightning Source LLC
Chambersburg PA
CBHW022004090426
42741CB00007B/885